# The Political Experience

# The Political Experience
## A Preface to the Study of Politics

WILLIAM J. MEYER
*The University of Michigan—Flint*

**Holt, Rinehart and Winston**
New York   Chicago   San Francisco   Dallas
Montreal   Toronto   London   Sydney

**Library of Congress Cataloging in Publication Data**

Meyer, William James
  The political experience.

  Bibliographies.
  Includes index.
  1.  Political science.  I.  Title.
JA66.M45   320      76-17254
ISBN 0-03-036306-3

Printed in the United States of America

890      090      987654321

# Preface

The question of how students should be introduced to political science is a troublesome one, and political scientists may be excused if they look with envy on their colleagues in other social and behavioral sciences where—at least from the outside looking in—a certain consensus seems to prevail on gaining access to the discipline. In the teaching of introductory sociology and macro/micro principles of economics, the question of approach seems more a matter of form than content. In political science we are still wondering about content and, in many colleges and universities, about whether a comprehensive introductory course should be mounted at all. This situation has produced a varied and sometimes exotic assortment of introductory texts. Some tend to be more personal statements than would be found in related disciplines; some attempt to deny the dilemma I have mentioned and courageously introduce students to the "science of politics"; and others finally settle upon conventional textbook formulas. Though the disarray in our introductory materials may be irritating and disheartening, the bright spot in all of this is that our better introductory texts provide a lively forum in which the very identity of the discipline is at stake, and that is something other disciplines might profit from.

This state of affairs makes it difficult to enter upon writing introductory materials for political science at large without being to some degree apologetic or apprehensive and without providing at least a partial answer to the disputed question of approach. The most explicit commitment I make is that the preferable way to introduce the uninitiated to political science is first to tell them what politics is all about. Beyond regular references to why and how political scientists are concerned with certain questions and the explicit treatment of the discipline in the last chapter, there is no discussion of the discipline in its formal intellectual finery. To stress at such an initial point methodological devices and a recondite analytical patois is neither essential nor useful, and some attempts at doing this are merely symptomatic of insecurities about whether we are really scientific at all. A certain familiarity with the subject matter should precede formal theory and intricate abstraction in entering a new field of study. Prior to a formal study of political systems and processes, students should know something about the state, nationhood, power, roles, public offices, institutions, parties, political groups, socialization, political resources, change, and so on. They should know what these things are, how to identify them in their own observation of political experience, why they are characteristic of political life, and what it is about them that may be useful in trying to interpret politics.

This introduction is also committed to the notion that politics is best understood and defined as an activity through which society exerts control over public affairs. I feel this definition has the advantage of encompassing other thematic approaches, of effectively distinguishing politics from other social and behavioral phenomena, and of being responsive to the student's intuitive association of politics with public issues and government.

It may seem a bit presumptuous to try to orient the student to the phenomenon of politics without introducing an explicit or formal theoretical perspective. I do not assume that one can merely "let the facts speak for themselves" in a thoroughly neutral, theory-free presentation; indeed, one will find here what Abraham Kaplan has called a "theory-in-use" and some general conceptualization of political systems and processes. Systematic, critical theorizing, on the other hand, is beyond the bounds of this book.

Finally, as the subtitle indicates, the book is useful mainly for what it leads to, for the direction and bearings it gives the student. It is designed to move him or her from the point at which politics is a blur of disjointed events, issues, and personalities to the point at which it emerges as a more or less comprehensible web of activities, relationships, and institutions directly related to the maintenance of life in society. The intent is not to provide students with an overall knowledge of politics, but to prepare them for further study through readings and formal courses. Topics are introduced and discussed for the purpose of alerting the new student to what to watch for, what questions to ask, what information is worth having, and what it might reveal. This objective is pedagogically basic but critically important, and if I am able effectively to lay the groundwork for the student's further study of politics by meeting this objective, I will have achieved my purpose in writing about the political experience.

W. J. M.

# Contents

# Introduction

There is something a bit odd about the title of this book. It indicates that we are going to be talking about "political experience." For most of us a subject probably becomes easier to grasp if it is related to our own experiences—immediate and personal events, matters that touch our lives in a direct way. This is presumably what was meant a few years back when many American students were demanding "relevance" in their education. However, this book will deal with a variety of ideas and make reference to actual events and situations which, most likely, have *not* been part of the personal experiences of the reader. Some of what will be covered may not even directly touch the experiences of Americans in general, for our country has not been torn apart by war as have the countries of Europe in the twentieth century, and political conflict in America has not normally involved ongoing confrontation between political parties and movements promoting basically different values and philosophies. Thus, talking about politics in a broad and general way necessarily means going beyond our immediate and probably narrow range of experience.

The reference to political experience has at least a double meaning here. As someone interested in the study of politics, you are not only being invited to refer to your own life and experiences but you are also being invited to expand and broaden your appreciation of the wide and diverse range of political events in the world. In other words, you should become more attuned to the variety of political experiences in the world, including those not directly your own. The study of anything so basic to human life as politics involves both making the subject relevant to you and opening yourself to a broader range of experiences.

There is something else to be said about this idea of experience. Our personal contact with real politics may be very narrow; it may barely exist. But the very nature of politics is such that to be involved in politics is a broadening experience. Involvement in politics means dealing with people you might not normally encounter, people different from yourself. It means acting and speaking in public situations and dealing with issues that may be quite important to you but are also of importance to a large community of others. When you get into politics, for whatever personal motives, you are unavoidably affecting other people's lives as well as your own. It is probably fair to say that political experience, by its very character, is not a narrow or restricted experience and that in studying politics we are not studying something that is purely personal or "relevant" only to you or to me. The world is a maze of different human experiences; we are one small part of this world, and politics is one vital activity that brings us in touch with the rest of the world or some part of it.

## CAN WE DEFINE POLITICS?

Beyond this matter of experience there is a much thornier issue: what do we mean by *politics?* In pondering this question, probably the first thing we would seek is a definition; definitions are handy, usually brief, and they give us something to hang on to in approaching an unfamiliar subject. However, we should not be too dependent upon definitions or exaggerate their value in understanding a very complex subject. The ancient Greek philosopher Aristotle offered a definition of man as a "rational animal," and though such a definition attempts to capture the essential character of human nature, our real understanding of man requires a much fuller and more elaborate description and explanation of his behavior, thoughts, and social interaction with others. It is much the same with understanding politics; we can define it—and we will try to develop a definition here—but really knowing what politics *is* involves much more than that.

Despite these reservations (and some apprehensions), it is worth trying to define *politics.* In considering what politics is all about, we might make reference to those direct experiences we mentioned above. An array of images may pass through our minds. Politics has to do with governments run by public officials, like mayors, governors, presidents, congressmen; it has to do with law and people who work with the law, like lawyers and judges; it has to do with political parties, elections, campaigns, and speeches; it has to do with conflict, arguments, quarreling, debating, and people talking, yes, a good deal of talking; and, of course, it has to do with power, with powerful people, with power over people, with people who want power. These images provide us with fair impressions of what politics is all about, but if we want to define politics we must get beyond impressions to what is basic and general about politics. Like an iceberg, these impressions reveal but the tip of the complex human relationships of politics. Thus, our immediate experiences and impressions give us guidance but are not sufficient to answer the question. In attempting some general understanding of politics, we want to be able to weave these piecemeal images together, to see how they interrelate. We also want to develop some conception of politics that makes sense for several different countries even though their actual way of practicing politics may differ considerably from our own. Defining politics will itself require—and provide—a broadening of our outlook.

## THE TWO FACES OF POLITICS

Of the wide variety of human experiences, politics is one of the more special and paradoxical. It can be rewarding and ennobling as well as frustrating and destructive; it has produced the most impressive and the most terrifying results. Strangely enough, the political community is the most comprehensive group we belong to, it encompasses all of us (with a vengeance, when it comes to paying taxes), yet, even in a democratic society, politics represents a substantial experience for only a small fraction of the community. It is politics, perhaps more than any other human endeavor, that has made history.

To get down to basics, we can say this much about politics: it is an activity which human beings engage in together and it involves relationships of power and control, decision and action, which affect the common aspects of our living together in society. In trying to extract from these thoughts a definition, we must be aware that defining politics has been a source of some controversy among political scientists who spend time worrying about such things. A variety of definitions have been put forward and they do not all say the same thing. It would, I think, be tiresome for us to review these different positions, but I think it is possible to identify two basic outlooks toward politics which go a long way in telling us what much of this controversy is about.

The first outlook views politics as an activity through which people are organized to exert control over affairs of common concern to them by maintaining, altering, or creating new conditions under which they live together. This may be called the *public purpose* view of politics. There are various ways of saying much the same thing: politics concerns the way in which people set down and pursue collective goals, the way they decide their fate; politics is the steering mechanism in society which attempts to direct the course of events. This view assumes that there is a range of "public affairs" that constitutes the concerns of politics. Public affairs consists of those aspects of life in society that people share an interest in but that they are incapable of controlling and managing by themselves. Consider, as a very basic example, the matter of crime. Successful living together in society requires that some people's use of their power over others, by stealing or assault, be controlled. If it is not, the fundamental forms of individual and social activity are threatened, for example, the acquisition of the needs of life—food, clothing, and shelter—or beyond this, engagement in art or industry. Controlling crime individually is a rather risky proposition, and for a healthy and secure social life political communities assume the responsibility of controlling such behavior (though they may not always be successful). Like the matter of crime, there are a number of issues that may be looked on as areas of public concern: the defense of the society from threats by other societies, the general health of the people, the character of economic relationships (the exchange of goods), and perhaps the condition of the physical environment. Whether any such matters are considered public in nature has to do not only with how they commonly touch people's lives but also with whether the members of society think of these things as matters of common concern and share an interest in regulating and controlling them.

One of the best explanations of these shared concerns was provided by the American philosopher John Dewey. If we look at the way in which we live and interact with other people in society, explained Dewey, we can see that these social relationships lead to two types of consequences, *direct* and *indirect.* Let us say that a group of us starts a small business to make soap flakes. Starting up and running the business involve organizing people—managers, stockholders, workers—to work together and deal with each other in the process of production. This business activity will have various consequences for the people involved in it at various levels. A decision of the managers might determine how much the workers get paid (a consequence) or whether the business is successful in making a profit for the owners (a consequence), or the workers may organize to promote better wages and working conditions which could lead to a strike (a consequence). Now in this example all the consequences we have mentioned are what Dewey would call *direct* consequences; that is, they are consequences that directly affect the participants in the organized business.

Now let us add to our example the fact that as our business goes about producing soap flakes it throws some of the waste involved in production into a nearby stream and this waste material creates so much pollution of the water that a small town several miles downstream finds the water no longer healthy to use for swimming or fishing. This pollution is also a consequence, but Dewey would call it an *indirect* consequence because it affects people who were not a part of the original enterprise that produced the pollution. The townspeople experience the result of the pollution but they are not members of the corporation and had nothing to do with making soap flakes.

What does all of this mean for politics? We may wish to say that it is the job of the soap flake business to worry about those direct consequences we mentioned, but Dewey raises a rather important question: Whose job is it to worry about the indirect consequences, the pollution? In the example we used, there is no identifiable group of people who have that as their responsibility. Those affected by indirect consequences, the townspeople, Dewey calls "the public" and in reacting to the need to exert control over those indirect consequences the public becomes organized politically, governments are formed, and a political process develops to give energy and direction to the tasks of government. Dewey's distinction and the example we have used here are not intended to describe the origins of political life literally but simply to show the significance of the idea of public affairs and its relationship to politics. Political experience not only derives from the need to control and regulate certain consequences but also from the need to decide *how* this is to be done and what goals are to be pursued in doing it.

Seen from the *public purpose* point of view, then, politics is a process by which people bring some order to their collective life in society and try to remove some of the insecurity and unpredictability of social living by mastering their own common affairs.

In the very process of dealing with public problems, however, governments make laws and rules and enforce them, and this too has consequences for people's lives. These actions of government are varied; they touch the lives of people with different needs and interests and with different qualities of life; they touch different people in different ways. This brings us around to the second outlook on politics, the *conflict* view. Harold Lasswell, a contemporary political scientist, vividly expressed this view in suggesting that we look at politics as a question of "who gets what, when, and how."[1] This view is captured also in the widely used definition of politics as the "authoritative allocation of values for society,"[2] which says much the same thing in more technical language. In other words, the variety of things that people value— health, security, riches, social status—is allocated or distributed through politics, and this allocation follows processes or rules that cause people to view the allocation as authoritative, that is, as the right thing to do. Politics involves the attempt to influence this allocation for whatever purposes, including seeking your own advantage. Far from being simply a question of united association for shared purposes, political experience seems very much a matter of human competition and struggle, of various segments of society seeking power and authority created by the whole society, of political values and beliefs being extensions of a number of purely particular and individual outlooks. This view finds its way into our common language, for to say that someone is very political or is playing politics has come to describe clever opportunism and active concern with one's position of power in relation to others. Going back to our example about the soap business and the polluted river, the interpretation of the *conflict view* would be that the business represents one set of interests and the townspeople another set of interests and that the study of politics is the study of how these interests collide, how the conflict between them is dealt with, and who tends to come out on top in the struggle. Looking at matters this way, we can think of politics as involving various "stakes" that people compete over. Formal government represents the main setting within which this competition goes on and the main instrument through which the competition is regulated. It is not surprising that people speak of the "game of politics."

These two views on politics—the *public purpose* view and the *conflict* view—would seem to be quite different and, indeed, political thinkers have often debated which is the more accurate picture. One view makes politics appear to be a question of imposing some correct order on human events for the good of the community and the other makes it appear to be a question of managing or coping with inextricable human differences and conflict. We should not feel, however, that we must choose between one of these views or the other; indeed, the position that will be taken here is that these two views simply represent two perspectives on the same experience, or the "two faces" of politics. Political experience encompasses both conflict and unity. The attempt to manage public affairs will necessarily lead to "allocations." When a government passes a tax law, it is allocating among the people in society the burden of giving financial resources to support the business of government; that is a kind of allocation, and it has a different impact on different people depending on how much money they have and how the tax burden is figured. Such allocation decisions become the basis for interpersonal conflict, and thus it is that politics presents us with an array of competing interest groups, political parties, and movements. The public's pursuit of the common interest thus leads to conflict because (1) the basic values and interests of the society are themselves subject to debate and have to be determined by people in society with different values and points of view and (2) how public decisions affect each of our lives is a matter of personal interest and concern. Yet just as the public's attempt to manage its affairs provides the basis for conflict, it is also the case that the conflict itself follows some process or order and results in decisions people consider legitimate. In other words, conflict is not pointless or unlimited (if it is, then political relationships among people have probably broken down entirely); it takes place within organized society. It does not make much sense therefore to think of politics as merely conflict and struggle; if we do we are not getting the whole picture. The conflict view is often thought of as being more "realistic" because it stresses how things happen in politics as a result of the power of some people over others. However, other realities must be accounted for: the fact that millions of individuals share a loyalty to the same nation, or accept the broad principles of the same constitution, or can join together in support of state projects (such as the United States' sending a man to the moon or Cuba's attempting a record harvest of sugar). Such behavior represents continual evidence of concerted political action and allegiance. (Indeed, rather than worry about too much conflict in politics, we may have as much reason to worry about man's willingness to submit to a common political order with excessive and uncritical zeal.) Politics has been pursued as a human attempt to remove some of the uncertainties and dangers of social conflict by creating means to achieve security and order.

The point of this discussion is that the unity and conflict of politics—the two faces of politics—are very much tied together in actual experience. In fact, it is the interplay between the forces of human conflict on the one hand and the drive for order on the other hand that gives politics its dynamic quality. In thinking about the two faces of politics, it may help to recall the insight of the eighteenth-century French philosopher Jean Jacques Rousseau, who said, "While it may be true that the antagonisms which exist between the divergent interests of different individuals make it necessary to establish a social order, yet, it is no less true that only because those interests are, at bottom, identical, is a social order of this kind possible."[3]

For those who would feel comfortable with a definition out of all of this, the following statement may best reflect the two faces of politics: *Politics is an activity in which people organize themselves for the purpose of exerting control over their common affairs by authoritatively allocating values for society.* There is a good deal in that definition; some things may even sound contradictory, but then, that is the way politics is. It is both interesting and challenging to study because, unlike eating, sleeping, or many of the routines of life, it is one of the larger and more complex areas of human activity.

## POLITICS AND HUMAN ASSOCIATIONS

Politics has been referred to here as a social or interpersonal activity; it concerns ways in which people interact with each other, not simply with the way they act as individuals. This raises questions about the differences and similarities between politics and other forms of social life. People in society form associations, which means that they group together for the purpose of pursuing some common objective. A labor union is an association of workers designed to protect and promote the interests of the workers, a church is an association formed to propagate a particular religious faith and organize common worship, a school is an association created for the purpose of education, and a factory is an association organized to engage in manufacture of a product. There is much more to these associations than this, but it is possible to compare associations according to the objectives they have. Politics also involves people in an association; government itself is the ultimate political association—but, speaking of government for the moment, is this association really like the others? Is it simply an association with a different set of objectives, or is it somehow a different *type* of association altogether?

Again, if we refer to our own experiences, there is much about government to suggest that there is something very different going on, that this is perhaps not an association like others. Consider that those born in the United States of parents who are citizens are themselves citizens, it is like being a "member" of this large political association we know as the United States of America. This citizenship has certain practical consequences; you can vote at a certain age, you will need a passport from the government to travel abroad, and, if you are male, you may be drafted into the army. But if you reflect upon your citizenship, it seems to be something that merely happened to you. You were born in a particular country; you did not choose your citizenship; you cannot recall consciously joining with millions of other American citizens for common objectives. Most other associations—unions, clubs, churches— at least appear to be voluntary extensions of our interests; but if you try to make a choice about citizenship (as many protestors to the Vietnam war did during the 1960s), you find that you must move to another country which may be very different from your own in language and culture and you must get your government to recognize the fact that you have changed citizenship. Moreover, your country may interfere with your leaving. Even all of this does not get around to the question of whether you can choose *not* to be a "member" of any governmental system or whether you can avoid the reach of government over your life. Belonging to a system of government seems quite different from belonging to the variety of other kinds of human associations.

Let us look at some further examples. Often our attempt to make an analogy between our relationships to government and our other relationships in society does not work very well. We pay taxes to government and we receive services in return, and it is tempting to think of this as similar to the way we operate in the marketplace where we pay a certain price to someone in exchange for certain goods or services. But paying taxes is not exactly like purchasing groceries or buying a car. For one thing we receive many benefits and services from the taxes we pay to government which we might not bother to purchase if we had a choice; we might not even want these services. In the United States there have been substantial government resources (your taxes) put into the construction of super highways, but you may not care very much about the opportunity to drive around the country efficiently and comfortably. You may enjoy the highways, but, if it were up to you, you might prefer some other governmental service, such as government-supported health care. Beyond this, we may also find that our taxes go to support benefits that we do not even receive. In the case of the highways, for example, you might not even possess a car or a driver's license and have little occasion to use this facility. Governments operate schools, but this benefit seems to go only to those people with children, though the schools are supported also by the taxes of those without children.

Finally, we should think about the way governments control citizens. Most all associations have certain means of regulating the behavior of the members. If you decide to leave a religious group, the church may condemn you or your family, and friends may pressure you to change your mind; or if you fail to pay your dues in an organization, the group may withdraw its benefits. Governments, however, are capable of exerting, and are allowed to exert, ultimate methods of control over those who violate its rules or threaten its existence: imprisonment or death. Its means of control can be final and compelling, and it uses means which no other group in society is allowed to use.

What these practical reflections are intended to show is that political association is somehow a different type of association, and perhaps these examples can be summed up best by our saying that political association is more *comprehensive* and more *compulsory*. Politics deals with a larger variety of concerns with a greater range of effects, and it leads to action which is backed by force and authority. Political association is more inclusive than other associations and stands above the rest. And, thinking back to Dewey's explanation, it deals with the consequences resulting from the activities and interactions of those other associations.

In addition to the comprehensive and compulsory character of political association, there is something else that makes it distinct. Politics involves different goals pursued in a different way, but these goals are not nearly as predetermined or preset as in nonpolitical groups. Indeed, as we have seen, the very purpose for politics is to define or discover or perhaps create common purposes or at least common rules and values among a population marked by numerous disagreements and divergent opinions over even basic political goals. In political struggle nothing need be taken for granted. Why should we have a "free-enterprise" economy? Why should criminals have rights in courts of law? Why should the Supreme Court be allowed to tell me where to send my children to school? Why should I fight this war? Such questions as these may not come up all the time in politics, but they may be thought of as essentially political questions. People in politics try to control and regulate their common affairs, to determine what their fate will be, but how they do this and what kind of society they want are political questions. Nonpolitical associations are more commonly characterized by defined goals: General Motors manufactures automobiles for a profit, the American Medical Association protects the professional interests of doctors, and the like. In the normal course of things, these fundamental goals are taken for granted and a substantial change in the goal might effectively mean a change in the very character of the organization. When such associations do engage in an internal struggle over their goals, we may speak of the "politics" that goes on within the association. Thus, many political scientists speak of politics not merely as an activity related to the operations of governments but as a general human activity that may occur in numerous human situations where power and control over a group's fate is at issue.

Thus, politics involves people in associated activity but in a way that is critically different from ordinary association by virtue of being more comprehensive, compulsory, and directly involved with the determination of goals.


## STUDYING POLITICS

In talking about political experience, our purpose in what follows is not to tell you everything about politics but to provide you with the kind of knowledge you can use to learn about politics yourself. The full range of information about man's political experience deals with about two thousand years of history and with societies all over the globe, and the information itself can fill a library. Some of that information will provide useful examples in our discussion, but the main objective is to provide certain basic ideas and principles, and a framework for thinking about politics that will be helpful in understanding and using that information as you encounter it. The approach of the book will not be to say "This is how politics works in this particular situation," but rather "If you want to understand how politics works, here is what you should consider, what you should look at, what you should keep your eye on."

The organization of the book consists of first looking at specific aspects of political experience, the elements that make it up, and then looking at the general relationship of these elements. The first task will be met by examining the boundaries of the political system, the human relationships and roles that occur in politics and the type of governmental machinery that has been commonly employed. The second task will be met by examining the political system as a whole in relation to several major concerns: the form that the political process takes, the types of political systems that we encounter in the world, the phenomenon of political change, and the ways in which people think about politics.

## NOTES

[1] Harold Lasswell, *Politics: Who Gets What, When, How* (New York, 1958).
[2] David Easton, *The Political System,* 2d ed. (New York, 1971), pp. 129–31.
[3] Jean Jacques Rousseau, *The Social Contract,* ed. Ernest Barker (New York, 1962), p. 190.

# 1

# The Body Politic

The immediate problem we face in trying to study politics systematically is finding out where to begin. Even in attempting to define politics it has been necessary to refer to a number of ideas—power, government, association, public decisions—that have not yet been explored. Organizing the study of politics is not like following a straight line from beginning to end; it is much more like following the path of a closed circle in which every avenue of investigation turns you back where you were before. The problem is finding out where to break into this closed circle.

## THE POLITICAL SYSTEM

A reasonable way to break into this closed circle is to gain some familiarity with the terrain of politics, with the setting in which political experience occurs. To make sense of man's political experience, we can first take note of the human collectivities that have formed as the basis for a common political life and of the organized expression of political activity in the form of various governmental jurisdictions and units. Politics consists of an activity that takes place within a large collection of people. However, the world does not consist of a single political collectivity, despite the dreams of certain people in history and the rudimentary efforts in the twentieth century in creating the League of Nations and the United Nations. A most basic reality of civilization is that the world is divided into a number of political collectivities; in this broadest sense there are a number of political units or "publics" or what we would ordinarily call countries or nations. There are presently in the world about 150 countries (as we will see, even the number of countries is not stable—it, too, is affected by politics). This political division of the world is familiar enough to the man on the street, and he can easily identify a number of countries with their own governments. This, indeed, may be the most fundamental aspect of our political experience; we are Americans, members of a separate political unit conducting our business in our own manner and, thereby, distinct from the politics of Germany, Zambia, or China.

Several terms have been used already—collectivity, unit, country— but it is useful to settle on one general term to convey this idea of a political division of the world. In the long history of political thinking the term *body politic* was used to convey the idea of the distinct political unity and identity of a people, and the term still has a nice classical ring to it. However, in contemporary political analysis such terms as *body politic* have been replaced with the now widely used term *political system,* which should serve quite well but which requires some explanation.

In the broadest and simplest sense a *system* refers to a set of interacting parts capable of being distinguished from the surrounding context or environment in which these parts interact. An engine in an automobile is what we would call a mechanical system consisting of a set of interacting parts—pistons, valves, gears, and electrical currents; the parts interrelate in a way that is not haphazard but rather, we might say, systematic. The human body is a biological system, again with numerous parts that work together, and with a boundary (our skin) that distinguishes the system from its environment. Although systems interact with their environments, they are capable of being analyzed as distinct from the environment; thus, the biological system takes in food and the mechanical system takes in gasoline. Of course, what we are interested in is not these types of systems but a type of social system, a system of human behavior. To get closer to the idea of the political system, consider the family as a system of human relationships. The various members of the family display forms of interaction with each other that serve to set this family apart from others who are not members of the family. The parts of this system are not determined merely by the biological relationship of parent and child but by the fact that there are patterns of interaction among the members of the family, expectations about how the members should behave that are distinguishable from relationships with nonfamily members. These may consist of a parent's authority, love, or protectiveness, or a child's dependence. Someone who has a particularly special relationship with an elder may say "He was like a father to me," which is a way of associating a pattern of behavior with familial relationships.

By analogy with such cases as these, we should be able to appreciate what is meant in referring to the various political units in the world as political systems. All that is really being indicated is that political man operates within a system of political relationships and that these relationships are bounded in some way. When we speak of the boundaries of a political system, the first thing that comes to mind are the geographical lines that separate one country from another, and indeed that is one tangible form that a system's boundaries take. Boundaries also refer to a population of people and, beyond this, boundaries should be thought of as encompassing interactions or sets of behavior. The idea of a system refers not only to a group of people but, perhaps more importantly, to the relationships that occur among that group of people. Going back to the family system, it is not the existence of a parent and a child that fully defines it as a system, but the peculiar ways in which parents and children behave toward one another.

To continue to be abstract for a little bit longer, consider this question: What do the boundaries distinguish a political system from? First, and most obviously, they distinguish the political system from other political systems, and this is why the concept of a system should be of use in discussing the political division of the world. Somewhat less obvious, however, is that these boundaries distinguish *political* relationships and behavior from *nonpolitical* aspects of our life in society, such as our behavior as consumers, students, or factory workers (though these other aspects may have political implications to them). People deal with each other politically, but politics is not all that they engage in; a political system is distinct not only from other political systems but, for purposes of analysis, it can also be distinguished from, for example, the economic system or the educational system.[1]

Many of the following chapters will concern what goes on within a political system, but for the time being our attention will focus on identifying the political system and the pattern by which the world is broken down into numerous such systems.

The idea of a *political system* has been introduced because in reading contemporary political analysis it is an idea that will be continually encountered. The term is very theoretical and abstract in the way that it sets down the general characteristics of political collectivities, but it is important to appreciate at the outset that the identity of a political system is not merely technical or academic; on the contrary, it is often itself a political issue of great consequence. One way to measure the political importance of this issue is to reflect on the tremendous amount of violence, bloodshed, and death resulting from the wars and revolutions of history that have been fought in the name of the identity of the political system. During the Vietnam war in the 1960s, considerable attention was given to the question of whether North and South Vietnam should be treated as a single country or as two separate countries. The dispute resulted from ambiguities originating several years earlier with international agreements which had temporarily divided the northern and southern parts of Vietnam; the process of reunification which was supposed to occur did not occur, and the two parts took on more and more of the attributes of separate political systems. How people perceived America's role in the Vietnam conflict was closely related to this issue. If the two parts of Vietnam were actually separate countries, then it made sense for the United States to say that it was militarily intervening in order to help an ally (South Vietnam) defend itself against another country that was trying to invade it; however, if north and south were only temporarily divided parts of the same country, then the behavior of the United States could be seen as an intrusion into an internal (civil) war of another country or as an aggressive move against that country. In a case such as this, the integrity and coherence of a political system, and the determination of where one leaves off and the other begins, are political issues as well as academic questions.

To the Vietnam example, numerous others can be added. In our own historical experience, we fought the American Revolution to defend our Declaration of Independence from Great Britain, asserting our belief that the thirteen colonies should no longer be viewed as part of the English political system. Later, of course, at the time of the American Civil War, we were confronted with the question of whether the United States of America would remain one nation or become two separate and independent nations. This issue of integrity and identity of the political system has been particularly vivid in the middle of the twentieth century; since World War II, we have witnessed the birth of dozens of new nations and the proliferation of national political systems throughout Asia and Africa as dependence on colonial nations like England and France has been thrown off.

Before examining these kinds of examples more closely, we should look at this idea of the political system in a more concrete way. We are trying to identify that collectivity or group that we are a part of and to determine why it is so important to our understanding of our own political experience. The notion of a *set of interactions* among people is terribly vague and obscure. To gain a fuller sense of what is meant by political systems, it may be helpful to consider the three concrete ways in which the system manifests itself in our experience: it appears as a *community*, as an *association*, and as a *jurisdiction*.

## COMMUNITY

In the first place, a political system appears as a type of community. But what is a community? Human beings tend to identify themselves with other human beings with whom they share certain characteristics or experiences. This sense of feeling comfortable with certain other people, of belonging to a group, is a very natural thing and it may be called a *sense of community*. If we live in a neighborhood for some time, we may see the development of this sense of community and we may become a part of it ourselves; if the population of the neighborhood is fairly stable, this sense of community may become very strong. People who live around you then become not just any other people but people with whom you share time, concerns, and perhaps even attitudes and values. The neighbors may be sorry to see someone leave the area and may be concerned about the kinds of people who move in. In the neighborhood, therefore, we do not merely see people living geographically side by side but also see the neighborhood as a kind of community. The American small town is another instance in which we see this community feeling, which we may call a "cliquishness."

It is not necessary, however, for a group to live close together to form a community; people belonging to the same racial or ethnic group may feel a common bond of attachment with each other even though they all do not know each other personally. People may possess this sense of community with an ethnic or racial group not merely because of common origins but perhaps because of the feeling that their experiences are similar as a result of these origins and because of customs and life styles which the group shares. Beyond this, it may be fair to speak of a professional community—of teachers, doctors, or architects—as a group of people sharing a common professional experience.

As these examples suggest, we can think of a *community* as a *group of people bound together by commonly identifying with each other as a result of some shared characteristics or experiences.* The key idea here is that a community is not a group with some commonly defined goals or purposes; rather, it is held together by common attachments, loyalties, and feelings. The experience of belonging to a community has to be examined by looking for the ways these attachments are expressed in our conduct, speech, and social relationships. In the contemporary world the major form that the political community takes is nationalism —allegiance to and identity with a particular nation. And a people's claim to nationhood represents an important political claim. Many of the trappings of politics are intended to help symbolize this sense of national community or to help foster it in the first place; thus, flags, national anthems, public ceremonies, appeals to patriotism, and pride in the accomplishments of a political system are ways in which this sense of nationalism is expressed. The feeling of national identity is enhanced by the fact that people over time share the same history, culture, and traditions; it is reinforced by common language, ethnicity, art, and values. Thus, in trying to make the idea of the political system more concrete in our minds, we can refer to this sense of political community that people feel as one aspect of their political life together.

The idea of community not only should make it easier to understand the idea of a political system, but further examination of this idea may also reveal some of the dynamic forces that operate in politics. A vital concern within a political system may be whether the feeling of political community is strong enough, and if it is not, whether this may damage the unity and coherence of the political system. Related to this concern is the fact that our allegiance to a political community is only one of many loyalties we experience, and these various loyalties may compete with each other. Among the more frequently encountered competing loyalties are race and ethnic groupings, social-economic class, religious affiliation, and attachment to a region within the larger system. When a particular system encompasses different racial or religious groups or serious conflict among different classes, we may find that loyalties to these groupings conflict with or even outweigh loyalty to the political community. Such conflict may become particularly severe where the feeling exists that one's race or class is the victim of unjust decisions or actions of the body politic. This whole problem of conflicting loyalties should be present least in societies where the population is generally quite homogeneous and in a period of stability; but the social and cultural pluralism, creation of new nation-states, and powerful forces of social and economic change which have tended to characterize recent history increase the likelihood that problems of this sort will arise.

The problem of competing loyalties has been a familiar difficulty to Americans throughout their history. After our independence from Britain, there was considerable dispute about whether loyalty to a state like Massachusetts or Virginia came before loyalty to the federal government, and the idea of *state's rights* that we occasionally hear of today is a remnant of that early dispute. The American Civil War was certainly aided and encouraged by the strong regional attachments people had acquired in the north and the south and the fact that these regional differences, over such matters as slavery, had become of political importance in governing the nation as a whole. Much more recently, the call for "black power" highlighted the conflict between the growing sense of community among a racial group and the larger political system that was alleged to be treating the group unjustly. Divided loyalties to different kinds of community identification are by no means limited to the American experience. Canadian politics has been frequently torn by the split between French-speaking citizens, living primarily in Quebec, and the majority of English-speaking citizens in the rest of Canada. French Canadians identify strongly with their own language and culture, and adding to this the charge that their language is not treated equally in such areas as education, business, and politics, it should not be surprising that their identification with and allegiance to the Canadian nation as a whole are thereby weakened.

One of the catalysts behind these competing loyalties is something called *cultural pluralism,* the existence within a society of people with different cultural backgrounds as indicated by language, ethnicity, religion. Cultural pluralism represents one of the more important forces in the world today posed against the solidarity of the political community. Since language patterns offer some indication of the degree of pluralism in a society, it is interesting to look at the various nations of the world in terms of the number of languages spoken within each and how many people speak them. For the most part we probably assume that in Germany people speak German and in France, French, and that that is pretty much how the rest of the world works; this, however, is not the case. If we consider the percentage of people in a country who speak the predominant language, we find several countries in which this is under 50 percent, for example India, the Philippines, Indonesia, Ghana, Nigeria, Peru, and Bolivia. Most of the countries of Sub-Saharan Africa and many countries in East and South Asia have less than 75 percent of their population speaking the most common language.[2] Language patterns are but one indication, but they do suggest the kind of difficulty that may confront a sense of political community within a nation.

In human experience this feeling of belonging to a community is for the most part a natural and healthy thing, but an extreme sense of community can have its harmful side; particularly in a society like ours which stresses the value of individualism and ingenuity, there is often distaste for the limitations and constraints communities can put on individuals. Any attempt, for instance, to instill and virtually enforce political loyalties threatens the autonomy of the individual and the other nonpolitical bases for community identification in society. In short, there is such a thing as a suffocating and stifling stress on political community. Probably the most dramatic and dangerous example in recent history has been in fascist regimes such as German Nazism in the 1930s, in which the appeal to German greatness and superiority was explicit, insistent, and pervasive and ultimately supplied psychological fortification for the systematic murder of millions of Jews. Not merely political conduct but all aspects of life were made susceptible to the judgment of whether or not they sufficiently expressed the German character or way of doing things. Political community clearly can become an unhealthy form of social attachment.

Identification with a political community, then, is one of the ways in which the existence of the political system is expressed in our experience, and the strength, weakness, or character of this community identification are themselves matters of political consequence to the system.

## ASSOCIATION

Clearly, the political system is not held together merely by the fact that its members may share some sense of *belonging* to a group; they also *do* things together as a group, and to this extent the political system must also be regarded as a type of association. In the most general sense, we can define an *association* as a *group of people organized for the pursuit of common objectives.* Where a community is formed out of common experience, an association is formed out of some shared task and is, therefore, more the product of human action and will. We have already referred to political association in the very process of trying to define politics earlier, but it would be useful to explore further some of the prominent features of political association.

When people pursue a task together, some coordination of their activity is required; organization tends to develop as a means of shaping and directing this activity toward a purposeful and efficient pursuit of the objective. Thus, human associations, like clubs, unions, and businesses, can be examined primarily through the mechanisms that are established to achieve this coordination, the most tangible mechanisms being the rules and offices of formal organization and the particular responsibilities they involve. A union of workers, for example, is an association founded for the purpose of protecting and promoting the interests of those workers. In order to guard those interests, the workers must function together, coordinate their activities, articulate what those interests are, and pool their energies and resources. Their mode of organization is designed to make possible and to facilitate this associated activity. Membership in the group is determined in some way, perhaps by working in a particular factory; dues are collected to provide the financial resources needed to support the union's program of activities; a system of rules is written to lay down the method for making decisions and using the group's common resources; and offices are defined and filled by particular people as a way of distributing the various smaller tasks that have to be carried out.

Politics consists of people doing things together and thus must be studied as a type of human association. Just as the term *nation* indicates the primary expression of political community in the world today, the term *state* indicates the primary form of political association. (*State* is used here to refer to national states such as France, Germany, or the United States and should not be confused with the fact that we use the same term for the subunits in our federal system.) In addition, government may be thought of as the specific, practical device through which the activities of the state are organized. We may now be in a position to appreciate the relationship between government and politics. *Politics* is the more general term, encompassing all facets of people's experience in trying to manage their common affairs through the authoritative allocation of values, while *government* refers to one aspect, though a very central aspect, of that experience. Politics goes on within government, but it also goes on outside of government and is more than just government.

Recalling our discussion of the two faces of politics, when it is said that political association means people are organized to pursue common objectives, there is no attempt to deny the conflict inherent in politics nor to assume that the objectives are predetermined or can be taken for granted. It merely indicates that the existence of political association assumes some recognition that there are political tasks to be carried out. Indeed, one of the central tasks for which political association is designed is the very determination of its objectives in the first place. Government is not a place where objectives are merely taken for granted and implemented; rather, it contains numerous forums—councils, cabinets, advisory groups, legislatures, committees—where deliberation, debate, and conflict take place over objectives.

As with community, the existence and character of political association are not only of academic concern but of political concern as well. How the state is run and organized, whom it includes and what roles it gives to those it includes, how power is distributed within it, what principles and rules it operates by—these are all central concerns of political life.

## JURISDICTION

In many ways this last mark or practical indication of the existence of a political system should need the least explanation and elaboration because the slightest reflection should reveal it to be the most direct and immediate way that we experience politics or what is done in politics. Politics is a system of human relationships in which people control their common affairs and the practical upshot of this is that decisions are made and actions taken in politics which touch our lives directly. *By the jurisdiction of the political system we simply mean that it exerts control over a particular territory and population and thereby regulates people's lives.* Examples of these controls, both great and small, would include such as the following: requiring a license to engage in certain activities from driving and fishing to selling prescription drugs; the outright prohibition of certain activities, such as theft or assault, with penalties for violators; hiring, training, and equipping a police force to insure obedience to the law; taking steps to encourage employment or control inflation; delivering mail; raising an army; operating a television network; deciding what can or cannot be published; determining how natural resources should be used or preserved; operating major utilities such as gas or electricity; requiring individuals to serve in the military; taking part of people's income in the form of taxes; determining when and under what circumstances a person can travel out of the country or even travel around within it. Not all of these things are done in all political systems, but they represent the ways in which various systems exert control over a particular territory and population. Thus, one way we experience the existence of the political system is through the range and boundaries of this network of controls, that is, through the system's jurisdiction. A simple and effective way of appreciating this is to drive across a border from one country to another. You may find yourself being examined and questioned in various ways by officials of the country you are leaving and officials of the country you are entering; you will find a change in the form of money you need to use; you will find out that there are certain things you cannot transport across the border. All of these occurrences are ways of telling you that you are leaving the jurisdiction of one political system and entering the jurisdiction of another.

## THE SHIFTING SANDS OF THE POLITICAL SYSTEM

We have looked to our loyalties and identification with a group, our associated activity with others, and the range of control over people's lives—the three ideas of community, association, and jurisdiction—as ways of bringing the abstract idea of a political system more down to earth and putting it in terms that can be more easily studied. The temptation at this point is simply to equate the political system with the boundaries of political community, association, and jurisdiction and to assume that they all fit each other exactly, that they are identical or coterminous (as in Figure 1–1). That may be the case, and indeed the

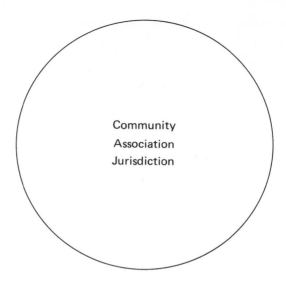

Community
Association
Jurisdiction

**Figure 1-1  Idealized Relationship of the Three Features**

forces in modern politics may incline in that direction, but unfortunately politics is not so simple (or fortunately politics is not so uninteresting). There are two types of situations in which an exact convergence of these various boundaries does not occur: (1) where one of these marks of the political system appears without the other two and (2) where the boundaries generally converge but also overlap in various ways.

Taking the first situation, is it possible to have a national community without an association (state) or jurisdiction? For many years before the nation of Israel was established as a state, many Jews around the world thought of themselves as belonging to a national group; indeed, it was the very strength of this feeling among other things which influenced the latter development of a Jewish state. Can jurisdiction exist without a state? When one country invades another with military forces, it effectively exercises jurisdiction over it, though the state of the invaded country is destroyed. These examples may be extreme or highly unusual situations, but they do show that we should not assume that community, association, and jurisdiction will always coincide.

The second situation takes us away from such extreme examples to those cases where there is some convergence but where this convergence is either not complete or a matter of political dispute. When Adolph Hitler ruled Germany, he insisted that a part of Czechoslovakia populated by German-speaking people was a natural part of the German nation and therefore should be taken over by the German state.

He exploited this apparent lack of convergence for his political objectives of conquest. Further, there are numerous cases of states that are not well integrated as national communities, and one of the best indications of this is the intensity of internal conflict that often results. Nothern Ireland is split between Protestants and Catholics who find it impossible to live with each other as fellow citizens; Nigeria experienced a civil war between groups split along old tribal lines. A frequent historical situation is the relationship between a "mother country" and a "colony" in which two countries are bound together by a common state structure and a common jurisdiction, though there is considerable reluctance to look upon themselves as a common nation. During its great age of empire, Great Britain had expanded its political control to the four corners of the globe but it would certainly be incorrect to view all the parts of that empire from Africa to South Asia as constituting a coherent nation. Thus, as Figure 1–2 shows diagramatically, the fit between these different components may be such as to give the boundaries of the political system a ragged, ill-defined quality.

The point of getting into this whole matter is not to try to make confusing an otherwise tidy affair, but to argue that we should not fall into the trap of thinking the political system is like a physical object with clearly observable, fixed, stable, and rigid boundaries. The system is not like a table or a car, for we are not describing a material thing but a complex set of human relationships that is susceptible to change and

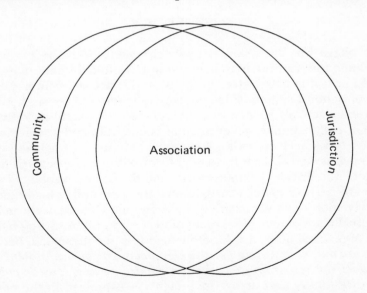

Figure 1-2  Realistic Relationship of the Three Features

alteration over time. However, we must also be careful to notice that although we should not expect always to find community, association, and jurisdiction coinciding, this does not mean that the relationship among them is random or insignificant; in fact, this relationship represents an important set of political forces in the modern world. The evidence of modern history is that they *tend* to coincide, and the predominant conception of the political order in the world today suggests that they *should* coincide. This is why each of the examples used above describes an unstable and dynamic political situation. Hitler's claims on Czechoslovakia led to annexation and ultimately to World War II; the claims of colonies to a national identity has brought about the destruction of empires and the creation of dozens of new states; in 1948 the Jewish claim to nationhood found its full political expression in the form of the state of Israel. If we look at the political system not at one point in time but in historical perspective, we find the birth and death, expansion and contraction of political systems. Through this historical movement the guiding principle for the modern age would seem to be the achievement by various distinct peoples of national statehood. Thus, a close identity among state, nation, and political jurisdiction (what is captured by the term *nation-state*), though it may not be in every case an accurate description of reality, nonetheless represents a vital political aspiration in the world today.

## SOVEREIGNTY

We began this discussion of political systems with the purpose of examining the political division of the world into different units, and it has led us to the nation-state as the most distinct and comprehensive form of political system. If we go back to where we began, however, experience actually reveals that the individual is caught in a complex maze of political units, governmental boundaries, and jurisdictions of various types such as cities, townships, counties, provinces, states, boroughs, as well as such strange entities as the European "Common Market," the British Commonwealth, and the United Nations. Some of these are parts of nation-states, others are large and actually include several nation-states (for example, the Common Market). Is the individual actually a member of several political systems? In sorting out this array of political units, it will help to consider the distinction between *sovereign* and *nonsovereign* systems. *A sovereign political system is one that does not recognize any decision-making power, law, or political authority higher than itself.* Sovereignty is expressed in the government's claim of a right to rule independent of any states or organizations above or beyond it and in its claim to being the ultimate source of authority for other units contained within it. A city or town in the United States, despite the extent to which it may run its own affairs, is still subject to our national constitution, and the United States as a whole may enter into a number of agreements with other nations without, in the process, surrendering its right to determine its own national interest. The United States of America is a sovereign political system, just as the nation-state generally is the sovereign form of politics in the modern world. There are several indications of such sovereignty: the sovereign state is the basis for citizenship, it maintains armies, it conducts diplomatic relations with other countries.

The idea of sovereignty is often equated with power or independence from outside forces, but these should not be confused. For to say that a state is sovereign is not the same as saying that it is all-powerful or that it is completely autonomous in how it operates in the world. A fundamental limitation on the power of any sovereign political system is the existence of other sovereign political systems, just as the power of the United States is limited by the power of the Soviet Union or of China. The power of a system will depend on many factors—the strength of its economy, its size, its relations with neighboring countries—many of which are not altogether within its control. The term *sovereignty,* therefore, is not used to describe the actual power that a state has but to refer to the recognition of its claim of a right to rule as the highest political authority over a particular jurisdiction.

The claim to sovereignty and the attempt to achieve sovereign statehood are fundamental concerns for any society and can become vital political concerns. As a minor example of how this issue of sovereignty can find its way into ordinary politics, we might examine an issue raised by Governor Reagan during the 1976 Presidential primary elections. Reagan seemed to be advancing the idea that the Panama Canal Zone, which contains the Panama Canal and is occupied and controlled by the United States under a treaty, should be considered as much a part of the sovereign United States as any one of our fifty states. In a television interview the following exchange occurred between Senator Paul Laxalt, a leader in the Reagan campaign, and Tom Pettit, a reporter:

SENATOR LAXALT: Governor Reagan has not advocated going to war over the Canal at all. He simply indicated that the matter of sovereignty, of title, is not negotiable, and that comes straight from the record. It comes from statements that have been made by prominent public figures in this country for a long time, including the President, including Barry Goldwater, and so over the years it has been uniformly felt here with the exception of the State Department, which has

been playing its own game in this thing, it has been uniformly felt
that we had sovereign rights in the Panama Canal.

MR. PETTIT: I am a little confused by that. If the Canal is sovereign and
you believe the Canal is sovereign, would you, say, advocate statehood for the Canal Zone?

SENATOR LAXALT: Oh, I don't think it is the type of situation which would
call for—

MR. PETTIT: Advocating full citizenship?

SENATOR LAXALT: No, I don't think so.

MR. PETTIT: Then how can you say it is sovereign?

SENATOR LAXALT: Well, it is sovereign from the standpoint that from the
first time that we went in there we were treated as a sovereign. We
were given title to the property in fee simple, and we have since that
time performed all the attributes of sovereignty.

MR. PETTIT: But you don't advocate giving the people who live there the
same rights that people who live in the States do—

SENATOR LAXALT: They have basically at the present time some of the
same rights as people in the States do. They have rights to citizenship
under their special act. But the fact is, we have within their country
our property which distinguishes it as far as I am concerned.[3]

Is the Canal Zone a part of the sovereign United States? Notice the
criteria that are introduced: statehood? citizenship? This exchange of
views may not settle the matter of Panama—indeed, it may confuse it
more—but it does suggest how the issue of sovereignty finds its way into
political debate.

The purpose of introducing the idea of sovereignty is to help sort out
the array of political and governmental units that are actually encountered in our experience. Thus, in addition to sovereign political systems
(the modern nation-state) that exist side by side in the world, there are
nonsovereign political units which can be divided into two types. First,
we can speak of *international* bodies which operate above the level of
the nation-state and through which various nations carry on relations
with each other. Second, we can refer to political subdivisions within
sovereign nation-states—such as provinces, cities, towns, and the fifty
American states—and, technically speaking, these can be called *subsystems,* meaning subsidiary parts or components of the larger system.
Thus, the world is not just cut up politically among different systems
living side by side; rather, taking into account the complex of political
units, it would be more accurate to imagine the political world as numerous boxes within other boxes (see Figure 1–3). We can further
examine the political division of the world by looking respectively at
these two nonsovereign political levels: the international and the subnational.

Subsystems

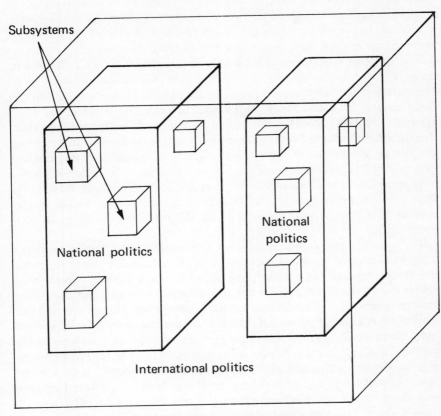

National politics

National politics

International politics

**Figure 1-3  Various System Levels**

## INTERNATIONAL POLITICS

The various nation-states of the world have numerous occasions and considerable need to deal with each other. Though they run their own affairs, this, of course, stops at their own boundaries, and to exert control in the environment beyond these boundaries they must interact with other nation-states. Nation-states share common boundaries, they engage in commerce and trade, they may need resources (such as food, minerals) that are controlled by other countries, and all of these situations present the opportunity for conflict and the need for relations among nations. These relations are what is being referred to in speaking of international politics. International politics and the handling of international conflict traditionally have been carried on in two ways: diplomatic agreements and war. Through diplomatic agreements—treaties—specific nations concur in writing to particular solutions to particular problems between or among them. Treaties, for example, involve agreements among the participating nations to partially disarm themselves, to assist each other if attacked, to allow each other's citizens to travel in the other's country, to exchange certain commodities or technical knowledge. Diplomacy refers to the whole process by which nations relate to each other, typically through the vehicle of such agreements. But nations also conduct relations, if it can be called that, through the conduct of war. Where diplomacy is ineffective in resolving conflict or where there is an unwillingness to use diplomacy, nations may resort to force to control a situation. Nations maintain armies not only to defend themselves against threats from other nations but also to extend their own power over others. The history of the world vividly reveals that war among nations is an all too common international experience.

The specific and fragile character of treaties and alliances and the frequent reliance on warfare demonstrate a critical difference between the internal politics of a nation and politics among nations. The central actors in international politics are not individual people but organized governments, and the relations among these governments are not controlled or regulated by an established governing body among the nations themselves. Agreements among nations hold only so long as the parties involved want to abide by them and there is no enforcement mechanism to insure compliance with such agreements; it is as if citizens obeyed laws only when they felt it was in their personal interest and there were no government to compel them to do otherwise. It should hardly be surprising that such an international system would produce considerable military conflict and that the risks of such a system have encouraged attempts to supplement limited diplomatic agreements and war with international organization as a method of conducting international relations. Though the notion of a *world government* has occasionally appeared in western political philosophy, the need for a comprehensive international organization began to acquire quite practical importance by the twentieth century, with war becoming an increasingly dangerous and destructive enterprise and with industry, technology, and communications drawing the various cultures of the world closer and closer together. After World War I a step in this direction was taken with the League of Nations, an experiment that was not particularly successful except possibly insofar as it prepared the way for the formation of the United Nations after World War II.

The United Nations is by no means a world government; it does not destroy the sovereignty of the member states, indeed the United Nations Charter recognizes such sovereignty explicitly, and its powers of enforcement have been weak. Nonetheless, its more modest objectives of providing an international forum for the airing of disputes and putting international relations on a politically more secure and predictable basis have truly introduced a new element in politics among nations. The organization was officially created by a charter signed in San Francisco on June 26, 1945, for the purpose of maintaining international peace and security. The three most prominent features of its organizational structure are the General Assembly, in which all member states have a seat, the Security Council, which is dominated by the larger and more powerful states and is designed to deal with urgent matters of security, and the Secretariat, which is the chief administrative arm of the United Nations under the direction of the Secretary General.

The United Nations, however, is not the only contribution to international organization. In recent history a number of organizations with regional concerns or with particular economic, technological, or cultural interests have been founded. To mention a few, there is the Organization of African Unity (OAU), established by charter in Addis Ababa, Ethiopia, in 1963 and consisting of forty-two member states from the African continent. The OAU is a result of attempts to seek unity among the independent states of Africa, oppose colonialism on the continent, protect a member's sovereignty, and aid in the development needs of the member states. Another example is the European Economic Community (EEC), better known as the Common Market, which is concerned with matters of trade and economic growth and stability among its members. The new and still struggling Asian Development Bank (ADB) was founded in 1966 with forty member states for the purpose of aiding the development of the region. An example of a more specialized body would be the International Whaling Commission (IWC), established in 1946 for the purpose of managing whaling activity and resources.

Despite the development of such international bodies, politics at the international level is still very much a matter of the competing power and interests of nations differing greatly in their values, power, and size. Among the nations of the world some are as wealthy in resources and industry as the United States, others as poor as Haiti; some are as old as France, others as new as Angola; some as open and democratic as Great Britain, others as totalitarian as China; some with the military might of the Soviet Union, others with the modest forces of Burma. The nations of the world do not deal with each other as equals; major powers, such as the United States, the Soviet Union, and China, necessarily have great impact on international events. Control over oil production has given several of the oil-producing states of the Middle East tremendous influence over the world's economy through their management of the price and supply of this vital resource to other countries. Thus, the study of international politics involves the study of the conflict and balance within this complex of unequal forces.

The international system clearly is shaped by the primacy of the modern nation-state and, therefore, the future of international politics is very much dependent upon the future of the sovereign nation-state as we know it today. Though the nation-state may appear to be a stable and permanent part of our political experience, it is worth reflecting on the fact that, in historical terms, it is relatively new. We think of recorded history as spanning, say, two or three thousand years, yet most of the sovereign states of the world today have achieved their present status within the past two hundred years and a good number of them within the last generation. A broader historical view allows us to appreciate that we are in the midst of a very dynamic set of events and, just as history reveals other types of political formations—the ancient Greek city-state, the Roman Empire, medieval feudalism—we may be led to speculate about what future forms may be used to organize political life when the nation-state no longer seems as effective and credible as it has been. Our attachment to the idea of the nation-state and its sovereignty may lead us to dismiss international bodies as weak, nonsovereign organizations which survive only as long as the foreign policy of many states allows them to. Though this is a realistic appraisal of such organizations, we should not forget that their very existence and the functions they are intended to serve pose something of a challenge to the idea of state sovereignty. The significance of such experiments may not be found in their present influence but in what they may hold for the future.

## SUBNATIONAL POLITICAL UNITS

If international politics seems to be an exotic and alien world of diplomats and generals, the nonsovereign political units at the subnational level are quite the opposite, for they likely constitute our most direct and personal experience with the world of government and politics. Mayors, city councils, tax collectors, water and sewer commissions, policemen, firemen, represent the presence of government in our immediate environment, the most localized level of government. As we said earlier, these units are not sovereign, for they are in some way merely parts of a larger national political system, though we may find that many of the most ordinary ways in which governments touch our lives occur at this level.

Again we are confronted with a maze of facts to sort through, for at the subnational level there are innumerable types of political jurisdictions with different functions, different degrees of autonomy, and different names from country to country. Yet there are ways of sorting through this maze of different governmental bodies to determine how a national political system may be subdivided. A primary consideration is the degree of autonomy which the subunit exercises in relation to the national government, for despite being nonsovereign and lacking ultimate authority, these units may possess a considerable amount of independence depending on how they have been legally established and on political circumstances (see Figures 1–4 and 1–5).

Some national systems are subdivided at a particular level into units —states (United States), provinces (Canada), or *Länder* West Germany) —which in certain areas of public affairs have more power and responsibility than the national government. Typically, this state of affairs is spelled out in the basic or organic law of the land and formal alteration of the situation may require constitutional change. This is the system Americans commonly know as *federalism.* The degree of independence of the subunits may vary from one federal system to another, though a common pattern is for national government to concern itself with such matters as defense, foreign policy, and currency, and for subunits to handle services relating to health, education, police protection, and so on. This picture, of course, leaves a number of matters which could be handled at either level or partially by both levels. Also, the independence of subunits may increase to the point where we have what is called a *confederacy,* of which Switzerland (with its various cantons) is an example. Unlike federalism, confederation may allow for the secession of a subunit or for the nullification by these units of laws made at the national level. Not all national systems are internally divided in these ways, and those that are not are referred to as *unitary states,* such as England and France. In these systems, the subunits (such as towns, counties, or cities) are considered extensions of the national government. This is identical to the situation that prevails within, for example, a state in the United States where a city government is created through a charter with the state.

The federal arrangement is often thought to be most useful in very large national systems and in systems where there are regional differences of a cultural, linguistic, or economic sort. Hence, it is not surprising that federalism is employed in such countries as the Soviet Union, the United States, Canada, and Brazil. The presumed advantages of federalism are that it allows many governmental functions to be per-

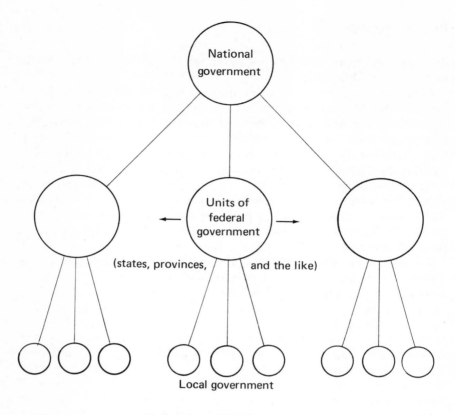

**Figure 1-4  The Federal System**

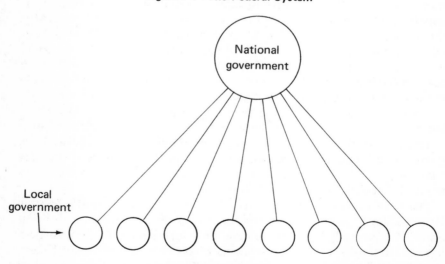

**Figure 1-5  The Unitary System**

formed on a smaller scale by being provincial or state functions rather than national and that it allows for some expression of regional differences. In addition to this somewhat autonomous level of government that occurs in federal systems, all national political systems contain a network of governmental units at the local level such as the cities, counties, and towns in the United States. Since these units are non-sovereign, they of course do not have armies nor do they conduct international relations or have their own system of currency, but they do provide on the local level many of the ordinary services of government such as fire protection, public safety, streets, water, and sewage.

In studying local governments there is another distinction that may be helpful. The local units that have been mentioned deal in a *comprehensive* way with the variety of governmental obligations at that level, but we may also encounter governmental bodies with *special* jurisdiction over a specific public service which appear to operate as separate governmental units. The best example of this in our country are boards of education which operate at the local level, often independent of city or county government, with their own tax base and their own election process. It is often the arrangement of these units and their overlap with other units that accounts for the complexity of governmental bodies and jurisdictions in which the citizen finds himself enmeshed, though it is probably the case that the United States is less tidy about these things than some other countries. For the student of politics, these various subnational units may be looked upon as *subsystems* of the larger national system which partially display an identifiable association, jurisdiction, and perhaps even sense of community. In this way it makes sense to speak of, for example, the politics and government of New York City or the state of Michigan.

There are a couple of very good reasons for beginning our discussion of political experience with this review of the nature and types of political units and governmental jurisdictions in the world. First, political experience operates within a given context, and the most fundamental part of our political experience is the very existence of public association, that is, of the body politic and its visible and practical extensions in the form of government. Politics is a human activity which goes on within a reasonably defined setting, and an understanding of this activity presumes some appreciation of the setting.

Even more important than this, however, is the fact that the very identity, existence, and sovereignty of defined political systems have been, historically, among the most serious and consequential political issues. The creation of sovereign states and challenges to their integrity have been at the center of much political violence in history. Civil war, international warfare, and rebellion have commonly grown out of issues relating to the boundaries and identity of political association, and many of the present political boundaries of the world are products of such events. Even where political violence does not result, people's self-perception as members of a public is a vital political consideration. As John Dewey has put it, "The outstanding problem of the Public is discovery and identification of itself."[4] This is most apparent in the case of the nation-state with its need for national identity, yet it may play a role at the subnational level where subunits may serve to recognize smaller publics. We can appreciate what is at stake here if we imagine the political consequences of, say, removing "home rule" from an American city or eliminating the French-speaking Canadian province of Quebec and uniting it with Ontario. Thus, the bounds of political systems are neither purely matters of administrative convenience nor accidental results of history, but political facts in themselves of no little importance.

## THE ENVIRONMENT OF POLITICS

In describing the political division of the world in terms of various systems and subsystems, we must also consider that each of these operates within a particular environment. Politics may be important to human life but it is not all that human beings do, and their other activities and other aspects of their life constitute the *environment* in which politics occurs, an environment consisting of various physical, social, economic, cultural, and religious circumstances and events.

The interplay between the political system and its environment is important because it reveals two important things about politics. First, political decisions and actions are greatly affected by the constraints and opportunities provided by the environment of the larger social system. The environment can control what it is possible and not possible to do in politics. For this reason it may be consequential whether a country's population is literate or illiterate, wealthy or poor, socially mobile or rigidly divided into classes. The environment can determine the resources that people are capable of bringing to politics and the subsequent influence they may have. But the second point is that while the environment may shape politics, it is also shaped by politics; the environment encompasses objects of political control, those aspects of life that people would like to govern and manage through politics, such as economic relationships, criminal behavior, or physical resources. Though the full range of this interaction between the system and its environment is an important matter of political inquiry, it is also such a large and expansive topic that it will have to suffice for our present purposes to enumerate examples of various environmental features, their consequences for politics, and the ways they may be affected by politics.

## Physical Features

Size, location, and natural resources are among the various physical features of a territory which are of potential political importance. Military security will be affected by such factors. Compared with, say, Great Britain, Germany's military needs and strategic thinking have been historically more affected by its land boundaries with the major powers to the east and west of it. Economic strength and independence will be affected by natural resources and are, in turn, of importance to the body politic. The size of a territory determines the reach that governmental organization will need to have and may explain why a federal arrangement may be developed to cope with this problem. Though such physical features as these may be so uncontrollable that the political system will merely have to live with them, the need to cope with the problems they raise and to exploit the advantages they offer makes them objects of political concern. The tendency of certain states to try to expand their boundaries and to create empires represents attempts to acquire more territory with its resources or at least access to greater resources. In a more commonplace way, governments have assumed responsibility for developing and thus altering the physical environment, as with roads, bridges, canals, in order to facilitate settlement and economic growth.

## Cultural Features

A variety of cultural features—language, customs, traditions, religious practices and beliefs, and perhaps even the elusive and controversial "national character"—may need to be explored for their political significance. The most apparent cultural consideration is whether the society is homogeneous or heterogeneous, that is, whether it contains commonly shared cultural patterns or encompasses very diverse cultural expressions. Where culture is very homogeneous we may expect to find that its values and beliefs are reflected in political values and decisions. For example, the predominant Catholicism of Italy helps explain the legal prohibition of divorce. Though this may seem quite understandable, the granting of political legitimacy to such cultural values becomes a real political problem in a society where such values are not universally accepted. The problem of *pluralistic* societies is one of the characteristic difficulties of the modern period. Cultural differences may lead to political strain if it is felt that such differences are the basis for prejudicial treatment by government. The feeling that one group is being treated unequally or unfairly by virtue of distinct ethnicity, language, or religious beliefs has been at the heart of many contemporary conflicts such as the struggles of Protestants and Catholics in Northern Ireland and French- and English-speaking citizens in Canada, and racial strife in the United States. One way government can react to these political strains is to try to take a position of neutrality between such groups. Though this may be an appropriate solution, it may not be as easy to do as it sounds. An attempt at neutrality or evenhandedness may not be very believable to those who have been treated unjustly in the past, and those who have been favored by earlier injustice may resist the new situation. Also, the very nature of political decisions may make it quite difficult to identify a position that will be recognized as neutral. In the United States, decisions *not* to have government entangled in any way in religious-affiliated private schools have often been interpreted by Catholics as an attack on their school system.

The United States has liked to think of itself historically as a culturally pluralistic and diverse society that has, for the most part, created original and effective political solutions to the strains involved. We should keep in mind, however, that the political difficulties relating to cultural pluralism are by no means limited to the United States and that they may be found in numerous modern nation-states. Thus, the problems of Asian minorities in certain African states, Ukrainians in the Soviet Union, Ibos in Nigeria, show that the question of minorities in the modern state is not a uniquely American concern.

## Social Features

Another aspect of the environment that may appear to be of even more direct relevance to the political system is the patterns of social life. Specifically we have in mind such considerations as whether a society is mainly rural or urban, the type of class structure that exists and the basis for class differences, how people make a living, and how occupations are organized. The different social situation of people may explain their different points of view or interests regarding the handling of public affairs. Differences in social class should be examined to find explanations for differences in people's political influence. Analysis of class and status in society has been one of the more prominent approaches to the study of politics and represents a cornerstone of one of the great political doctrines of our time—Marxism. The idea of class has also been taken over in political analysis to refer to a ruling class or ruling elite.

*Social class,* or social stratification as it is often called, simply means that various things that a society values—wealth, education, inherited position, religion—are unevenly distributed, resulting in a hierarchical ranking of people according to these differences.

The considerable emphasis put on social class in the study of politics derives from the fact that all modern societies exhibit significant and sometimes substantial differences among people as well as the fact that these differences affect both the amount of political influence people may have and the ways in which their lives will be affected by the actions of government. People, quite simply, do not enter the political arena as equals; indeed, their social circumstances may not allow them to enter it at all.

Though social stratification is a universal feature of the environment of politics, how this stratification is achieved and what it is based on will vary from one society to another. For example, one's place in society may be *ascribed,* determined by such factors as birth, or it may be *achieved,* determined by personal initiative. Ascribed social position is encountered in the case of hereditary aristocracy, where birth into the right family can give a person very high social position regardless of his own abilities or accomplishments, or in the case of racial discrimination. Achieved position, on the other hand, might be the result of a person's acquiring great wealth or developing a particular skill or talent.

Also important is the amount of *social mobility* in a society, that is, the degree to which people are able to move from one class to another. Though the United States still possesses a class structure, Americans would like to believe that class is based more on achievement within a society where there is a high degree of social mobility.

As was mentioned above, aspects of the environment not only affect politics but are affected by it, and the maintenance or transformation of the existing social stratification may be a critical political concern. Revolutionary regimes in the modern period have attempted to alter class structure dramatically in a short period of time, which explains why their political values are frequently dominated by professed faith in the worker and the common man—the lower classes in society. In much the same way the leadership of other political systems may be just as dedicated to preserving the particular social stratification that exists.

## Economic Features

Though closely related to social features, the production and distribution of wealth, the Gross National Product, and the type of economic base of society are worth mention as vital circumstances affecting politics. Such classical political concerns as equality and justice are commonly raised as problems of economic distribution. The humanly created material conditions of life in society invariably raise questions of public direction and control perhaps because the quality of life is at stake in such a fundamental way and because material resources are so closely tied to the wide range of needs and values that people pursue. We should realize, further, that the political importance of economic conditions is by no means limited to those political systems which believe in direct governmental management of the economy. What has been called "political economy" is critical to all types of systems; even in capitalism, the choice of achieving economic justice through the unregulated force of supply and demand must be understood as an important political commitment.

The relationship between politics and economics has been one of the more prominent areas of concern in modern political thought. Is economics such a vital factor in human life that it effectively determines political relationships? Should government manage and control all aspects of the economy? Should economic relationships, on the contrary, be allowed to develop freely with only minimal regulation by government? Such questions as these are very much at the heart of modern political conflict.

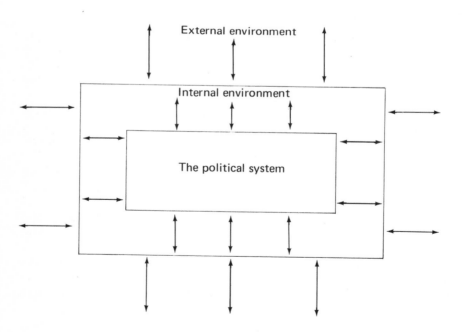

Figure 1-6  The System and its Environment

To this brief review of some of the environmental circumstances impinging on politics, it should be added that environmental factors can be distinguished according to whether they are internal or external to the society we are examining. By *internal* we simply mean those factors that are part of the larger social system; by *external* we mean those factors that impinge from outside the particular society being studied. For example, in studying the American political system, the amount of unemployment, inflation, and the Gross National Product in the American economy are part of the internal environment; whereas the availability of Middle Eastern oil, the international price of gold, and the strength of foreign currency comprise aspects of the external environment. The political system and its environment is portrayed in Figure 1–6. Just as the idea of a political system has been expressed in terms of a patterned relationship of certain elements or parts, so also the interaction between the political system and its environment assumes a certain definite shape or pattern that can be systematically studied. The arrows in the diagram point both ways to express the mutual interaction that takes place.

## CONNECTING ABSTRACTIONS AND REALITY

By this point, we cannot help but be impressed by the incredible generality and abstractness of such notions as "system" and "environment," and of how far all this seems from the particular features of concrete political experience. Yet for this very reason, the attempt to set the stage for our examination of politics reveals something very critical about the nature of political experience. Just as it is difficult to reflect upon the dimensions of the body politic in a way that can easily be grasped, it is equally true that modern politics in many ways lacks human scale. The individual is part of a massive and distant network of relationships, the effects of which he continually encounters but the dimensions of which are difficult to comprehend and, by necessity, are often condensed into abstract terms that may hide the intricacy of the reality they are intended to describe. Yet we do pay taxes to that distant government, we do identify with that nation and give voice to its political values in more pervasive ways than we might think, and many have gone to their death in defense of the state. The ability to grasp the significance of our immediate political experience is thus bound up with the ability to reach beyond that experience.

The difficulty in handling the idea of the political system may be a good omen as well as a frustrating problem. We have tried to observe along the way that the matters we are discussing often appear as issues in actual political conflicts and disputes. Nationhood, cultural homogeneity, the boundaries of the state, may all at one time or another be of political concern. Yet it is also true that these matters are not central to ordinary politics as we know it; elections are held, laws made, taxes collected without our being called upon to ponder the definition of the body politic and its environment. This is probably a good sign, for to the extent that the identities of the state and nation become central political concerns, politics tends to take on its worst features of instability, war, and violence. It would not be easy for a stable, peaceful political system to endure where there are deep-seated disagreements or ambiguities about its integrity as a system. Most of the wars and violent political struggles of recent years—whether the crisis in Northern Ireland, the Nigerian civil war, the Vietnam war, or the unrelenting conflict in the Middle East—have their roots in political conflict over the very identity of the political system. What are its boundaries? Who really belongs to it? Who holds allegiance to it? Is it a coherent nation? Is it an effective state? From the display of political hatred and violence stirred by such issues, we should feel fortunate if the same issues appear to us, with our relatively stable national system in the United States, as technical and abstract concerns.

Such observations do not eliminate the ponderous gap between the abstract scale of the political system and its environment on the one hand, and the range of concrete events and experiences on the other. One important connecting link, however, is *history*. To this point we have been talking about the political system, its traits, boundaries, and environment, without any reference to history, to the growth and development of the body politic over time. The notion of "nation-state" as a type of community makes little inherent sense until we appreciate how history reveals to us actual growth of the nationalistic outlook which has so decidedly sorted the world into French, Chinese, Argentinians, and so on. The notion of "economic environment" is also coldly analytical until we reflect on the periodic waves of economic expansion and depression and the conflict of rich and poor classes and rich and poor nations that have dominated political history. The concept of "political association" is again a bit impenetrable until we consider the rise and fall and evolution of governments and constitutions that have given birth to the particular structures we find in use today. Precisely because the idea of the political system goes beyond our immediate experience, we must look to history to uncover its practical meaning. It is the history of the body politic which must be added in to fully set the stage for our investigation.

## SUMMARY

Our purpose in this initial chapter has been to identify, in general terms, the setting in which political experience occurs. Politics brings its share of surprises, but it is not a totally spontaneous act of relationships or events and it is very much concerned with order. Thus, it is not inappropriate to begin examining politics by reflecting upon the most basic features of the political order that surrounds us. This has led naturally to a consideration of the systems and subsystems around which man's political life is organized and his political identity established. The phenomena of political community, association, and jurisdiction can be used to give somewhat more tangible reality to the idea of the political system. The internal and external environment rounds out this picture to its fullest dimensions. The next task is to return to the activity of politics itself, to fill the stage we have set with actors and plots. To pick apart the inner workings of the political system, attention will be turned in the next chapter to the human activity, roles, and relationships that characterize political experience and allow us to gain an understanding of it.

## NOTES

[1]David Easton, *A Framework for Political Analysis* (Englewood Cliffs, N.J., 1965).

[2]Dankwart A. Rustow, *A World of Nations* (Washington, D.C., 1967), pp. 284–86.

[3]Interview with Senator Paul Laxalt, "Meet the Press" 20, no. 20 (Washington, D.C., 1976): 5–6.

[4]John Dewey, *The Public and Its Problems* (New York, 1927), p. 185.

## FOR FURTHER READING

Crick, Bernard. *In Defence of Politics.* Baltimore, Md.: Penguin Books, 1964. An interesting, readable exploration of the nature of politics.

Dewey, John. *The Public and Its Problems.* Chicago: Swallow Press, 1927. A classical analysis which sees the roots of political experience in the existence of the public. Explores the relationship between political association and community.

Easton, David. *The Political System,* 2d ed. New York: Alfred A. Knopf, 1971. A sophisticated treatment of the nature of politics, the approach of systems theory, and the task of political science. Develops the idea of politics as "an authoritative allocation of values for society."

Morgenthau, Hans J. *Politics Among Nations,* 3d ed. New York: Alfred A. Knopf, 1960. A classic work that has done much to shape contemporary thinking about the workings of international politics.

Rustow, Dankwart A. *A World of Nations.* Washington, D.C.: The Brookings Institution, 1967. An overview of the dynamic forces shaping the contemporary system of nation-states, focusing on the problem of modernization in underdeveloped societies.

# 2

# Politics and Human Relationships

The study of politics, as we know, leads us into the study of large institutions and complex organizations, of constitutions and laws, and of the intricate workings of national systems. At the bottom of all this, however, is the fact that politics is a form of interaction among people directed toward the management of public affairs. The consideraion of politics in its most basic form—as human behavior, activity, and relationships—provides an appropriate next step to our study of politics. Within the body politic that we have described, what roles do people play? How do they behave? What does political conduct look like? We might think of this set of questions in this way: where we see political events going on—at a political convention, during an election, in the United States Congress, or at the United Nations—what are people doing and how are they relating to each other that makes their behavior so characteristically political?

A couple of fundamental observations will help in studying political behavior. First, even the most cursory look at political life reveals considerable variety in political behavior. Not all people are engaged in politics in the same way, to the same extent, or with equal success. People do not all know the same things, have the same objectives or beliefs, or have similar levels of interest. It is this variety which must be examined and which provides the dynamic element of politics; indeed, some may argue that it is this variety which makes politics necessary. The second observation is that political behavior is not random; political activity is not a haphazard jumble of events. There is a certain predictable and patterned aspect to political behavior, just as there is to human behavior generally. This does not mean that human behavior is as regular and predictable as the boiling point of water or the movement of the planets—man is not a machine. But there is sufficient order and pattern to behavior that we can generalize and make predictions.

## THE IDEA OF POLITICAL ROLES

There are several ways we can begin to study the various patterns of political activity, and the purpose of the present discussion will be to introduce some of the more basic ones. One type of pattern is found in the *roles* people play. By role we simply mean the behavior expected of a person as a result of his position in society. The idea of roles is widely used by sociologists, as in talking about one's role as a parent or employer or student; what we wish to look at are roles peculiar to political relationships. Two observations can be made about roles before turning to specific types. First, any particular individual most likely plays several roles, and we can thus speak of a person's "role set." Several years ago the political scientist Clinton Rossiter identified several different roles that the president of the United States plays (hats that he wears, as Rossiter called them) including commander in chief of the armed forces, chief diplomat, head of his party, and chief legislator.[1] Second, the existence of a role set creates the possibility of "role conflict" through contradictory demands placed on an individual by virtue of different roles he or she plays.

In order to see the importance of this in politics, consider the following example: Imagine that you are on a committee in an organization which distributes funds for various projects proposed by the members and that a close friend of yours puts in a proposal which is very weak and poorly prepared. You may feel inclined to support his proposal because of friendship, for the "friend" role involves being helpful and supportive; yet you recognize the weakness of the proposal and in your role as "officer of the organization" you recognize an obligation to serve its purposes in the best way possible. Your two roles are in conflict. Role conflict can be quite significant in politics since one of the major tensions in public life is between private interests and public responsibilities, something more familiarly known as conflict of interest. The study of how people cope with such conflicts would draw us deeply into psychology, but one political technique for handling the problem is to remove the significance of one of the roles. This is why in the United States it has become common practice to ask people who assume major positions in government to abandon their ties to corporations or institutions doing business with the government. Thus, the ideas of role set and role conflict should be kept in mind in studying various political roles.

## Subject

What sort of political roles do people play? If it is useful to begin by looking at very general and basic political roles, one could hardly find a more appropriate starting point than the role of subject. The most widespread experience with politics occurs through being subject to the jurisdiction and laws of the state by virtue of the simple fact that political decisions and actions govern various aspects of our lives. As with any role, there are certain expectations about how people will behave, and for subjects these expectations consist of obedience to the rules and directives of government such as the paying of taxes, military service, and licensing of vehicles. The subject role does not appear critical to the making of public decisions, but it is still the most universal role in politics. Though it had been thought at one time that the king was above the law, the modern idea of "rule under law" means that *all* are subjects, even including presidents and prime ministers. The notion that certain top political figures are not effectively subject to laws is typically associated with dictatorship or arbitrary rule of some sort. The other interesting feature of subjects is that one does not have to be in any way a recognized member of the body politic to be subject to it. Those who have lived in foreign countries are well aware of being subject to foreign governments in certain respects, and not being a good subject can lead to expulsion or punishment.

The exact expectations placed upon subjects will vary according to the character of the political system (indeed, we will see that this is true of political roles in general). These expectations may range from the minimal demand for abiding the law to the demand that all subjects publicly express support for very specific political doctrines, such as the expectation in the People's Republic of China that people will be dedicated to "Mao's thoughts." Whatever the expectations, this role is clearly one of the most widespread in any political system, particularly since it is acquired in an essentially passive way. One does not have to do much to become a subject, and for many people it is simply a question of living under a political jurisdiction by accident of birth and not by choice. Also, for many people, even in political systems that are considered democratic, political experience may be summed up in their role as subject; we may say that such people are *mere* subjects.

While the top political leaders at certain times have tried to divorce themselves from the responsibilities of being subjects by thinking of themselves as above the law, the subject role may also be questioned and resisted from below. The political rebel or revolutionary challenges the legitimacy of the expectations put on subjects. Such challenges also may be related to role conflict, as when a person's moral conscience collides with the demands of government. This has been the experience of pacifists whose moral views do not allow for participation in the military and this has caused them to seriously evaluate their role as subjects.

## Citizen

Another common and fairly general political role is that of citizen. This role is not easy to define broadly since the practical significance of being a citizen may vary greatly from one system to another. In the broadest sense citizenship refers to officially recognized membership in a political association and thus necessarily involves something more than being a mere subject (for a subject need not be a citizen). Official membership suggests an allegiance of the individual to the state and an entitlement to certain privileges of which the most basic is the security and protection offered by the state. Expansion of the rights and privileges of citizens has been one of the historical objectives of certain systems (such as our own) throughout history, and the result has been that citizenship may carry with it, for example, the right to vote, to criticize the government, to petition one's grievances. In such systems formal privileges of citizenship often imply expectations about appropriate behavior of citizens—for example, not only *may* you vote, but you *should* vote. Aside from privileges, citizenship suggests responsibilities that may go beyond those of a subject—in addition to obeying the law, upholding, supporting, and defending it.

For most people the citizen role, seen as official membership, is acquired in a passive way—we become citizens by birth. Yet becoming a citizen or even giving up one's citizenship may be the result of specific actions of the individual or state involved. One can become a naturalized citizen of the United States by meeting certain legally defined requirements and taking an oath of allegiance. On the other hand, there may be provisions recognized by the state for renouncing one's citizenship as well as those allowing the state to remove citizenship from people. In addition to these formal rules, there are a number of less formal expectations of good citizenship, met not in a passive way but by the activity of the citizen. In democratic societies this consideration is particularly important, for the citizen role may be a function of the individual's tendency and ability to engage in political activity.

## Political Actor

The roles of subject and citizen are basic, widespread, and familiar but they are not usually central to what goes on in politics. When we talk about key political roles, we are necessarily talking about a much smaller number of people. Even in those societies considered the most democratic, only a narrow segment of the population is regularly engaged in political activity. We can speak of the *political actor* as one who displays an active concern with public affairs or, more concretely, who attempts to influence the outcome of public decisions, whether or not he is successful. Though loosely defined, the category of political actors seldom accounts for more than a minority of citizens. The expectations associated with this role include such things as joining a political organization or party, attending political meetings and rallies, discussing politics with fellow citizens, donating money to a candidate, working in an election campaign. In studying American political participation, one political scientist has summarized the situation in this way:

> Only about 4 or 5 percent are active in a party, campaign, and attend meetings. About 10 percent make monetary contributions, about 13 percent contact public officials, and about 15 percent display a button or sticker. Around 25 to 30 percent try to proselyte others to vote a certain way, and from 40 to 70 percent perceive political messages and vote in any given election.[2]

What accounts for the fact that certain citizens become political actors and others do not? As a result of our own political experience in America, we are inclined to think that the role of political actor is adopted voluntarily, that is, that people are interested and active in politics because they want to be. Political activity may be engaged in as a result of individual interests, drives, and motivations, but it may also result from involuntary factors. In many societies throughout history people have been recognized as members of a particular social class merely by being born into it, and the tradition of these societies included expectations that members of the upper class would assume responsibility for political involvement and explicitly exclude those from lower classes. Our society has a less rigid class structure and is guided by the belief that power and influence will result from personal effort and achievement, not from accident of birth; but even here there are a number of constraints and limitations which will affect the inclination or ability of people to become engaged in the political process. Being interested and involved in politics means being active, and activity suggests effort, which, in turn, suggests the use of time, energy, and various kinds of resources and skills. Helping in a political campaign assumes a certain amount of information about the candidates for public office and the positions on issues that distinguish them, access to the sources of such information (newspapers, TV) and the time taken to use them, time and energy to seek out and contact the campaign organization, and the time and energy to actually work for the organization in some capacity. To the extent that political activity requires material resources and effort, it means that the individual must possess these resources and must be willing to channel them into political activity rather than into some other pursuit, such as his or her education, professional advancement, or recreation. Beyond material resources there are other considerations, such as personal abilities and skills. To help on a political campaign, the individual may need to have a certain amount of self-confidence in dealing with people and a certain grasp of how an organization of this type works; he will have to be literate and articulate. Not only must our political actor have the necessary skills and resources but also the inclination to use them and the belief that there is something of value to be gained. Every degree of participation has such corresponding constraints, whether it be the minimal literacy required to read a ballot, or the time, money, and social standing to run for an important public office. Thus, clearly we must take into account both voluntary and involuntary factors that determine people's political activity. (The ancient Greek philosopher Aristotle appreciated the importance of political resources enough to offer a clever suggestion for encouraging the citizens' attendance at popular assemblies. He proposed that if poor people were paid to attend and rich people were fined for not attending, the situation would be much more equitable.)[3]

These various considerations lead into a set of questions vital to political scientists: Who is active in politics and who is not? Why do people become politically active? What percentage of the population is active and what explains this? Is the activity intense or relatively mild? Furthermore, what some of these questions reveal is the importance of what was discussed in the previous chapter, that is, the effect of the environment on the performance of the political system. How is the level of political activity related to the amount of literacy, the distribution of wealth, or the social class structure in a particular society?

In thinking about the broad category of political actors it should also be kept in mind that activity may be either supportive of the existing political system or in opposition to it. Supportive activity operates within accepted rules of politics and law and employs means which are considered legitimate. Political rebellion or dissent, which may be a very significant form of political activity, involves an attack on accepted rules and institutions or employs means generally condemned as illegitimate. Political activity is not merely that conduct which is thought acceptable.

## Political Elite

Our observations about political activity naturally lead to another consideration—of those who are active some will be successful in pursuing political objectives and some will not. We are concerned not merely with who is active in politics but with who is effective; who has power, influence, authority; who controls decisions; who makes things happen. These considerations shift attention from the political actor to the political elite. The role of the elite brings us closer and closer to more vital political roles and, not surprisingly, a considerable amount of political analysis deals with the roles and behavior of elites. This requires making careful distinctions among different levels or strata of the elite according to who is more or less powerful. It leads to the study of such particular individuals or groups as mayors, labor union leaders, legislative bodies, courts, political party leaders, dictators.

The acquiring of an elite role may be explained by extending many of the same considerations regarding political actors. Constraints, resources, personal ambition, and desire will also play a role, but indeed a much larger one. In addition, many personal qualities of the individual will need to be taken into account to understand political leadership. The exercise of influence requires not only the right resources and the right situation but the ability to use them in an effective way. The study of political elites gets to one of the most fundamental questions of political science: Who rules?

## Public Official

Finally, we should mention official roles played by those who hold public office. In this case the expectations associated with the role are quite formal and involve the powers and duties associated with the official position. The official is a subject of laws perhaps in an even more strenuous way than the nonofficial; he is a citizen of the state, but he need not be a political actor or leader. The reason for this last observation is that public office encompasses everyone from a prime minister or a president to the most minor governmental clerk. The whole range of public offices relates to politics in that it involves people doing the public's business (or at least that is what they should be doing), but while top officials may represent critical political actors and leaders, numerous lower officials will merely be involved in the machinery of administering the public's business.

Officials' roles in a stable governmental situation are filled by some formal, accepted process, and there have been a wide variety of such processes in history. Such a process may consist of election, and this may be by the citizenry at large, by "popular election," or by some narrower body of electors. Appointment of one individual by another already in official position is a widespread and necessary method of filling the varied offices of government. Heredity has also been used to fill offices, as with hereditary monarchy, in which the child of a king becomes the future monarch. In instances of political instability we cannot ignore the fact that public offices are acquired by force, as when leaders of a rebellion or revolution become governmental leaders upon successfully overthrowing established officials.

## THE MULTIPLICITY OF ROLES

This discussion of political roles has led to the identification of five basic types: citizen, subject, actor, elite, and official. There are various combinations of these roles; indeed, we find substantial overlap among them mainly because they are such general roles. Analysis of political behavior, however, ordinarily deals with much more specific roles, depending upon the exact situation or event being examined. Even the "elite," though it constitutes only a small fraction of the population, still encompasses a large number of significant political actors without distinguishing carefully among them. But since our main purpose here is not to study every conceivable political role but to familiarize ourselves with the idea, some brief examples may help you appreciate what the multiplicity of more specific roles might look like (see Figure 2–1).

If we were studying the behavior of a group of legislators, we might find that some of them consistently advocated the point of view of some interest group; we might find others always concerned with trying to get all the members of their own political party in the legislature to vote the same way; yet another group of lawmakers might vote mainly on the basis of a careful sampling of the opinion of the voters who elected them. All of these people are officials and they may all be regarded as elites, yet their particular behavior reveals different expectations about their jobs. These differences imply different roles. Some are acting as "interest-group advocates," others as "party men" or "constituency

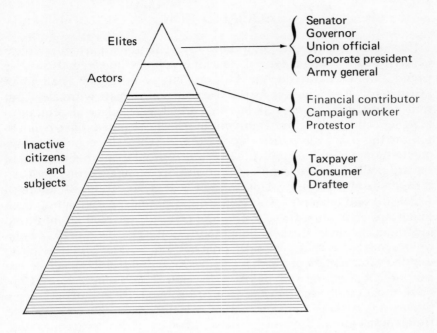

**Figure 2-1  The Variety of Political Roles**

delegates." Even this represents only a fraction of the complex role structure that might be found in a modern legislature.[4]

Let us say we are studying the top executive officers, or "cabinet," of a particular government. To begin with, they all have different official roles because they are each running different parts of the government and performing different duties. In addition, imagine that some cabinet members are old political friends of the prime minister, whereas others do not know him at all on a personal basis. Further imagine that some cabinet members feel that their proper role is continually to make dramatic suggestions for new policies and decisions and vigorously try to advance them within the group, whereas others prefer sitting back and sensing the mood of the prime minister and the whole cabinet before committing themselves to a position. In order to study how such a group makes decisions, it will be important to take account of what is actually a complex network of roles including the roles of old friend, head of a major department, vocal advocate, and so on. Thus, beyond the general roles described here, there is a multiplicity of specific ones encountered in the analysis of specific political situations.

## SOCIALIZATION

How is it that people know how to act in their particular roles? Clearly, there is some type of learning process involved. How else would I know what to do as a voter or a city councilman? The type of learning involved is not the formal learning we associate with school but rather an informal process of learning which takes place all around us in society and occurs throughout our life. Social scientists have come to refer to this process as *political socialization,* which, in technical terms, means the way in which individuals acquire orientatious (beliefs, values) toward politics and government. Put in more familiar terms, we learn through experience and adapt, to some extent, to various situations in which we find ourselves. The young adult has heard that voting is an important civic duty, that "every vote counts," and that an informed judgment should be made in going to the polls. These views have been reinforced by parents, friends, political candidates, and the civic-minded commentary of the mass media. An individual so socialized has learned about voting and, in effect, learned about being a voter. Consider also an individual elected to a city council. He will experience a process of learning the behavior of a councilman, the customs and rituals of the group, the way one does and does not deal with colleagues, the expectations for one now in the public eye. Our new councilman has adapted his behavior; he has learned about being a public official.

Socialization can occur throughout our lives and will be particularly prominent when we find ourselves in new situations—for example, taking a new job or moving to a different city. Nonetheless, socialization tends to be most important in the early years of life because it is then that there is so much to learn and that so many basic orientations toward politics in general are established. What do children learn? From school, parents, and the culture generally, American children begin to learn that there is someone called the president and the mayor who are perceived as benevolent, helpful figures. Later they may begin to identify different political parties and even ideological labels.[5] As this type of learning proceeds, children gradually develop more and more elaborate orientations toward the surrounding political environment. They are being socialized.

The process of socialization may become a matter of considerable political concern. As described here, the process appears natural, spontaneous, and lacking in conscious control; yet politics itself is profoundly concerned with control and social order, and inevitably ruling groups throughout history have taken an active interest in consciously influencing the ways in which people adapt to politics and the political orientations they acquire. In the present People's Republic of China it is hardly left to chance whether young children will respect the thoughts of Mao and gain a keen awareness of their duties to the state. It is the explicit purpose of Chinese social and educational institutions to insure "proper" socialization. The process of political learning, we might say, has become a matter of public policy and governmental action. This type of socialization might be called, more accurately, indoctrination.

Western democracies presumably reject this type of indoctrination by stressing the value of free speech, tolerance of diverse political views, and the primary responsibilities of parents in raising children. Yet even democracies hardly leave socialization to pure chance, for they must be attentive to the acceptance and promotion of those very democratic values that sustain freedom and tolerance. Thus, even here we will find an active concern for proper socialization expressed through such practices as good-citizenship awards in school, frequent recitation of the oath of allegiance, and playing of the national anthem. Indeed, in American school districts it is normal for the promotion of civic virtues and values to be cited as an explicit goal of the educational program.

Socialization is also vital to understanding politics because of the substantial problems that may derive from inadequate socialization. This is particularly relevant for political systems experiencing instability or change. What will happen to a system in which the predominant political orientations of most of the people are inconsistent with existing political arrangements and governmental structures? Will there be political conflict, weakness in people's support for government, inefficiency, disorder? Imagine the introduction of a liberal, democratic constitution into a society with a tradition of strong, centralized political rule with little political liberty. The people would expect a kind of direction and order from government that would not be provided, and the government might expect patterns of responsible, active participation in politics and tolerance of competing views which would not occur. It may be argued that something very much like this occurred in Germany after World War I, when the Allied powers imposed on Germany a very open, democratic constitutional structure even though German society and culture had been shaped by the experiences of more hierarchical and authoritarian social and political relationships. Among the various factors that contributed to the instability of Germany during the 1920s must be listed the incongruity between earlier patterns of socialization and the existing formal structure of government.

What this discussion of socialization should also reveal is the importance of a point made earlier—that the political system is affected by the general culture. In the general culture, will people be raised to believe that they should have a hand in public affairs and speak freely about their government or feel that they should be told what to do by more important, intelligent people and not discuss political matters for fear of saying the wrong thing?

## AGREEMENT AND INFLUENCE

Politics, as we have seen, concerns people dealing with their common affairs and concerns, those matters that have an impact on their living together. The art of politics, therefore, is concerned with giving direction to a group, of identifying common courses of action and pursuing common purposes. This, in turn, suggests that politics requires some degree of agreement or consensus for successful political direction to occur. In theory, society can try to proceed on the basis of voluntary and spontaneous political agreement, and the prospect of such agreement may be aided by widely shared customs, traditions, and habits. Yet we are drawn back to the fundamental fact that political objectives and ends are inevitably the source of human conflict and struggle, indeed the very purpose for the art of politics in human relationships is not to give expression to voluntary agreement but to manage the ceaseless competition over values and goals. This fact suggests two vital characteristics of political relationships. First, political direction and purpose result primarily from the influence of some people over other people, influence which may be exerted in a wide variety of ways. In other words, some consensus or common basis for action in a group has to be created and is created through political influence. Second, the basis for common action that is achieved necessarily will be partial and incomplete, at least in the long run. Complete and permanent unity in politics cannot be achieved, and it is inappropriate to try to achieve it. The art of politics is very much the art of finding solutions to human conflict that are less than perfect but nonetheless practical in meeting the political needs of people. Thus, the study of the behavior of people in politics naturally leads to an examination of the ways in which they influence each other in their political dealings and thereby produce practical, if not permanent, decisions and actions.

## POWER

The term *influence* describes a kind of relationship that occurs among people. The simplest and perhaps most widely accepted definition of influence describes it as a relationship which consists of one person getting another person to do something he would not otherwise do.[6] A parent strenuously encourages a child to eat his food and the child does so; a mugger points a gun at you and you hand over your wallet; you vote for a particular candidate because of the convincing arguments of a friend. Take away the parent, the mugger, and the friend, and the presumption is that the child would not eat, you would not hand over your wallet, and you would vote for a different candidate.

Influence is a very general concept, but there are different types of influence depending on the means used to get a person to comply. Terms such as *power, force* or *coercion* indicate the exertion of influence through control over a person's access to things that he or she values (as in the case of the mugger). Power relationships can be understood by analyzing key elements, such as the values that are being controlled and the resources used to control them. Consider, for example, an employer's ability to determine whether an employee continues his job, a policeman's ability to impose punishment on someone he finds breaking the law, or a union leader's ability to deliver a collection of votes to a particular candidate for office. In each instance the person who is being coerced places a value on something: his job, freedom from fine or imprisonment, or the votes that will win an election. Thus, this method of influence builds on human values, and the values at stake may include not only such basic considerations as self-preservation, security, and wealth but also less tangible values such as respect, self-esteem, and happiness. When one person is able to control another's ability to enjoy these values, he then has the capacity to exercise power over him. The employer can control the job, the policeman can control one's freedom, and the union leader can control the votes. Where values are extraordinarily vital, as in the case of a direct and credible threat to one's life, the power relationship may be thought of as a case of coercion, force, or violence. The other part of the analysis of these power relationships is the explanation of a person's control over these values. The thing to be looked for here are the *resources* of the powerful person which provide this control; these may include a person's wealth, social position, education, or strength. Power requires the possession of resources.

Perhaps the most frequent misconception about power is the notion that it is a kind of commodity, something you can accumulate and store up to use whenever you like. This is the connotation in saying that someone has a great deal of power; it is as if we are saying he has a great deal of money. Power is not a commodity like money but rather it is a type of *relationship* among people. For this reason, the ability to exercise power is relative to particular contexts, to particular sets of relationships. As these relationships change, the relevant values or resources change, and consequently one's power changes. For example, you may be quite wealthy and your money may provide you with economic power in the marketplace, but when you go to college you find that (assuming you cannot bribe your instructor) your money is of little use in getting good grades. It seems that intelligence (possibly aided by a bit of flattery) is much more influential in getting good grades. Consider also the case of the husband and father who at home is the king of his castle (assuming this is one of those old traditional homes) but at work is the lowest-ranking person in the factory. His influence changes dramatically with the change in context. In other words, if we look at power as relative and contextual, a whole host of questions become important in understanding it: Whom is the power exercised over? Which values can be controlled? What resources does one have that can be applied? Under what circumstances can the power be used?

The idea that power is not tangible but is a relationship shows that the analysis of power is much more complex than we might have suspected. Perhaps nothing reveals this more than the attempt to answer the one question about power that has intrigued political scientists more than any other: How do we know that one person has more or less power than another, that is, how can we measure power? There are pitfalls even to what would appear to be simple or obvious ways of answering this question. If one person can influence a greater number of people than another person, we might be prepared to say that he has more power; that is, the ability to influence 1000 people indicates more power than the ability to influence 10 people. However, what if the 1000 are ordinary voters and the 10 are, say, the department heads in a municipal government; influence over the 10 officials would translate into considerably greater political power. It may also be thought that the amount of influence is greater if the amount of change that can be induced in another increases. If I can get my father to lend me $100, my influence is greater than if I can only get a $5 loan. Here even we encounter one of the messier problems in talking about power: How do we reliably identify this change that the person being influenced supposedly undergoes? The following example shows the problem.

If I am squabbling with a salesman over the price of a used car, it may be fair to measure the influence of my bargaining by reference to how much I can get the salesman to reduce the price of the car from his original stated price. But we are all familiar with the practice of a seller setting an initial price high in order to create bargaining room, and this means that the effective measurement of influence must take into account an individual's real attachment to a particular position he takes. The problem results from the fact that it is in a person's interest not to reveal his or her real position. Though a seller, for example, feels a need to get $100 for his product, it may serve his interest to make possible buyers believe he must get $150. In this way he may bargain away $50 and still get the price he needs, and the buyer's influence in lowering the price could not be said to actually be as great as it would have been if the seller had really felt a need to get a price of $150. Indeed, if you went into the situation really wanting to pay no more than $90, but settled for the price of $100, we have a situation in which it appears you got the better deal, when, in fact, the salesman technically got the better deal if all of the conditions of our example hold true. Who influenced whom?

This example resembles yet a broader problem in discussing power. When someone claims that something has happened as a result of his influence, it begs the question of whether or not the event would have occurred had he done nothing at all. To make the point with an absurdity, imagine the fellow who rises in the dark of morning and orders the sun to come up, and sure enough it does! Though his claim to mystical powers might make us question his sanity, more commonplace versions of the same principle occur in politics all the time, except that it is more difficult to test the claim of power. A public official wins an election after being endorsed by a local newspaper, but would he or she have won without the endorsement? A diplomat threatens military action and extracts a settlement from another country, but could the settlement have come without the threat? The point of these remarks is to show that the specific measurement of one person's power over others is much more complex than it appears on the surface, but the best way to avoid these pitfalls and to appraise power sensibly is to keep in mind that power is a characteristic of human relationships and is relative to the context of those relationships.

We are, of course, interested in knowing not only what power is but how it is used. In analyzing power we must watch for the difference between *potential* power and *actual* power. In the case of potential power, the conditions and resources for power are available but there is little or no interest or willingness to employ power; when power is used we can then refer to actual power. Wealthy people are not politically powerful simply because they are wealthy; rather it is a question of how and when they use their wealth as a political resource. If their wealth itself is threatened through proposed new tax laws or regulation of the source of their wealth, an interest in and willingness to use political power may appear, though they might not exercise their influence on a totally different set of public issues. So also the citizen in a democratic society does not have power because of the right to vote, but only because the right is exercised. What all of this means is that often it will be the case that the actual power of individuals or groups in a political system may be noticeably less than their potential power, and this will result from the level of concern they have for public affairs and the extent to which their interest in politics competes with family, job, religion, hobbies, and the variety of other concerns in their life.

There is an ironic quality to the use of power. Often the greatest effectiveness is achieved by threatening to use power rather than by actually using it. The threat to use power is itself a form of power in that it may be sufficient to gain the compliance of the other person, such as when the parent says to the child, "If you don't eat your dinner, you can't watch television," or a civic leader says to a legislator, "Vote against this bill or I won't support you in the next election." What is interesting here is that in certain circumstances the threat accomplishes something that would not be accomplished if it had to be carried through. Thus, if the legislator ignores the threat and votes for the bill, the civic leader's withdrawal of future support still does not accomplish what he wanted, that is, opposition to the bill. This explains why so much importance is placed on how credible or believable it is that the threat to use power will be carried out. Even if the legislator considers the political support (the thing he values that is being controlled by another) important, if he happens to believe that the threat will not be carried out, it will lessen its influence over him. There is another aspect to this irony. The actual use of power involves literally using up resources of power that cannot be used again; thus, if the civic leader carries through on his threat, he may weaken his own ability to exert influence in the future. Indeed, the need to carry through on a power threat may be viewed as a sign of weakness as much as a show of strength. When police have to be called in to subdue a riot, it can be taken as a display of the power of government in maintaining order, but it may also be taken as a symptom of the inadequacy of other less severe and destructive means for maintaining order.

The purpose behind these various observations concerning the use of power in human relationships is to dispel a frequent misconception about the behavior of powerful people and powerful governments. We may be inclined to think that power is always expressed through giving commands, heavy-handed threats, and the capricious use of physical force. Our stereotype of personal power may be contained in the image of Adolph Hitler or the town thug. Yet power in general is more complex than that, and political power is acquired and enhanced by those who know enough to use power in resourceful and subtle ways, who know that squandering their influence may be as bad as not using it at all, who know that power may be most effective when it is not apparent immediately that it is even being applied.

As observers of politics we are interested in the general phenomenon of power because it enters politics as a factor in the making of public decisions. The use of the vote, economic reprisals, the boycott or strike, or, on an illegal level, the bribe, all represent ways in which public decisions are affected by power. Power relationships may burst forth dramatically and violently where dispute and conflict become the occasion for physical struggle such as internal rebellion or civil war (as we have seen in recent years in Northern Ireland, Angola, and Rhodesia). Whether in its more subtle and controlled form or in its more coercive form, there are generous examples of the use of power in political experience, a fact which is critical in trying to understand political behavior. But there is another important way in which power is of interest in the study of politics, for one of the prime characteristics of all governments is that they are allowed to use instruments of power that would not be allowed or available to the private citizen. Governments organize military forces for both external (armies) and internal (police) application and administration of laws and policies. Through these instruments of force, governments engage in taking people's property, jailing people, and killing people, through war and by means of capital punishment. In order to do this government has been said to exert a "monopoly" over the tools of coercion and violence. This has been such a sufficiently disturbing aspect of government that it has led numerous political thinkers to condemn the very existence of government as illegitimate—these thinkers are called *anarchists*—and other thinkers to propose schemes of government in which this coercive element is as limited and controlled as possible. Though these latter thinkers have had some historical success in limiting and harnessing governmental coercion, the universal character of this coercive element cannot be ignored. Governments, indeed, do control some of the most basic values of life including life itself.

## POLITICAL AUTHORITY

We have examined power as a common way in which people influence each other and thereby advance certain political objectives or goals, but there are other ways in which influence occurs and one that is extremely central to politics is *authority*. What is distinctive in an authority relationship is that people are not only influenced by others but they treat this influence as something which they ought to accept; they see the influence as rightful or legitimate. Indeed, the very acceptance of this influence is precisely what allows it to work. The orders of a judge, policeman, or public official are something we may obey not only or primarily because of their ability to force us but because we think of them as possessing a right to tell us what to do. If we reflect a bit on this general idea of authority, it should be apparent that all political order rests on some authority and that it would be difficult to imagine a durable government at all which was not recognized as having some right to rule. Perhaps a prison is as close as we could come to such a system.

In studying authority we should note that it has two aspects, *informal* and *formal* authority. Informal authority refers to authority which is possessed by an individual as a result of some personal qualities, recognition, or achievement. It may be said, for example, that Ralph Nader is an authority on consumer affairs. We presumably mean by this that not only does Nader influence us on consumer issues but that we accept his influence, seek out the direction he gives, and consider it right that we take his advice. Now in a case like this, of course, Nader holds no office that gives him such authority, nor is he invoking any law requiring us to follow his advice; rather he exercises influence purely because of who he is and what he has done. If he is an authority on the topic, it is purely because of something about him as a person. This informal aspect of authority must be taken into account in politics, for it is clearly the means by which certain political leaders wield great political influence. In the case of a Franklin D. Roosevelt or a Gandhi or a Napoleon, we must look to the aspect of informal personal authority to explain their great influence.

In contrast, the *formal* aspect of authority refers to instances in which authority is felt to reside in certain principles, laws, and official institutions—the source of authority is impersonal. It is in this sense that people recognize that constitutions and statutes, the Catholic church, the offices of president, governor, or prime minister, possess authority. Presumably this authority is an attribute of the office itself or the written law or tradition, not of the individual person who holds the office or enforces the law. Thus, a policeman possesses authority not because of who he is as an individual but because of the sworn duty he has and the badge which symbolizes it. One of the features of formal authority is the use of symbols as a way of indicating that the authority is being used—the policeman's badge, the judge's robes, the bureaucrat's official stamps and seals, oaths of office. It is this formal aspect of authority that people frequently have in mind in appraising public acts. Was an individual properly empowered by law to do what he did? Was his order or decision pursuant to his public duties? Did he have the right?

Both the formal and informal aspects of authority are important in politics and often closely connected in actual experience, sometimes so closely that it is difficult to separate the influence of a president or prime minister that derives from the office he holds from that which derives from the personal support he has among the people. One way these two aspects of authority are relevant to the study of politics is that they can be used to compare different political systems according to whether formal or informal authority is predominant. The fascist dictatorships of Adolph Hitler in Germany and Benito Mussolini in Italy represented instances of extreme dependence on informal or personal authority of the single leader. In contrast, the United States has developed a tradition of "rule of law," in which the authority of formal institutions, offices, and processes is stressed. The reason societies develop structures of formal authority is so that governmental order does not depend exclusively on the leadership of one person or a group of persons; formal authority serves to establish principles and rules which will outlive one generation and bind future generations of political leaders. Informal authority is important because it provides immediate direction and leadership for the solution of immediate problems and thereby represents the active and dynamic element of political authority. Though both aspects of authority are inevitable and natural parts of political experience, dangers can arise if one is exaggerated over the other. An excessive dependence on personal authority, as seen in the case of dictatorship, often generates arbitrary, capricious decisions and fails to provide a strong foundation for governmental authority when the dictator is gone. It may even be the case that no process is agreed upon for even selecting a successor and, as with the disturbances following the death of Mao Tse-tung in China, the succession of new leaders to power may bring political violence and disruption. The dangers of excessively formal authority may seem tame by comparison, but they are real nonetheless, for such a political system may so strap itself with legal networks and processes that its ability to respond efficiently to crises may be limited.

There is one further point about authority that should be mentioned. The formal authority which sustains the idea of a government's right to rule carries with it the idea of the people's *obligation* to obey government. It is by playing on such commonly recognized obligations that public authorities are capable of exercising influence. This sense of obligation or duty on the part of citizens is sufficiently strong to override purely personal desires and objectives, as in the paying of taxes or serving in the military. More cynical observers are inclined to argue that it is rare that a person would act purely out of support for authority and recognition of obligations, that it is really the coercive power of government constantly standing in the background that insures compliance. Such cynicism is popular, but it probably serves to ignore the tremendous power of recognized authority over our lives and it exaggerates the ability of governmental coercion to maintain law and order. If we look at the reaction in the United States to the Vietnam war, even as the enforcement of draft laws and military codes were becoming ineffective in containing real opposition to the war policy, we see that the bulk of the American people still supported that policy as the legitimate execution of governmental authority. Those who dissented not only went through the crisis of suffering criminal penalties but the crisis of turning against institutions which they had been raised to respect and obey, and this second crisis was often as great as the first.

The idea of obligation reveals also an important distinction between force and authority. Force (what we have called power, in general) constitutes a one-way relationship—someone applies force to someone else; but authority suggests a two-way relationship, that is, someone gives directions and commands and someone else accepts them. But without the acceptance there is no authority, and people in authority are strangely dependent upon the subjects of that authority. There is nothing inherently influential about the things that public officials tell us to do, the influence comes from the fact that we believe they should be able to tell us such things and that we are obligated to follow. As we will see later in discussing political institutions, it is as important to provide government with sufficient authority as it is to provide it with sufficient soldiers and police.

## DELIBERATION

In sorting through the ways in which people act to influence each other, where we assume that some natural agreement among them is not present, we have dealt only with *hierarchical* relationships, that is, situations in which one person plays a role that puts him above the person he is influencing. One person is the superior and the other is the subordinate. Although politics seems to be dominated by this superior/-subordinate type of situation, we should not ignore the fact that influence also occurs among people who normally think of themselves as equals or peers. A group of peers who approach an issue from different points of view may find it possible to discover agreement through rational discussion, exchange of information, and expression of their differences. This may still be called a kind of influence, in the broadest sense, since it results in people doing something they would not otherwise do were it not for their involvement in such processes.

Many governmental institutions and political situations operate on the basis of collegial relationships among such equal participants. Committees, legislative bodies, courts consisting of a group of judges, and average citizens at a community meeting—all represent examples of this. We do not wish to argue that the use of deliberation excludes the role of power and authority, but only that the collegial character of such groups makes possible, and may actually encourage, reliance upon deliberation as a method of forming common decisions and actions. Deliberation calls upon one to exert influence through the force of logic, evidence, and convincing reason. The design of the American system of courts, for example, is explicitly intended to emphasize the influence of deliberation over all else. We may complain that this form of influence plays all too little a role in public affairs, but we would be mistaken in trying to study politics without giving due consideration to it when it does appear.

## ORIENTATIONS AND CONSTRAINTS

American voters elect Jimmy Carter President of the United States; Protestants and Catholics in Northern Ireland are involved in constantly escalating political violence; Prime Minister Ian Smith of Rhodesia agrees in principle to a plan to reorganize government so as to put political power in the hands of the black majority. How can we better understand the behavior of the participants in these events, beyond a mere analysis of the roles and influence relationships involved? What are the particular dynamic elements that account for people doing what they do in politics?

We began this treatment of political behavior by discussing certain patterns of conduct that are possible to identify and can be of assistance in studying the human relationships that occur in politics. Along this line we have looked at different roles, at the existence of leaders and followers, and at the power, authority, and deliberation that occurs among people in politics. Through all of this we do not want to lose sight of our original purpose, which is to learn how we can study what people do in politics and why. In order to explore this matter more directly, we have to go further than we have gone, mainly because to this point the discussion has been very abstract and general. The elite role, socialization, authority occur generally in politics, but an understanding of a particular situation or event requires an understanding of the particular circumstances in which politics goes on. After all, people differ and political systems differ around the world, and at some point these differences and particular circumstances will have to be recognized in political analysis. What will be suggested here is a handy way for someone new to the study of politics to approach this problem.

To analyze something simply means studying it by breaking it down into its various parts, and that is what we need to do with political behavior. In relation to any particular political situation or event, the study of people's behavior and conduct can be organized by breaking the situation down into two elements: first, the person's own *orientation* to the situation, and second, the opportunities and constraints presented to the person by the political system and society at large (for convenience, these will be referred to simply as *constraints*). As these ideas are developed it will be clear that orientations and constraints are not altogether separate and unrelated, but the very purpose of analysis is to look at things separately and distinctly so that they can be properly related later on.

*Orientations* simply refers to what the individual person brings to a particular situation, that is, what he brings to it in regard to his psychological state of mind, his objectives and purposes, and the concrete and material conditions of his life. These orientations include a person's values, beliefs, attitudes, personality, objectives and motives for his actions, interests, knowledge, skills, wealth, and a particular quality of life, occupation, profession, and religion. Any or all of these orientations may help explain his role in politics and what he specifically does or does not do. This individual confronts a world of constraints which, in the most general sense, refers to those elements external to the individual which affect his behavior in a particular situation. These constraints are provided by the political system itself and by the environment of the general social system which was discussed in the previous chapter. These constraints encompass such things as the political values, attitudes, and beliefs of other people in the society, governmental institutions, the class structure of society, and the society's general level of wealth. Any or all of these constraints may also serve to explain what a person does or does not do in politics. In thinking about our own orientations and constraints and how they might differ from other people's, we will consider some of the more prominent items we have listed here, beginning with those factors that make up our orientation to politics.

## Sense of Efficacy

Do you think that the decisions of government are important and that you can do anything about those decisions? The feeling of being able to do something about what goes on in politics is called, by political scientists, a *sense of efficacy*. A person with a low sense of efficacy may hardly be inclined to bother with political matters at all. A sense of efficacy can be the result of an individual's own personality make-up, the amount of personal self-confidence and positive feeling about himself or herself; but, it should be noted, it may also derive from a realistic appraisal of one's own place in the political system. In other words, one reason a person may *feel* he cannot do anything about political decisions is because it's true. It would hardly have occurred to a serf in the Middle Ages that the manner in which his life was governed was something for him to alter or change. This does not mean, however, that even where you can be effective you will think of yourself as being so. Sense of efficacy may determine whether one is inclined to assume any active political role in the first place.

## Ideology

What system of beliefs and values do you have about politics? Are you liberal, conservative, fascist, or communist? nationalist or internationalist? militarist or pacifist? Let us not worry about what all these terms mean for the moment. We simply wish to make the point that one element of a person's political orientation consists of a system of political beliefs which that person finds useful in guiding and shaping his or her response to political issues. People will differ according to how clear and systematic an ideology they have. If a person brings to political experience a fairly conscious ideology, an understanding of this belief system can help explain his conduct. Even where an individual may be said to lack an ideology, it can still be said that everyone approaches a political experience with some values or beliefs about it. Patterns of values and beliefs taken at large make up what is known as the *political culture* of a society. Such ideas, whether strictly ideological or not, serve to answer many critical questions for the individual: Does he feel that government should have a right to regulate all aspects of his life, that he should have a say in government, or be able to criticize it, or that it is better for common people to stay out of political affairs? Is it the job of government to maintain order, improve the quality of people's lives, or just leave people alone? Should government be trying to expand the size and power of the political system through war, or avoid getting involved in international conflicts? What kind of conduct should be considered criminal? A person's answers to these kinds of questions constitute an important part of his or her orientation to politics.

## Interests

What particular interests do you have as an individual that you consider relevant to what you do in politics or to what government does to you? Are you an avid fisherman who might be concerned about the price of fishing licenses or about governmental programs to preserve natural lakes and streams? Are you an architect concerned about how governmental planning departments will regulate the design and engineering of buildings? Are you a student concerned about the tuition increases or budget cutbacks in your state-supported institution? Each of these examples points up some particular interest an individual may have and the way in which it may be considered politically relevant. The importance of these interests is that they point up the way in which government ultimately can affect our lives in the most practical way.

## Quality of Life

What is your particular quality of life? What are your wealth, income, state of health, education, profession, occupation, neighborhood, creature comforts? One thing each of us brings to political experience is a particular quality of life. Indeed, it is this which frequently shapes our interests and other orientations toward politics and it is this which can be altered or protected by the actions of government.

## Other Social Roles

What general roles in society do you play? Are you a parent, student, employee, political party member, homeowner? Again, each person's role set can have a bearing on his or her political experience.

These various particulars represent what we mean basically when we refer to a person's orientation to politics and, if you have answered the questions for yourself along the way, you may have a pretty good notion of your own orientation. We should notice that these various ingredients of a person's orientation interrelate with each other. For example, someone who lacks any sense of efficacy will likely not possess a cogent ideology; someone whose ideology supports the idea that politics ought to recognize the importance of individual interests will likely consider his own interests to be legitimate political objectives; someone who has an extremely poor quality of life may possess a very low sense of efficacy when he considers the prospects of "fighting city hall."

Another observation about these orientations is that they differ from individual to individual within the same political system as well as differing from one system to another. But before we take a closer look at this, we should consider some of the major types of constraints which confront the individual.

## The Political Culture

This term has been mentioned already to refer to the general pattern of beliefs, values, and attitudes about politics that prevails in any particular political system. It is other people's psychological orientation to politics that operates as a constraint for a particular person. Is a person's ideology similar to widely held ideological views in the society? Is he energetically interested in public affairs, while the general attitude of people around him is one of boredom and apathy?

## Political Institutions

One of the more tangible constraints (to be treated at length in the next chapter) is the type of political institutions operating in the system. Here a number of questions are relevant: How are public officials selected? Are they elected by popular vote? Are there political parties? Is criticism of the government allowed? How are governmental decisions made? Is it possible to have individual grievances heard by public officials?

## Quality of Life

Again, just as the individual's quality of life shapes his orientation to politics, the general quality of life in the society as a whole constitutes a set of constraints on the individual. This is defined by much of what we earlier identified as the environment of the political system: the state of the economy, the degree of urbanization and industrialization, the technology in use, the state of health and education, and so on. The ability to read and write, for example, might not be taken as a critical political resource in the United States, but in a country where 80 percent of the population is illiterate, this skill might be quite relevant. By the same token the high degree of illiteracy would represent a constraint on acquiring this skill in the first place and using it to communicate with large numbers of people who cannot read or write.

## Social Structure

Lastly, the general social structure should be considered as a constraint. Of special interest is the social class structure or what sociologists call the *stratification* of people in society. Societies in general all include some distinction among people based on such variables as wealth, life style, and intelligence, which allows us to speak of an upper class and a lower class or of several classes in between. One's position in this class structure, or perhaps what one thinks one's position is, represents a political constraint or opportunity. It is also important whether this class structure is highly rigid (thereby making it difficult or unlikely that one could expect to advance to a higher class), what the size of the respective classes are (for example, is the poorest class in society very small or very large), and how much of a difference there is between the upper class and the lower class.

A good deal of political analysis consists of a more detailed study of such constraints and their effect on people's behavior.

## CASES

The idea of orientations and constraints has been introduced here as a device to assist us in describing and analyzing people's conduct in politics (Figure 2–2 presents this diagramatically). In order to show how these ideas might be applied we will develop some specific cases as examples.

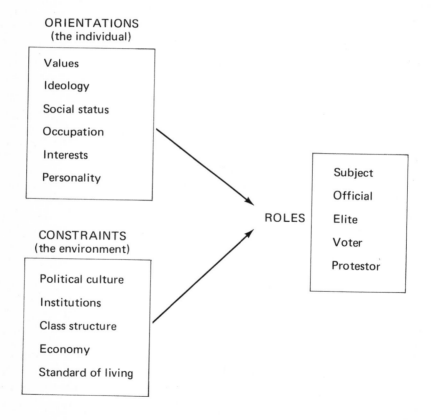

ORIENTATIONS
(the individual)

Values

Ideology

Social status

Occupation

Interests

Personality

CONSTRAINTS
(the environment)

Political culture

Institutions

Class structure

Economy

Standard of living

ROLES

Subject

Official

Elite

Voter

Protestor

**Figure 2–2  The Elements of Political Behavior**

## The War Protestor

This case involves an American in his early twenties at the height of the Vietnam war. The war represents a government policy to which this individual has become opposed on the grounds that the war is unconstitutional and immoral. The government attempts to draft him into the army and he refuses; in the process he burns his draft card at a public demonstration. He is subsequently prosecuted for violating the draft law, found guilty, and he must serve time in jail.

What might make up the orientation of this protester? His socialization has taught him to respect public authority and that violation of the law brings with it not only punishment under law but the disapproval of his family and peers. But his socialization has also provided him with certain expectations about the democratic character of the American political system, its foundation in popular consent, and the legitimacy of criticizing the government. As a college student he is exposed to social issues through his academic studies, has more time to think about them, and, perhaps more than many his own age, is beginning to feel a certain self-confidence about expressing his political views. As a student he is also aware of organized resistance to the draft which is centered on the campus, and this environment provides support for his own resistance. Aside from his attitude and general outlook, his orientation is also shaped by the fact that he is the right age to be drafted into the army and that most of his friends, also the right age, have had experiences with the draft. He may have defined for himself an interest in staying out of the army, and his ideological outlook may now be telling him that the war represents a seriously wrong policy.

Now look at the constraints on him. The most dramatic constraint, of course, is that the government is conducting a war and does have the formal authority to draft him into the army with criminal penalties for refusal. Another constraint is that most of the American people seem to be in support of the war policy and much of this more vocal support has branded draft resistance as treason and disloyalty. The major political parties, which have not taken the organization of college students seriously since most of them have not been old enough to vote, do not appear to represent a useful or convenient channel for expressing dissent. Numerous organizations opposing the war and the draft have begun to spring up around the college campus and have begun to provide moral and material support for student dissenters. Charges against resisters can be heard in a court where they can have legal representation and where known legal processes will be used.

These orientations and constraints do not all point in one direction, which is frequently the case in politics. The fellow in our example could have ended up not resisting the draft at all, thus following the inclination of much of his socialization, the pressures of society at large, and the punitive power of the government. An important aspect of this example is that this protester is experiencing *cross-pressures*, forces inclining him to behave in different ways; some forces incline him to obey, some to resist. Recall the earlier mention of role conflict. Here the individual may be experiencing a conflict between his role as an independent moral person and his role as a dutiful citizen, roles which seem to be pointing him in different directions. The much greater force seems to be on the side of compliance with government, and this means that the decision to resist is quite consequential and is fraught with personal and social tension. The decision to burn the draft card is important in serving to make the ultimate decision to resist clear and articulate both for himself and others by expressing it in a dramatic form. He deals with the powerful impact of the consequences by a resolute and public acceptance of them.

This particular action involves political roles—the subject and citizen being drafted, the public official issuing draft orders. It also involves relationships of power and authority, for the government has certain power to back its orders and presumably is acting pursuant to law. But the actual event—the resistance to the draft order—has to be understood in terms of how these roles and relationships are played out, that is, in terms of the orientations of the individual and the constraints of the system. One way to appreciate this is to examine the impact of a change in the circumstances. Instead of going to college, the person gets married, acquires a good job, and has a medical deferment from the draft. He might go through the war wondering why college students are such a quarrelsome lot or, if the war is such a bad policy, why they do not just organize to defeat the president at the next election. What if the government is a dictatorship which has never allowed public disagreement with decisions? Would the individual keep his doubts about the war to himself? Or, if he could not, try to leave the country quietly or, with even greater strain and feeling of alienation from society, go through with the protest and suffer severe and arbitrary government punishment and harassment of his family and associates?

## The Communist Party Official in the Soviet Union

Let us look at another quite different example. This particular person is a local official of the Communist party in the Soviet Union in the 1950s. The party chairman, Nikita Khrushchev, makes a speech to party officials indicating that there is going to be a departure from the tactics and policies of Joseph Stalin, who had ruled for almost three decades. Stalinism can now be disregarded and officials of the party should conduct party business accordingly. Our particular official subsequently begins to openly oppose old Stalinist supporters in the local party and uses Khrushchev's new policy as a tool in doing this.

Again, the individual brings certain orientations to this political situation. He has made a career out of his party job; he has been raised with the doctrines of Marxism and Soviet communism which he very much believes in; he has learned that successful advancement through the party requires compliance with party leadership. He has also developed over several years an attachment to Stalinist attitudes which were always taken to be unquestionable guides to proper party policy.

This individual confronts a political system which allows only for the operation of a single political party—the Communist party. In this system political support does not depend on ability to muster mass appeal through popular elections, but on the recognition of ability and loyalty by those higher up. Government not only possesses the usual power to punish but in this case this power is unrestrained by an open legal process with reliable rules of fairness.

As in the previous example, there is an element of cross-pressure. Our official had viewed Stalin for years as a national hero; he is now being told it is appropriate to criticize his leadership. Again, what if the set of circumstances were different? What if, for example, there were more than one political party? (In this respect it is interesting to note that abrupt shifts in the policy of the Soviet Communist party often had disastrous effects on Communist parties in Western European democracies where people could switch party membership or form new parties altogether.)

## The American Voters in an Election

The two examples above consider specific individuals, but the kind of analysis suggested here can be applied also to the behavior of large numbers of people. As a brief example of this we can consider the behavior of the American voter in the 1976 presidential election. What were the voters' attitudes and concerns? They may have been interested in seeing some new faces in government, in more directly attacking the problem of unemployment, in taking ideologically a reasonably moderate approach to these problems which would not immediately swell the size of the national government, or in rejecting a party touched by the major scandal of Watergate. This voting population had also been experiencing a period of peace and the absence of the social unrest that had marked the previous decade. They operate within the formal constraints of a presidential election that occurs at a fixed time every four years in which only two major parties that appear to have a chance of winning compete. Voting behavior is also shaped by the methods used in communicating information about the candidates and the campaign—televised news, campaign appearances, advertising of the candidates, and so forth.

How did these voters behave? By a narrow margin, they elected one of two candidates who had not appeared during the campaign to be radically different in their positions on the issues, The voters' choices resulted from a combination of their own political attitudes and predispositions and the character of the options that confronted them.

## STUDYING POLITICAL BEHAVIOR

The analysis and examples above are intended to show the things that a political scientist is going to be interested in looking for in trying to explain political behavior. What kind of people are we talking about? What do they think? What do they believe? What are their interests? What is their condition of life? What kind of a political system are they living in? What is permitted? What kind of political organization goes on? What is the political culture in general?

The objective of the political scientist is to use this type of analysis as the basis for generating and testing certain propositions or explanatory statements about behavior. It is in this way that we develop systematic knowledge of political experience. What might we learn? That lower-class individuals participate less in politics than upper-class individuals; that too great a gap between our values and expectations and reality can lead to rebelliousness; that the physical intimidation of the state can be effective in inhibiting political criticism; that one's political effectiveness can be enhanced through the proper kinds of socialization.

Using a general strategy such as this, political scientists can go a long way in explaining political behavior and, perhaps, even in predicting it. People respond in fairly consistent ways to similar situations and factors in the environment, and looked at collectively, a good deal of their behavior is sufficiently repetitive that it can often be predicted quite well. Techniques have now been developed which make it possible to predict within a few percentage points how large numbers of people will vote in an election and whom they will vote for. It can be determined what kinds of people are more likely to be engaged in politics or what the reaction will be to a particular decision or event. The effects of socialization and early education on adult political behavior can be carefully examined.

A basic factor which makes these types of explanations possible is the *replicability* of certain kinds of action. The casting of a vote, for example, is a political act which is engaged in by a large number of people under certain identical conditions. All the votes are cast on the same day and the choices on the ballot are the same for each voter. In a system that has popular elections, the act of voting is continually recurring. With a political act such as this, which is continually replicated, it is possible to discern broad patterns of behavior that can become quite predictable. The beliefs, values, and ideology of the voting population can be studied as well as such factors as age, sex, income, and religion. From this, certain statistical findings reveal the impact of the voter's orientation: that middle-aged people and those with higher incomes are more likely to vote than younger people or those with lower incomes, or that Jewish voters tend to be more liberal than other religious groups, or that blue-collar workers tend to vote Democratic more than Republican. This same tactic for studying political behavior can be applied to numerous group situations in which there are replicable types of decisions; political scientists have similarly studied the voting behavior of the members of legislative bodies and have even applied the technique to the decisions of the nine-member Supreme Court of the United States. Thus, where political behavior has this replicable or common element we can go a long way in studying the elements of behavior with a fair degree of statistical precision, and indeed, much of our knowledge of political behavior derives from this approach.

## THE PROBLEM—UNIQUE EVENTS

At the very beginning of this chapter it was mentioned that one of the things that helps us in approaching the study of political behavior is that behavior is not totally random, that it often follows discernable patterns. We have taken advantage of this by exploring some of the major types of patterns: political roles, political influence, individual orientations to politics, and the variety of constraints on individual conduct. If all political behavior were patterned and routine and if we could go out and collect all the information we wanted about people in politics, we could use the approach considered here as the basis for a very thorough and scientific explanation of political behavior. It might not be exactly simple to do, but it would make this subject quite manageable; in fact, it has been the hope of contemporary political scientists to increasingly refine our ability to study behavior scientifically.

Unfortunately, at least for these political scientists, the study of political behavior cannot be limited to such a tidy approach, primarily because man's political experience is not altogether routine and patterned. Man is not a machine and his life reveals varied, unique, unexpected, sometimes surprising decisions and actions which suggest the working of human imagination, creativity, and originality. For the political scientist this situation is both problematic and fascinating— problematic because it interferes with the manageable development of a science of politics, and fascinating because it is precisely the unique and the novel occurrences that make political experience rich, interesting, and intriguing.

Our problems begin with the fact that much political behavior occurs on the part of distinct individuals in situations that are not replicable. Consider what is perhaps the most dramatic instance of this, the behavior of a chief executive such as a prime minister or president. He has certain individual responsibilities for making policies and decisions, and the issues he confronts and the situations he must deal with are not identical to those faced by his predecessors. There is no way to generalize statistically about how presidents might behave in the way that we can generalize about how millions of voters might behave. The type of analysis called for in this situation requires a familiarity with the president or prime minister himself, how he works with cabinet or staff, his relationships with legislative bodies, and the peculiar circumstances of the issues that come up during his administration. Of course, even in a situation where there is a replicable set of circumstances to examine, we are still able to talk only about the whole group of people being studied, not any single individual in the group. A political scientist may be able to tell how an election will come out without knowing how you are going to cast your single vote. This problem will be aggravated by those cross-pressures that were mentioned in the examples above. If the individual's circumstances are such that there are some factors inclining him in one direction and others inclining him in a different direction, it will be all the more difficult to assume anything about individual behavior from the behavior of the group. Our war protestor was a very torn individual and even looking back on his actions it may prove difficult to ferret out what it was that made him turn in one direction rather than another.

In addition to the individuality of certain political conduct that has to be accounted for, there is another consideration. Political action displays what would appear to be original and novel initiatives on the part of political actors that could not have been successfully anticipated through the normal means of studying political behavior. What do we mean by such novel and unique events? Consider some examples. During his first term in office President Nixon proposed to the Congress of the United States the passage of a bill which would have created what was known as the Family Assistance Plan. The purpose of this plan was, in effect, to provide every American household with a "guaranteed income," that is, money from the government which they would receive if they did not work or money which would supplement an extremely low income even if they did work. Nixon was, of course, a Republican president who had built his public career around a commitment to the values of hard work and free enterprise, and belief in the unjust and debilitating effect of massive government "handouts" to the individual. His political support over many years had come from groups in society of like opinion. In fact, proposals for a guaranteed income had originated primarily with Democrats, and even within that party such ideas had not received widespread or energetic support. In addition, there did not appear to be substantial public pressure for such a proposal that might have caused the president to deny his previous stands for some practical political benefit. The novelty of this initiative on his part is best seen in the general surprise and the outrage of many Republicans that followed his announcement of the Family Assistance Plan. Looking at his role as a moderate-conservative spokesman of long standing, looking at the orientations and constraints of the situation, one would think that this plan is the last thing that Richard Nixon would be proposing.

Consider other examples. In 1939, Joseph Stalin, the leader of the Soviet Union, agreed to a nonaggression pact with Adolph Hitler, the leader of the new Nazi state of Germany. Stalin was the leader of a regime in the Soviet Union dedicated to the principles of communism, the creation of a classless society, and the destruction of nationalism and militarism as the corrupt result of capitalist societies. Fascism was perceived by communism as the ultimate extension of nationalism and capitalism and, therefore, in complete opposition to Soviet ideology. Again, the action seemed to shock and surprise most everyone; a less likely alliance was difficult to imagine. The unexpected and surprising is very much a part of political experience. The Japanese surprise attack on Pearl Harbor which led to American entrance into World War II seemed to violate expected, rational military calculation. In the 1968 election, Eugene McCarthy mobilized thousands of young political amateurs in support of his antiwar campaign for the presidency, thereby contributing to Lyndon Johnson's decision not to run for another full term. The McCarthy effort seemed to run counter to most of the accepted truths of the day about the requirements for a successul or influential presidential campaign.

We do not wish to argue that these actions cannot be explained. Presumably, if we dig deep enough and get close enough to these events we can understand why people did what they did. What we are saying, however, is that people in politics do not merely react to events in predictable ways; they also want to make events, to create new situations, to initiate new possibilities. Unlike eating, sleeping, and making a living, politics is a realm of human activity that is not totally controlled by necessity. In other words, the political world is not a natural and unchangeable force to which man merely reacts; rather, it is something of his own creation. Indeed, one thing that is created is new modes of political expression and new kinds of political relationships that would not make sense at all in terms of old ways of doing things. In the Middle Ages, the notion that the mass of people in society might collectively vote for public officials in competitive elections and actually pass laws at the ballot box would have struck people as absurd. Several hundred years later it has become common practice in several democratic societies. What is a commonplace in one era of history seems an impossibility in another. It is because politics is dynamic, changing, and man-made that this is able to happen.

If the novel and unique make it difficult to know exactly what lies in wait for us in political experience, it must also be said that it is often the unique event that is most important and interesting in the political life of a society. Such events should not be seen as bothersome factors which refuse to fit into an otherwise neat picture of political reality, but as central elements in what politics is all about. Thus, the study of political behavior invariably will involve us in the examination of conduct and action that are distinctive and historical as well as mundane and ordinary.

## NOTES

[1]Clinton Rossiter, *The American Presidency* (New York, 1956).

[2]Lester Milbrath, *Political Participation: How and Why Do People Get Involved in Politics?* (Chicago, Ill., 1965), p. 19; see also Angus Campbell et al., *The American Voter* (New York, 1960), and H. T. Reynolds, *Politics and the Common Man* (Homewood, Ill., 1974), p. 127.

[3]Aristotle, *Politics*, ed. and trans. Ernest Barker (New York, 1962), p. 127.

[4]See M. Jewell and S. Patterson, *The Legislative Process in the United States* (New York, 1966), ch. 16, as an example of a more elaborate analysis of legislative roles.

[5]See Fred Greenstein, *Children and Politics* (New Haven, Conn., 1965).
[6]Robert Dahl, *Modern Political Analysis* (Englewood Cliffs, N.J., 1965), ch. 5.

# FOR FURTHER READING

Dahl, Robert A. *Modern Political Analysis.* Englewood Cliffs, N.J.: Prentice-Hall, 1963. A useful book for pursuing the study of roles, power, and legitimacy and the frameworks of analysis that political scientists have used.

Elms, Alan C. *Personality in Politics.* New York: Harcourt Brace Jovanovich, 1976. A lively and interesting review of psychological perspectives on political behavior, particularly in regard to the psychological orientations of elites and activists.

Greenstein, Fred I. *Children and Politics.* New Haven, Conn.: Yale University Press, 1965. A study of childhood political socialization based on empirical research.

Lane, Robert E. *Political Life.* New York: The Free Press, 1965. Though the book is dated, it is an extensive review of the empirical findings of social scientists concerning political behavior and a valuable guide to the questions and concerns that have dominated this area of study in the discipline.

Mulcahy, Kevin V., and Richard S. Katz. *America Votes.* Englewood Cliffs, N.J.: Prentice-Hall, 1976. A current review of findings about the behavior of the American voter with a readable and comprehensible style.

# 3

# Government: The Blueprint of Politics

Politics has been defined here as an activity by which people exert some control or management over public affairs, and initially we have approached the study of politics by looking at the behavior of people in politics. But we know quite well that politics is not a formless, shapeless kind of activity in which people spontaneously arrive at decisions. Politics is an activity, but more precisely, it is an organized activity. Indeed, the most immediately visible part of our political experience consists of the numerous and varied ways that the political task of society has been formally organized: laws, public offices, courts, police departments, tax collectors, city councils, parliaments, armies, or, in other words, what we commonly know as *government*.

Perhaps the function of government in man's political experience can be appreciated by a hypothetical example. Imagine a group of people shipwrecked on the proverbial desert island. In order to feed themselves they must resort to the gathering of foods growing on the island. This requires a considerable amount of work and effort, and the stockpiling of food begins as a way of getting ahead of their needs and providing themselves with some security. A problem develops; some people begin to take food from stockpiles which they did not help to collect and this happens often enough that it becomes a matter of general concern to the group. One person is caught taking food in this way and he is physically attacked by some of the active food gatherers who charge him with being lazy and with threatening their survival. Others in the group become quite upset that the thief is so severely punished and argue that he really should not be treated as a thief at all, that not everyone will be able to be as productive at gathering food, and that the stockpile should be considered a supply for the whole group. Perhaps, they suggest, those who have been a bit lazy at gathering could be useful to the group in some other way. A meeting of everyone is arranged and the stealing incidents and the issues involved are all discussed. At this point, the group has already begun to think of itself as sharing—as a "public"—certain problems that must be dealt with; we might say that they have already recognized a "political task." Let us further imagine that as a result of the meeting the group decides to meet again at regularly scheduled times and agrees that at these meetings various rules about the collection and distribution of food will be established by majority vote. They appoint one of their number to organize the meeting, recognize people to speak, and record the decisions that the group makes. At the first of these meetings they draw up some initial rules regarding food and choose three members to take on the job of making sure that people follow these rules. If there are any questions about what the rules mean or whether someone was really violating them, the whole assembly will listen to the arguments and issues in the case and render a judgment.

Our isolated, shipwrecked group has engaged in one of the most fundamental acts of man—they have created a government. In doing so they have responded to basic political needs: the need for the political task to be handled in some more or less predictable, orderly, regular way, the need for some formal method by which decisions can be legitimized, judged, applied, and discussed. The formal institutions of government might be thought of as the stage set on which political action takes place. In our little island group, decisions have to be made about the handling of the food, appropriate means of enforcement, and the assignment of tasks. And all of these decisions are the focal point for disagreements, for differences in points of view, and for conflict of interest. Their miniature government does not solve all these issues or even guarantee enough food supplies; what it does provide them with is some dependable and legitimate machinery for handling these questions. Each problem that comes up is now not handled individually in a case-by-case, spontaneous way but referred to the common forum of governmental process. Their political task as a group is now put on some organized basis.

We can also see in this example the presence of certain key building blocks in the design of governmental institutions. First, there is the existence of *public officials,* that is, people who hold a formal role in government as defined by a particular set of duties, responsibilities, and powers. For example, our island group has chosen a form of government which makes all of them legislators or lawmakers when they meet in their assemblies; they have made one person a meeting organizer, or chairman, as we might call him; and they have made yet other people enforcers of the rules. We alluded to these roles in the previous chapter when we noted that certain people exercise authority by virtue of the public office that they hold. Second, there is the existence of *rules*, a very general term which is used to encompass laws, official orders, decisions, and the like. Our example shows the group making rules regulating food, determining enforcement, and for that matter, creating their government in the first place.

## RITUAL VERSUS REALITY

The formal institutions of government represent a key component of any political system and perhaps the most obvious and universal part of political experience, for it is through what government does to individuals that people commonly gain initial experience with political reality: zoning laws, speeding tickets, social security, taxes, and so on. But it must be stressed at the outset that a grasp of formal institutions and of the mechanics of how they work should not be taken as a satisfactory understanding of politics generally. There are two basic reasons for this. First, as most political philosophers through history have appreciated, the capacity of laws and institutions to put the governance of society on a predictable and secure footing is limited and partial. Solutions to every future problem that may arise could not be spelled out ahead of time in explicit laws and rules even if we wanted to; the factors to be accounted for are too complex, the appearance of new crises and dilemmas too unpredictable, the consequences of each decision too difficult to anticipate. Thus, governmental decisions are a mixture of formal rules and the judgment and discretion of individuals. It would be impossible and undesirable to try to reduce to definitive rules all the conditions under which we should declare war with another country or have someone found guilty of breaking a law. Thus, when these decisions are made, they are partially the result of the rules and official duties of government, but they are also the result of the judgment of the particular people involved, the president, Congress, a judge and jury. This is why the study of formal government must be linked to our previous consideration of what people do in politics.

There is, however, another reason why we have to be careful about treating the study of institutions as our only line of insight into politics. This is a somewhat more complex reason which has to do with what might be called the problem of "ritual versus reality." This problem results from the fact that formal institutions are not always what they seem to be nor do they always do what they seem to do. In the Soviet Union, the constitution gives complete and ultimate power to the Supreme Soviet, a huge two-house legislature. A complete picture of Soviet government and politics reveals, however, that the Supreme Soviet really exercises very little decision-making power; in fact, the top leadership of the Communist party is much more central to decision making. In Great Britain, it is the queen, the reigning monarch, who officially names the prime minister, yet in reality the selection of the prime minister is a product of the electoral support achieved by his party possibly combined with supporting agreements with other parties (called a coalition). In the United States, the Constitution explains that a president will be selected upon the vote of something called the electoral college, which consists of certain electors chosen from each state. Surprisingly, Article 1, Section 2, of the U.S. Constitution does not even explicitly require that these electors be chosen by popular vote of all adults. As we know, what is considered the effective election of a president actually occurs in a popular national election and the meeting of the electoral college still occurs later as an almost unnoticed ritual. In each of these examples there are certain rituals or formalities of government which do not seem to square with reality, that is, with the reality of who is really governing and who is not.

The problem of ritual versus reality is not only a complication that the political scientist must deal with; it can also be a source of frustration and cynicism for the average layman trying to make sense out of political experience. He may begin to think of government as a grand deception, in which laws do not mean what they say, public rituals of decision making are hollow, and real decisions are made by powerful forces we never really see.

Is government a sham? Is this cynicism justified? Yes and no. Yes, it may very well be the case that the outward forms of government are meaningless, out of fit with reality, and a disguise for what really goes on in politics. Quite simply, it may happen that official rules and roles are ignored in practice or that they were never intended to be anything but rituals. This country fought a painful and controversial war for several years in Southeast Asia without ever having a declaration of war from Congress, as the Constitution calls for. The official doctrine of equal protection before the law does little for the fact that hundreds and thousands of people spend time in jail in this country only because they cannot raise bail money. Though this may provide the basis for quite legitimate cynicism, we can also answer no to the above question. Some cynicism is based on a misunderstanding of the role of formal institutions in the political system. Such institutions are not designed with the intention that they actually describe political reality and there may be nothing wrong if they do not. Sometimes they serve a useful symbolic function, like the taking of an oath of office, which hardly is capable by itself of making a responsible public official out of an unethical, irresponsible person. If oaths of office were taken absolutely literally, there would never be any governmental corruption. But, both good men and bad men will find their way into government, and the purpose the oath serves is to put on record what the public expects of officials and what standards it will consider relevant in judging their conduct. Also, certain institutions, like the British monarchy or the American electoral college, simply outlive their usefulness but remain as a tradition of the political system.

We have to be alert to the fact that what we dismiss as empty outward forms and rituals of government may actually serve some real political function. Many historians have pointed out that the values and principles contained in our Declaration of Independence and Constitution have not accurately described the realities of American politics. We say that all men are created equal, but it was not until recently that the principle of equality was effectively recognized by insuring the right to vote for all adults. Nonetheless, the language of the Declaration was not a *mere* ritual for it has served the purpose throughout our history of defining an expectation that we were ultimately called upon to live up to. When organized segments of the population—women, blacks—pushed this principle to its obvious application by demanding the vote, the expectation and ideal of equality were powerful enough that they could not be denied. We may agree that it should not have been necessary for them to fight for this right, but where would this fight have led if the value of equality, at least as a vague ideal, had never been enunciated? Thus, the problem of ritual versus reality is not dealt with only by distinguishing between the two but also by watching out for how ritual itself can be a force in real politics.

The point of this problem of ritual versus reality is simply this: the study of formal government requires not only that we know about the workings of governmental machinery but that we carefully examine how these workings relate to the general process of making political decisions. To put it another way, we have to look beyond the *structure* of governments to examine the *functions* performed by that structure. In some cases the function may be merely ritualistic, in other cases it may be central to the political process. (One thing that will be discovered is that institutions in different countries that seem to resemble each other do not perform the same functions in the political system at all. The United States and the Soviet Union each have a national legislature, but we would be seriously misled to think that they serve identical purposes for the two systems.)

## STUDYING FORMAL GOVERNMENT

A thorough understanding of institutions really requires the study of specific governments. Since institutions reflect the peculiar history and experience of a particular political system, it is very difficult to generalize about them. But again, our more limited and modest intent is to provide a foundation for the further study of politics and not a definitive account of all of man's political experience. What we will take up here is a consideration of the more basic and common institutional building blocks that are encountered in the modern state. Even though institutions differ considerably in detail from one system to the next, there are, after all, a reasonably limited number of basic ways to design formal decision making. This is what we will examine here under Legislature, Executive Offices, Political Executive, Bureaucracy, and Courts.

## THE LEGISLATURE

A widespread but by no means universal component in the institutional organization of modern governments is the legislative assembly. These parliaments or assemblies are known by various designations around the world: in the United States it is called the Congress; in Israel, the Knesset; in Japan, the Diet; in the Soviet Union, the Supreme Soviet; in France, England, Germany, and Italy, it is known simply as the parliament. Within the United States, the existence of legislative bodies is common at all the various levels of government, from the Congress itself to state legislators, city councils, county commissions, town councils, all the way down to that fading, nostalgic tradition of American local government, the New England town meeting.

In the most general sense, a legislature is a formally organized assembly of public officials who, dealing with each other on a more or less equal basis, are charged with publicly deliberating over and collectively making certain kinds of governmental decisions. Prior to the growth of the modern legislature, kings would use councils or assemblies of aristocrats to advise them on decisions, but these assemblies came and went at the kings' wishes and were purely advisory. The development of the modern legislature really occurs when such assemblies achieve some formally recognized powers, a certain amount of independence from other organs of government, and thus become an important institution of government in their own right. The historical pressure for this to happen came from the increasing demand of new groups in society for a share in the process of government, and a restriction, if not elimination, of the personal power of the king. The push for increased democracy or "popular rule" encouraged this process of legislative power. The history of popular legislatures shows that the earliest often began either through the elite in society expanding the role of the legislature to respond to this popular push (the case with the British Parliament) or with the creation of assemblies from scratch upon the overthrow of the elite (the case with the French National Assembly at the time of the French Revolution in 1789). Today, the legislative arm of government is an essential element in political systems purporting to be democratic and has even come to appear in systems that we would not normally consider democratic. Despite this, there are many systems in the world (Iraq, Libya, Nigeria, and Bolivia, to name a few) that do not have any legislative body at all, or at least have not had one for several years.

Not all of these legislatures are doing the same thing or even doing anything integral to the processes of government, and this naturally leads us to consider what critical functions we might expect legislatures to perform before we consider the variety of ways in which they are organized. Any particular legislature may be performing several of the following functions.

## Lawmaking

The function most frequently associated with legislatures in most people's minds is the drafting and approval of laws for society. This has certainly been the main function traditionally envisioned by democratic thinkers. Accordingly, it is understood that what legislators do is propose bills, debate their merit, vote as a body, and thereby create the law of the land. Legislatures vary as to whether or not this is an effective function they perform, but even in those cases where it is, we should be aware of the number of factors limiting the exercise of lawmaking. To begin with, legislatures never totally control all lawmaking, even in a situation of legislative strength such as exists in the United States or Great Britain. Rules and decisions made in government which have the standing of law are made by numerous public officials in and out of the legislature. The reason it is inevitably this way is that although legislatures may be good at deliberating on general laws and policies where there is sufficient time, they do not possess the resources or ability to make decisions on an almost day-to-day basis where adaptable and quick response is called for. Thus, much of what legislatures do is to pass laws that essentially delegate to other officials certain powers to act within certain constraints or guidelines, which themselves would have to be changed by further legislative action. Thus, Congress might give the president power to draft people into the military, following a set of conditions, and the power to issue orders himself that are pursuant to the objectives of the draft. In doing this the president would also be engaged in a kind of lawmaking.

There is an even more basic reason why the legislature does not dominate the whole field of lawmaking: the basic law or authority under which the legislature operates typically specifies over what subjects it may make laws. Thus, the French National Assembly can pass specific legislation only in such designated areas as civil rights, penal code, amnesty, and electoral laws, and beyond these areas it may determine only general principles or not act at all.[1]

Another problem with this lawmaking function is the ambiguity in the term *lawmaking* itself. To "make" a law would seem to suggest that the legislature confronts problems by collecting information, actually writing possible laws, and debating and approving the final product. In fact, "lawmaking" in this literal sense, if it is done by the legislature at all, is seldom done by them alone. Turning to the U.S. Congress as an example, most of the major laws that it passes are based on proposals submitted to it by the president and drafted within the bureaucracy; rarely does it pass a major piece of legislation that has been completely initiated and designed by Congress itself. It may be argued that legislatures by their very character are better suited to discussion and approval of laws rather than to the initiation and researching of proposed bills. It might be a bit more accurate to say that legislatures do not "make" laws as much as they simply "approve" laws.

All of these remarks are intended to apply to legislative bodies in which some significant lawmaking function is being served, but it should be stressed that the mere presence of such a body in the government cannot automatically be taken to mean that it has a lawmaking function. Legislatures in communist systems represent a major exception.

## Representation

Another possible function of legislatures is to represent, through their membership, a group of people or assortment of interests in society. The legislature may very well be the single arm of government that can claim to mirror the views and attitudes of society as a whole, thus providing government with a forum in which the mood of the nation can be tested. All sorts of political leaders throughout history have liked to fancy themselves representatives of the people or the nation, but the peculiar claim of legislatures to this representative function derives from some combination of their election, diversity, and large number. One difficulty political thinkers have had with the idea of representation is determining what it exactly means to *represent*. We can appreci-

ate this difficulty by looking at two basically different conceptions of
representation: the one views the representative as a trustee, the other
views him as a delegate. A *trustee* thinks that he is representing other
people by virtue of being entrusted with the job of defining what the
best decisions would be for them; he may think of himself as being
selected to represent because of his regard for the public interest,
knowledge of public affairs, and general intelligence and responsibility.
The *delegate*, on the other hand, feels it is his job not to do what *he*
thinks is good for the people, but to do what the people want him to
do. In this sense the people have directly *delegated* their power to him,
and he assumes he is to act according to the directions they give him.
This is only one of several ambiguities about the word *represent* that
would have to be cleared up in studying the representative function of
legislatures.

## Service to Citizens

In American politics a particularly prominent function for the legislator is the provision of services to individual citizens. What might also
be called the "errand-boy" function involves the legislator or his assistants helping people in their dealings with government bureaucracy
and providing information about government. In the United States this
job is often energetically performed, with the legislator maintaining
offices back home where his constituents are, appointing a staff whose
sole responsibility is in the area of "constituency relations," mailing
periodic newsletters to the voters, and spending significant chunks of
his own time handling the more difficult or important constituency
requests that come across his desk. This function, of course, is reinforced
only by the opinion of his constituents that this is what he is supposed
to be doing.

## Deliberation

The legislative body may provide a forum for the discussion and
debate of public issues. Even where deliberation is not directly related
to the specific business of legislation, it is useful in giving public expression to major differences of political viewpoints and publicly airing
competing positions. The legislature can be looked upon as an open
setting in which those with dissenting views can have their say and have
as well an opportunity to sway opinions which might be more difficult
to hold to when submitted to public scrutiny. The power and importance of deliberation in shaping opinion and holding it up to public
examination can be easily underestimated.

## Conflict Management

Legislatures may be quite valuable as devices for managing and controlling social conflict. They are the main vehicle through which conflicting interests and political movements may actually get a foothold in government; at the same time, the legislative process calls for making agreements, building coalitions, bargaining, and compromise, which in one way or another tend to moderate the severity of these conflicts. Not everyone has seen this as a potential value of the legislative process, and legislatures have often been accused of causing instability and unrest as well as creating and legitimizing as much conflict as they resolve. It is not uncommon to witness the disbanding of the legislature as one of the first acts of a political leader bent on maintaining order through dictatorial control. The ability of the legislature to engage in conflict management depends on many factors, but most especially it depends on the willingness of the political factions involved to accept, to some extent, the processes of compromise and coalition building.

## Symbol of Legitimacy

The legislature may serve a whole host of symbolic or ritualistic functions, which may increase in importance as more substantial tasks, like lawmaking or conflict management, become less important. The main thing that is supposed to be symbolized is popular legitimacy and support for the government. For example, the annual meetings of the Supreme Soviet in the USSR last only a few days and are characterized by long speeches by government and party leaders, unanimous votes on government measures, and the lack of spontaneous deliberation and debate, the presumed value of which is to dramatize the base of political support behind the government. Aside from this extreme example, some symbolic functions are performed by even an active, democratic legislature. The U.S. Congress occasionally gathers to hear speeches by major public figures not immediately related to their ordinary legislative chores or to pass resolutions which merely express thanks or appreciation to some individual or civic organization. Even laws that are passed may have a primarily symbolic value, such as the Full Employment Act of 1946 which, among other things, mandated full employment as an objective of governmental policies and actions. This law probably did more to appease the labor movement in the United States than it did to create more jobs.

Having reviewed the range of functions the legislature may perform, we can now turn to an analysis of the structural design of legislatures as formal institutions, keeping in mind that this will have some bearing on which particular combinations of functions are relevant to any particular legislature. In other words, we want to be familiar not only with how a particular legislature works as a formal organization but with how this provides clues to what it *does* within the political system.

Let us imagine ourselves to be launching the study of some particular legislative body—our city council, our state legislature, or perhaps a legislature in a foreign country that we are quite unfamiliar with. As a starting point, the following questions would be worth asking.

*How are the members of the legislature internally organized to perform their governmental task?* The legislature has been described as an assembly in which the members are presumably equal in respect to their official duties and powers. In order to perform any task in an ongoing and efficient way, a group of people must coordinate their efforts, and, therefore, legislative bodies develop forms of internal organization. The two most typical elements of this organization are committees and official leaders. Committees are created by breaking down or subdividing the membership into a number of smaller groups that take on particular tasks; in other words, committees represent a division of labor among the members. A typical arrangement would have each committee dealing with some particular area of public policy. In the American Congress we find legislative committees on, among others, foreign relations, banking and currency, education and labor, agriculture and forestry, and commerce. Though committees may turn out to be very powerful, they are, in the final analysis, extensions of the whole assembly and thereby answerable to it.

The other element of organization is official leadership which, at the very minimum, means a post—usually called the Speaker—where responsibility resides for chairing meetings, enforcing the rules of the assembly, and generally managing the routine business of the body. In many parliamentary systems the position of Speaker is a distinguished but not particularly powerful office; in the British House of Commons the Speaker severs his ties to a party and serves as a neutral chairman with formal and innocuous duties. At times, our House of Representatives has been at the opposite extreme, with the Speaker wielding tremendous power over legislative work and acting as a major spokesman of his party. Indeed, Speakers of the House, like the late Sam Rayburn, became famous public figures in their own right. The explanation for this has to be found in the rules and traditions of the body which allow a leader to gain such power, and in the difficulties in dissolving the power once created. The Speaker, however, is not the only leadership position; the chairmanship of committees and the leadership of factions and parties represented in the legislature are the two other sources from which the body is able to achieve a certain direction and organization of its work. Achieving such positions of leadership is one of the prime ways of gaining power within a legislative body.

*Is the legislature bicameral or unicameral?* One of the curious features of modern legislatures is that such a large number of them are divided into two distinct assemblies, or "houses," a situation known technically as *bicameralism* (as opposed to *unicameralism*, where there is only one house). The Congress of the United States is a bicameral legislature consisting of the Senate and the House of Representatives; likewise, the British Parliament formally consists of the House of Commons and the House of Lords; the Japanese Diet consists of the House of Representatives and the House of Councillors; the German parliament consists of the Bundesrat and the Bundestag; and all but one (Nebraska) of the fifty American state legislatures have two houses. What is odd about bicameralism, in light of its widespread use, is that on the surface there does not appear to be any compelling reason why two houses are better than one. There are, however, some ways in which we can explain this situation. In a federal system it is sometimes the case that while one house is a popular body—one directly elected by the people—the other house is designed to represent the different states or federal subunits. This is the case with our own Senate, which is made up of two senators from each state regardless of population (and their election by the people was not guaranteed by the Constitution until the passage of the Seventeenth Amendment in the early part of this century); and it is also the case with the German Bundesrat, a body of forty-one members appointed by the state governments, with the group of representatives from any one state voting as a bloc.

There are other possible explanations for bicameralism. The two houses may have distinctly different powers and the existence of two houses ensures that one can check the tendency of the other to act in a rash or precipitous way if they both must approve a piece of legislation. Bicameralism may also reflect the traditions of the society and the way in which legislative institutions actually developed. This is most obvious in the case of the British Parliament, where the now relatively powerless House of Lords symbolizes the original role of the aristocracy in advising the king; while the House of Commons represents, in both name and function, the growth of the modern democratic legislature. Whatever the reasons for bicameralism, some have begun to argue in the United States that there is little reason any more for having two houses at the state level which almost exactly duplicate each other. The fact that only one state has chosen to change to unicameralism may show either the strength of our traditions or the natural tendency of politicians to resist eliminating employment opportunities in their chosen profession.

*How do the members get selected and whom do they represent?* In addition to internal organization and bicameralism, another important consideration is how the members get to be members, and, in conjunction, what is their formal constituency (that is, *whom* do they represent)? The characteristically democratic method is through popular election by the citizens. This can be done by dividing the whole population into districts with each electing one or more members of the whole body or by having the whole population elect all the members to "at-large" seats. These two methods can be mixed, with some seats being elected at large and some from districts. But whatever the exact method, popular election is designed to create a defined "constituency" of citizens whom the legislator, in one way or another, represents.

However, not all legislative houses are popularly elected. The British House of Lords consists of those who hold titles of nobility, though that body is no longer a working legislature. The French Senate is chosen by an electoral college consisting of an assortment of National Assembly deputies and local officials.

*How large is the legislature?* A national legislature might consist of anywhere from 30 or 40 members to as many as 700 or more. The Supreme Soviet is the largest legislature in the world, with the membership in both of its houses together totaling 1,443. Seemingly a minor consideration, size of a legislature may provide some clues about its operation. As a very general rule it may be said that the larger a legislative body is, the more likely it is that committees and internal leadership will be important centers of power. Our own House of Representatives is a case in point.

*Is the job of being a legislator a full-time profession or a part-time civic duty?* Though most national legislatures consist of people for whom the job represents a full-time responsibility, there are other cases, such as local legislative bodies in the United States, where the job is handled over and above other means of making a living. There are some clues that can help us to distinguish these two situations. One is the salary that a legislator receives. Is it the equivalent of a full-time professional salary or, indeed, is there any salary at all? American congressmen make over $40,000 a year, while members of local city councils may not get paid at all or may receive only a nominal salary which would have to be supplemented by income from some other occupation. Related to this is the question of how much money they receive over and above their salary for maintaining an office and hiring a staff. Another indicator is the frequency with which the legislature meets. Does it meet for ten months, six months, or only one or two months? One effect of all of this is that an unpaid or underpaid group of legislators, not meeting very often, with little or no independent resources, may very well be in a weakened position in relation to other offices of government.

*What are the formal duties and powers that are given to the legislature?* In so-called constitutional governments in the modern world, this may be the single most important factor in analyzing the role and influence of the legislature. Written constitutions will likely specify exactly what areas the legislature can set policy on, what areas it may merely advise on, or what areas it may not touch at all. Article 1, Section 8, of the United States Constitution explicitly lists the powers of Congress. Such formal grants of power are often the main tool that the legislature possesses in asserting its influence in the process of government, and in analyzing legislative institutions, this is one of the first things to look for. (We must, however, be cautious in sorting out ritual from reality, particularly where the grant of power is general and vague, as in Article 30 of the Soviet constitution, which claims that "the highest organ of state power in the U.S.S.R. is the Supreme Soviet" and which goes on to say that "the legislative power of the U.S.S.R. is exercised exclusively by the Supreme Soviet of the U.S.S.R."[2] Constitutional statements such as these, which would appear to grant more sweeping powers than those possessed by the U.S. Congress, actually provide a much narrower role in their interpretation and application.)

Having collected this kind of information about the legislature, we do not automatically know what its role is in the process of government, for we have only described it as an institution. But using this knowledge as a base, we can proceed to a fuller understanding of the legislative role. How can we put this knowledge to use? In the previous chapter it was argued that political behavior could be analyzed in terms of external constraints and opportunities confronted by the individual, with the formal institutions of government representing one category of constraints. Thus, knowledge of the structure of the legislature provides us with information about the constraints and opportunities facing the legislator, as an official of government, and the citizen, as one who may have dealings with government and wish to influence its decisions and actions. The legislative role can be analyzed from three different perspectives: those of the individual legislator, the citizen, and the legislative body as a whole. If the individual is a member of a large legislative body he will automatically have to compete with several hundred other legislators for influence and likely he will have to achieve this influence by gaining leadership positions (such as a committee chairmanship or head of his party members in the legislature) which will only come with some seniority. The opposite extreme would be that of a city councilman who might only be one of, say, nine members, and who would be in a position to exert immediate influence through his own energy and aggressiveness.

Though large size may be a negative constraint on the legislator, the citizen may find certain advantages in it. If the members are all elected from districts, then the larger the legislature, the smaller each district will be, assuming they are apportioned according to population. The smaller the district, the more likely it should be that citizens can communicate their views to their representative. Finally, the legislature itself is constrained in relation to the other offices of government by these various factors. If its members are not full-time legislators, if the law of the land gives limited formal powers, or if it meets infrequently, the influence of the legislature within the government will be weakened; the reverse of these conditions can provide important opportunities for the body to assert itself in government. Of course, opportunities and constraints operating on the legislature itself will indirectly operate on political actors who would wish to use it as a political forum.

The structural features of the legislature not only tell us something about institutional constraints and opportunities; they also, as was mentioned earlier, provide us with clues as to the actual function or functions of the legislature. Since effective influence through lawmaking is the dominant concern in discussing legislative function, it can be used as the prime example.

How would we design a legislature which we wanted to be an active force in lawmaking? There is no simple formula nor is there one type of such a legislature, but there are some specific factors that can help or hinder this objective. First, the lawmaking function should be supported by some fairly clear and specific mandate of legal authority. It is all the better if this authority operates long enough to be reinforced by tradition. The selection of members through popular, free, competitive elections provides legislators with a source of legitimacy that will strengthen their hand in the governmental process. Either a small enough size to be manageable or, in the case of a larger-size house, strong, coherent internal leadership would be desirable. Resources and technical assistance in researching and investigating public problems and developing proposed laws, combined with the full-time dedication of the members, will also help. If we want to know what a legislature does we must, in the final analysis, watch it perform, but an institutional analysis of it can provide both clues to and explanations of its function. The Supreme Soviet in the USSR and the House of Commons in Great Britain do different things within their respective governments and they are designed accordingly.

## THE EXECUTIVE OFFICES

Every government requires as part of its formal operation the existence of public officials whose job it is to execute or carry out laws and decisions and provide a sense of direction and purpose to the task of governing. The vast majority of people who work in government are officials of this type. They range all the way from presidents, prime ministers, and kings to accountants, lawyers, soldiers, policemen, clerks, and mailmen who are, in varying ways and to varying degrees of importance, all engaged in doing the public's business.

There are two striking and virtually universal features of the organization of these offices. First, each person is part of a *hierarchy,* which means that he is subordinate to and takes direction from people above him and is responsible for others who are subordinate to him. Unlike a legislature, a collegial body of people officially equals of one another, a hierarchy is an arrangement of people who are officially unequal (see Figure 3–1). Second, executive authority at the very top of these hierarchical relationships is put in the hands of a *single individual.*[3] This individual may be absolute and unrestrained in his authority or he may be carefully limited by law, by other branches of government (legislature, courts), and by a network of formal and informal advisors; but it is one of the most widespread principles of governmental design that the exercise of this executive authority is ultimately traceable to that single chief executive whether he be known historically as king, dictator, president, chancellor, prime minister, mayor, governor, chief, or prince. Indeed, the universality of this role and its usual preponderance of power in most systems has made it virtually synonymous with "government."

One reason for these two structural principles is that the executive represents the *active* arm of government, that part of government that gets the business of government done. Much of what the executive does is define objectives and carry out tasks to fulfill those objectives. The natural, efficient, and responsive way to carry out such tasks is through hierarchical organization in which the task is given coherence and direction through commands emanating from the top. The traditional explanation for the role of the single chief executive is that the mobilizing of people behind a defined task requires a unity of purpose which can be achieved only by a single responsible leader. This single *head of state,* as he is commonly known, is often relied upon as a symbol of the unity of the body politic.

For purposes of analysis the executive offices of government may be divided into two categories: the political executive and the bureau-

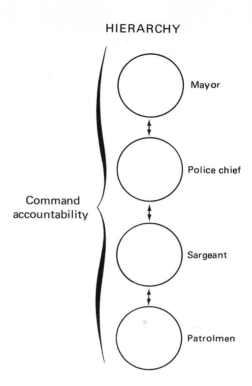

HIERARCHY

Mayor

Police chief

Command
accountability

Sargeant

Patrolmen

COLLEGIALITY

Deliberation, bargaining, voting

City
councilman

City
councilman

City
councilman

City
councilman

City
councilman

**Figure 3-1  Hierarchy versus Collegiality in Official Roles**

cracy, the first consisting of the top leadership and the latter consisting of the mass of public officials and the workers they direct.

## THE POLITICAL EXECUTIVE

We include under this heading the single head of state plus the immediate next layer of advisers and heads of major agencies and departments. As we have already suggested, the function of the political executive is to manage the overall task of executing public decisions, but this is by no means the only governmental function this top leadership may perform. The executive also performs certain kinds of lawmaking functions, and we can identify four ways in which this might occur.

First, the executive is typically charged with making those rules and regulations that are necessary for organizing administrative behavior. These will define who will be assigned what duties, whom they will report to, what approval is needed to take certain actions. Even where an active and powerful legislature is capable of getting into this kind of rule making, the bulk of it is done at the discretion of the executive. These types of rules constitute the internal law by which government itself operates.

Second, the executive can be a force in shaping law by virtue of discretionary powers that are either formally granted to it by the traditions and basic law of the land or given to it by the legislature itself. During World War II, for example, the president of the United States was given certain powers by Congress to control wages and prices, control which allowed room for presidential discretion to be employed without going back to Congress. In this way, the executive is allowed to apply a law to specific situations or adapt it to events and thereby represent, in a sense, a second step in the process of lawmaking.

Third, the executive will likely assume the task of extensively drafting proposed laws for legislative approval, what in this country we call a *legislative program.* This task inserts the executive, as a partner with the legislature, into the process of lawmaking. The executive can bring much influence to bear in this process for he can develop a single coordinated package of legislation and can tap the vast amount of information and talent available within the administration under him to design and defend such proposals. The power to sign bills into law puts this partnership role on a formal basis.

Fourth, all of the above ways of engaging in lawmaking, in varying degrees, apply to executives in political systems with active and effective legislatures. But where there is no legislature or where it is purely ritualistic, laws may be the product of executive decrees. The classic mark of dictatorships and absolute monarchies is the addition to the power of the executive of the unilateral power to make laws for society.

In considering the functions of the executive we cannot ignore the tremendous importance executive leadership has always had in serving, both symbolically and actually, as the focal point for the expression of public purposes and as an expression of the unity and action of the body politic as a whole. This *leadership function* fills as basic a need for political man as the need for deliberation, bargaining, and the representation of different interests. Recall that the very nature of politics and the purpose for formal government is to place the management of public affairs on a more or less orderly and predictable basis. Though deliberation and group decision making partially serve to do this, they may just as well bring conflicts to the surface without being able to resolve them decisively and use this resolution as the basis for action. The leadership function of the executive is designed to insure the ability of government to act decisively; one indication of this is the extent to which political systems turn to strengthening the political executive when confronted with political instability and social disorder. This is most apparent with the rise of dictatorships, as in the case of German nazism and Italian fascism in the 1920s and 1930s, but in more subtle ways it represents a tendency in all governments. Even in the United States those "great" presidents we speak of—Abraham Lincoln, Woodrow Wilson, Franklin D. Roosevelt—who have contributed so much to the power of the office usually governed during times of war when the nation was threatened by external enemies or internal division. Conversely, we have all but forgotten presidents like Millard Fillmore or Rutherford B. Hayes.

The executive functions of law enforcement, lawmaking, and leadership are generally structured along the lines of hierarchy, as we have seen, but beyond this there is considerable variety in the specific design of these offices. In approaching an analysis of the executive, one of the very first traps frequently encountered is distinguishing between *ruling* and *reigning* (just a more specific version of the distinction between ritual and reality). These terms represent two quite separate functions of the chief executive; the first refers to his governmental powers, the second refers to his ceremonial duties. We may say that the president of the United States is ruling when he is appointing cabinet members, signing bills, and giving orders to his subordinates; that he is reigning when he is giving a dinner for a visiting dignitary, attending the opening of a government building, or talking by telephone to astronauts on the moon. The main reason this is an important distinction to make is that even though the American president both rules and reigns, this is by no means the case in all political systems. Often these two functions are performed by two separate public officials. In Great Britain, there is both the queen and the prime minister, the former performing ceremonial functions as "head of state" and the latter performing executive functions as "head of government." Similarly, in Germany it is the president who reigns and the chancellor who rules. Though we do not distinguish these offices at the national level in the United States, if you happen to live in a city with a city-manager form of government, you can see the difference operating between the mayor, who may spend most of his time passing out keys to the city, and the city manager, who is directly responsible for running governmental operations. Obviously, where two separate offices are found it is important in analyzing the executive to take note of who is ruling and who is merely reigning.

The political executive consists not only of the single head of government but of other officials directly below him in the hierarchy. In this connection it is important to appreciate that, despite the concentration of responsibility and authority in the hands of the single chief executive, he cannot exercise power alone. Indeed, in terms of the exercise of power, it may be quite true to say that there cannot be such a thing as literal one-man rule, for every leader is inevitably and necessarily surrounded by advisors, aids, and department heads whom he greatly depends upon in exerting the full power of his office. The major reason for this is that, even in a relatively small political system, government quickly reaches a size and level of complexity that makes it impossible for one individual to thoroughly exercise control. The ability to know what is going on at all levels of the administration, and the ability to fashion rules and regulations guiding the myriad activities within these levels, clearly surpass the capacity of a single person. Thus, the chief executive commonly acts through others, and this is the basis for a layer of executive offices which stands between the chief executive and the general bureaucracy. They are considered here as a part of the political executive because their function more closely resembles the activity of the chief executive than the activity that goes on below them.

These officials are of two types: heads of departments and general advisors. The management of executive functions is broken down into a number of departments, which are simply subdivisions dealing with some specific area of public policy. At the national level there might be distinct departments dealing with such areas as foreign relations, military defense, agriculture, commerce, education, and public works; or at the local level we might find departments dealing with police, sanitation, housing, and mass transit. In national government the heads of these departments are frequently called ministers or secretaries. Along with their immediate assistants, they serve as the top officials within their departments and as the advisors, representatives, and arms of the chief executive in relation to their particular area of responsibility. Collectively they may be known as the cabinet or council of ministers, and as a group, depending on the particular style of government, they may engage in a certain amount of deliberation and advising. In addition to formal department heads, there is another loose category of such officials who have no direct responsibility for a department. These general advisors may receive appointments from the chief executive as assistants directly to him, with or without specific assignments. They will be engaged in a variety of tasks, such as formulating policy proposals, collecting and distilling information, and making recommendations to their superior.

Because of the visibility and public prominence of the chief executive in the eyes of the people at large, it is easy to mistakenly dismiss the importance of the rest of the governmental leadership. Carrying out the business of the executive is much more of a group process than it may appear on the surface, and tremendous amounts of power can be found among these officials. Therefore, it is important in studying government to consider not only the chief executive, but the kinds of people he surrounds himself with. The power of these officials can be seen in the fact that the chief executive cannot depend solely on the formal power of his commands and orders in dealing with them but must be able to assume their loyalty to him. He needs them as much as they need him, and he will attempt to choose people he can depend on.

How are these offices filled? How does one get to be a king, a president, or a mayor? One of the oldest means of filling the position of chief executive is *heredity,* meaning that the oldest child of a king would become the next monarch. This is found in more traditional or primitive systems and was prevalent in Europe during the later Middle Ages. Certain hereditary monarchies still exist formally even though they have long since lost their power in government and become ceremonial positions. Such is the case in Sweden and England. It is rare to find a ruling hereditary monarch in the world today, though the Shah of Iran is a notable instance.

*Popular election* is the typical democratic practice, whether it is direct or indirect. Direct election means that citizens actually mark their support on a ballot for one or another individual who becomes the chief executive. It is in this way that we choose all of our governors, many of our mayors, and (leaving aside the electoral college) the president. Indirect election is employed in what are known as parliamentary systems. Each political party selects, from among its members in parliament, a leader whom they will choose as prime minister, for example, if they have a majority. The voter does not vote directly for the prime minister, but in voting to support a particular party he or she is, in effect, helping to choose the prime minister. Note that one of the peculiarities of the parliamentary system is that the executive officers of government are chosen from the membership of the legislative branch but retain their seats in the legislature. We will be saying more about the parliamentary style of government later; here it serves to exemplify the method of indirect election.

Where neither of these methods is used, the system may rely on certain methods of *appointment*, or what may be, in effect, an election by a very narrow group. Thus, in the USSR the Supreme Soviet chooses the council of ministers and its chairman. Some such method is normal in contemporary communist regimes.

It is an unfortunate reflection on the lack of progress in man's political life that one of the more common means of gaining executive office within the nation-state is through *force*. The use of physical coercion to overthrow existing leadership and install oneself and one's followers in public office, known as a *coup d'état*, is still a widespread method of creating dictatorship. The existing regimes of such countries as Uganda, Cuba, Libya, Peru, Bolivia, and Nigeria are all led by individuals who achieved power through a successful coup. The difficulty that arises in these situations is that the coup tends to aggravate political disunity and usually requires the continued application of force to sustain the new leadership in office. If a leader has achieved office through force, usually he can be removed only by force. A further difficulty results from what is known as a succession crisis, the disorder and conflict attending the death of a dictator who has provided no institutional means by which his successor may be chosen. The phenomenon of the succession crisis shows why stable institutional means of generating new leadership is important.

Other executive officials are normally chosen by appointment of the chief executive, though he may be limited in making this choice. The requirement in our Constitution that the Senate advise and consent to cabinet appointments is one of the constraints on the president. A variation on this appointment method is found in parliamentary systems, with the cabinet as well as the prime minister selected by the party in power.

Finally, we should add that the role of the executive is affected by the orientations of the individual and the constraints of the system just like any other official or unofficial role in politics. One of the most important developments of the modern period has been the attempt to use legal and constitutional constraints to prevent the excessive concentration of power in the hands of the executive. This resulted from the traditional concentration of power in the hands of a small elite and from the inclination of the executive, given its control over the organized power of government and its leadership function, to expand its influence if not explicitly held in check. The variety of constitutional checks consists of such things as explicit legal restrictions on the executive, the requirement in parliamentary systems that the executive maintain the support of the majority in the legislature, and the distribution of governmental power among other branches of government independent of the executive.

## THE BUREAUCRACY

The other component of the executive that needs to be examined in studying the workings of governmental machinery is the administrative offices or, to use the term that characterizes the modern form of organizing administrative tasks, the *bureaucracy*. The bureaucracy is that part of the executive which operates directly under the authority of the political executive and is designed to serve primarily the function of carrying out policies already decided upon elsewhere in the government. To put it quite simply, the institutional purpose of the bureaucracy is to get things done.

Many years ago the German sociologist Max Weber described what a perfect bureaucratic form of organization would look like. Weber argued that the purpose behind bureaucratic design was to coordinate the work of large numbers of people to accomplish a defined task in the most efficient way. Such a style of organization would be built upon certain definite principles. To begin with, the total task of the organization would be broken down into a large number of very specific tasks; in other words, there would be a division of labor in which each bureaucrat would have specifically assigned duties. These various bureaucrats would then relate to each other as part of a very formal hierarchy such that at any one point in the bureaucracy an official would be accountable to a particular superior for what he does and for what goes on below him in the organization. This hierarchical division of labor, Weber argued, would then be held together and coordinated by a consistent system of abstract rules. People in the bureaucracy would deal with each other and with people outside the bureaucracy by an equitable and impersonal application of these rules and execution of their duties. Finally, recruitment into the bureaucracy and advancement to higher positions would be based exclusively on an evaluation of one's technical skills, knowledge, and merit appropriate to the official duties required of him.[4]

If you take a look at some familiar bureaucracy—and they are all around us—you may be able to discern the operation of these principles that Weber described. Consider, for example, a registrar's office at a college or university. There are several clerks and secretaries who each have some specific task: filing, verifying the accuracy of transcripts, mailing out requests for transcripts, feeding registration forms into a computer, and so on. If it is a large university, some of these clerks will oversee the work of several people under them but, in any event, they will all be accountable to a registrar who hires them, defines their tasks, and insures that the tasks are being performed. The registrar, in turn, reports to a higher official, a dean or the president. The activities of these people are defined and coordinated by certain set rules, such as the rule that only certain kinds of letter grades can be marked on a transcript, that every student must have some letter grade reported for every course he enrolls in, that when a student requests a transcript it will cost two dollars, and that transcripts will not be sent out for a student who owes money to the university. Presumably these rules will be applied to everyone without special favors so that even if a personal friend or relative of yours happens to work in the registrar's office you should not assume that you will be treated any differently from anyone else. Finally, the various workers in the registrar's office have supposedly acquired their jobs on the basis of some manifest skills which might be measured by their formal training, previous job experience, or successful performance on an examination. Taken as a whole, the office of the registrar, as a subdivision of the overall administration of the university's affairs, is designed for the efficient performance of a specific, predefined task, that is, the accurate registration of students into courses and the maintenance and handling of the permanent records of what courses students took and what grades they received.

What is curious about our experiences with bureaucracies, such as the one described here, is that many of the things we dislike about them are precisely the things which Weber tells us are their greatest virtues. We often come away from our dealings with bureaucrats complaining about their impersonal treatment of us, which we interpret as a lack of sympathy for our special problem or dilemma. The individual clerk in the registrar's office may show complete lack of interest in our personal financial problems which interfere with paying our debts to the university and thereby receiving a transcript. Yet Weber's theory suggests that it is precisely this kind of behavior on the part of the clerk that makes the bureaucracy work in an efficient and responsible manner. We also find it difficult to understand why the bureaucrat always argues,

"If I do it for you, I will be expected to do it for everyone," but this derives from the classic bureaucratic principle of applying a general system of abstract rules to all on an equal basis. One of the most irritating of these experiences is the answer, "Sorry, that is not my job," or "Sorry, I am just doing what I have been told to do." From the bureaucrat's point of view, of course, he is only doing what he is supposed to do and operating within the chain of command.

The purpose of these remarks is simply to explain the way bureaucrats behave, not to justify it. They do not behave the way they do because they are particularly quarrelsome people with deficient personalities; it is rather bureaucracy as an institution in modern society that has created certain kinds of behavior, that is, a *bureaucratic role.* Whether this behavior is justifiable, necessary, useful, or effective is another question and an important one for modern society.

The study of bureaucracy, however, involves much more than applying Weber's idealized picture of it. Perhaps by virtue of the very unnaturalness that we associate with bureaucratic behavior, bureaucracies seldom operate in exactly the way Weber described, and an accurate study of such governmental offices requires that we be alert to these variations. The ability to advance oneself through "making the right contacts" and ally oneself with the right people, the less favorable treatment of poor people and racial minorities by bureaucrats, the distortion of information that is passed up through the chain of command to make lower officials look good, the power of individual bureaucrats to be arbitrary and capricious in using their official positions, the passing over of real talent in favor of those who have gone to the "right schools" or are of the right social class—all of these are ordinary and commonplace ways in which modern bureaucracy falls short of the abstract model. This model may tell us about the purely formal principles on which bureaucracy is based, but this should not exclude from consideration the inevitable human and political dynamics that will help tell us what is really going on in a bureaucracy.

To put the matter quite simply, it is important to realize that there is politics going on in bureaucracy just as there is in every other area of government. The bureaucrat's formal mission may involve simply implementing policy but, looked at another way, he may also be viewed as a political actor with certain official powers and responsibilities and a certain political interest in protecting and expanding his influence. In this respect, as with other political actors, we can study the bureaucrat's behavior by reference to the institutional opportunities and constraints that characterize his situation in government. The institutional limitations on him may be quite substantial, especially the fact that his position in the administration is defined by a narrow field of duties. If he is to exert influence, he will be initially limited by the defined span of his expertise and area of responsibility. An expert in the Food and Drug Administration can hardly use his official influence to effect decisions in the area of national defense. His field of action and influence is also constrained by the formal rules and expectations of administrative behavior. A casual and unrestrained lobbying and public voicing of opinion would be inappropriate and might very well backfire by destroying the individual's credibility as an expert administrator who is supposed to be politically neutral.

On the other hand, there are many things the bureaucrat has going for him, and the most important is that just as the chief executive has a certain dependence on his immediate subordinates, the administrative head must depend on the loyalty and skill of the bureaucrats beneath him. The bureaucrat has an interesting advantage over everyone else in that he operates on the "front lines"—everything that government does must pass through his hands. Even if his range of duties is narrow, he will ordinarily have a more profound and thorough knowledge of his special area than anyone else. This gives bureaucrats a tremendous power over one of the popularly underestimated resources of politics, *information*. Indeed, what the bureaucracy is very much about is the use and management of information. This control over information does not mean that bureaucrats exercise power simply by lying to their bosses, though that may happen. The use of information is not just a question of gathering facts—it is also a question of analyzing, interpreting, and organizing facts in some meaningful way that makes it possible to deal effectively with the enormous and overwhelming amount of information that gets processed in government. This management of information is a job mainly for bureaucrats and one of the critical things that higher officials depend on the bureaucracy for. This offers a critical opportunity to shape policy by shaping the information on which policy is based. If the president or secretary of defense wishes to consider the addition of a new military weapon, or the choice of several new weapons, he must turn to cost analysts, weapons experts, engineers, and military strategists for the relevant information needed to weigh the decision in a rational manner. What they tell him about the expense and effectiveness of each weapon's option will influence the choice.

Bureaucracy and politics also come to be mixed together by the "politicization" of the bureaucracy, as the political leadership of the system replaces the bureaucratic principles and norms described by Weber with purely political norms. The most obvious version of this is found in totalitarian systems where dedication and loyalty to the specific political doctrines of the elite may be as important as or more

important than merit or expertise as the basis of achieving high bureaucratic position. Beyond its limited range of administrative duties, the
bureaucracy is expected to assume the larger role of displaying and
promoting the prevailing political doctrine. There is danger in this
approach of weakening the ability of the bureaucracy to perform in an
efficient way, and some observers have argued that Stalin's excessive
and violent purge of military leaders in Russia during the 1930s on the
grounds that they were political enemies threatening his regime is an
important explanation for Russia's military weakness at the outset of
World War II. Similarly, the civil service system in the United States was
created in an attempt to remove the political influence from the bureaucracy at a time when all administrative posts could be filled by the
supporters of whichever party won the election. The issue of the politicization of the bureaucracy also came up at the time of the Watergate
scandals, when it was charged that people on the president's staff,
perhaps at the president's direction, were trying to initiate Internal
Revenue Service audits of the income tax returns of people they considered their "political enemies." Such actions hardly fit with what we
would consider the proper role of the bureaucracy in our system of
government, which is to collect taxes in an equitable manner without
regard to which political party one belongs to.

The importance of these several observations is simply this: the study
of bureaucratic institutions necessarily involves us in the study not only
of the formal structure of administrative work but of the extent to
which such structures represent yet another setting in which we discover political experience.


## THE COURTS

Another major set of institutions encountered in the study of modern
governments is the *courts*. The essential purpose of courts is to judge,
interpret, and preserve the prevailing rules and laws of the political
system. Their function derives from the existence of disputes and the
need for a method to resolve them. The courts do not deal with any type
of dispute, but with those which question whether the law has been
properly interpreted or followed. If you sign a contract with a construction company to build a house for you and you feel that the company
has not lived up to its side of the agreement, your charges initiate a
dispute which, if not resolved by informal means, may be tested against
the legal terms of the contract. On the other hand, let us say you are
arrested for speeding. If you plead guilty you are raising no dispute or
quarrel with the police officer's action against you. If you plead not

guilty you are saying, in effect, that the policeman's attempt to enforce the law through application of his police powers was mistaken in this case. In order to deal with issues of this sort, the design of government includes numerous public bodies and officials, most commonly known as courts, that serve what may be called the judicial function. Thus, the dispute between you and the police or you and the construction company is heard by a court—a forum within which the dispute may be settled one way or the other. The general method by which courts do this is to match the facts against the law. Viewed in this way, the two general functions of courts are the *adjudication* of specific disputes and the *preservation* of the laws, norms, and traditions of the political system.

In studying courts as institutions of government, there are certain common structural elements to look for. The centerpiece of the court structure is the judge who administers the judicial process and is the ultimate official authority in the court. The exact tasks of the judge will vary, depending on the type of court and the judicial practices of the particular system. He may operate alone or he may operate as one of a group of judges sitting as a panel, in which case decisions will result from collective deliberation. Final judgments in cases may not be made by the judge at all if he is aided by a jury. The jury system involves the recruitment of a group of citizens empowered to make judgments in judicial disputes, while the judge administers the process of hearing the case and makes procedural rulings and instructs jurors regarding their responsibilities. Jurors and judges are not the only official participants in the judicial process; the other critical group is the lawyers who represent the disputing parties. Though his interest is in his client's case, the lawyer is typically thought of as an "officer of the court" who has responsibilities and expectations placed on him beyond those of the private citizen.

The other aspect of the courts to be examined is the way in which the judicial task is divided up and distributed among various courts within the judicial system. A common distinction is between courts of original jurisdiction and appellate courts. The former refers to courts empowered to hear disputes for the first time; this is the point at which the use of jurors is encountered. Appellate courts are those having jurisdiction over the appeal of an earlier court decision. The existence of an appellate process indicates that under certain conditions, the decision of the original court need not be treated as final, and the dispute may be carried on to a higher court. It is possible for the same court to have, under law, a mixture of some original jurisdiction and some appellate jurisdiction (such as the Supreme Court of the United States), though typically these functions are not mixed. Depending on the complexity of the judicial system, there may also be several layers of appellate courts, so that one may receive more than one appeal. In addition to the distinction between original and appellate jurisdictions, there are two other organizing principles that may be used in designing the court system. First, courts may be organized around a defined territorial jurisdiction, thus creating local, state, regional, and national courts, with each court being limited to hearing cases arising within its boundaries. Territorial jurisdiction creates several tiers as these boundaries become larger, leading up to the national level. The second organizing principle, encountered particularly at the local level, is the division of jurisdiction according to certain kinds of disputes, as in the case of a small claims court, a family court, or an administrative court.

One similarity between the courts and the bureaucracy is that courts are also thought to have a very restricted set of functions with no latitude for the political discretion and judgment that resides in the executive and the legislature. One of the great accomplishments attributed to the modern constitutional state is the removal of the courts from politics. Within our political culture, it is expected that judges will be wise, prudent, and objective, will merely apply the law, as handed down, to the facts as verified in court, and will not distort their judgments with personal or political prejudices. This explains why, for example, American judges are sometimes appointed for life (so they cannot be subsequently influenced by the politicians who appointed them) or, when elected, prohibited from identifying themselves with a particular political party (called a nonpartisan election). Whether or not this removal from politics works is an important subject of political analysis and again takes us back to the issue of ritual versus reality. Are the judges' robes and the hushed courtroom the symbols of an even-handed justice that does not actually exist? Though judges may be removed from politics, they are not removed from government. Their decisions can be as consequential in the life of the citizen as the decisions of any legislature or executive. Whether justice is really occurring or not is a vital political question.

By virtue of this attempt to remove courts from politics, there are numerous constraints which limit the influence of a judge. A major constraint is the very expectation of impartiality which is imposed by the political culture and may be institutionally reinforced by the appellate process which allows the decisions of one judge to be examined by other judges. The frequent overruling of a judge by appellate courts is commonly taken as a sign of a deficiency in a judge's professional ability or standards. Another very basic institutional constraint is that courts make decisions only when disputes are brought to them, which means that they are only passive agents in determining what issues they will be influencing. They cannot take up any public question they wish to; they must wait for a relevant case to arise.

Ironically, the very factor which seems to tie the hands of the court politically also provides it with its main opportunity to exert influence; that is, by being removed from politics judges can presumably make decisions according to their own interpretation of the law without being constrained by the attitudes of powerful elites or public opinion. Thus, in the American legal system, courts have been used by individuals and groups as an important governmental vehicle for the recognition of valuable civil rights that could not have found expression elsewhere because of their political unpopularity or controversy.

## HOW INSTITUTIONS FIT TOGETHER

While an analysis of these institutional components—the legislature, executive, bureaucracy, courts—is an important part of understanding the workings of formal government, it is equally important to consider how these various components fit together in the overall design of government.

For the political scientist perhaps the most important aspect of the way institutions fit together is the degree of differentiation and specialization—the extent to which governmental functions are divided among a number of somewhat independent branches of government. To understand this better, consider that in many traditional or primitive societies many of the governmental functions we have mentioned here—leadership, representation, lawmaking, administration, adjudication, conflict-management—were all performed by the same person. The king or tribal chief declared what the law was, enforced it, interpreted it, and saw himself as the representative of the whole society. There was, in effect, only one institution, which performed many functions. One of the characteristics of the modern state, it has been argued, is that institutions become more complex and specialized and the functions of government are not concentrated in the same hands. In order to see the different ways the components of government fit together and the extent of the specialization, we can consider three basic patterns that occur in modern politics.

### Separation of Powers

The United States is the prime example of this greatest differentiation. There are strict constitutional divisions among the three main branches—Congress, the executive branch, and the courts. The president and Congress are elected separately, with separate terms of office, and the president does not sit as a member of Congress. Even the bureaucracy is recruited under civil service laws—only a relatively few top posts can be filled by the president. The nonpolitical character of the bureaucracy and the courts is of great value in the political culture. We have even carried this diversification of institutions to the point of creating a number of so-called regulatory commissions to oversee particular fields somewhat independent of both the executive and the legislature. These include such bodies as the Federal Communications Commission (FCC), the Federal Trade Commission (FTC), and the Federal Securities and Exchange Commission (FSEC).

The explicit purpose behind such a design is to create countervailing powers in government or what is more popularly known as checks and balances. The idea is that this will make it difficult for power to concentrate in one office or branch of government. Though this is achieved to a certain degree, the value of such checks and balances must be weighed against the dangers of their working all too well and thereby making the coordination of governmental activities difficult and inefficient. This is an appropriate type of design when the main concern is protecting society against governmental corruption and abuse of power.

## Parliamentary Government

The main distinguishing feature of this format is that the executive and legislative branches are combined by having the members of the legislature choose from among their own members those who will fill the top executive positions of government. Thus, in Great Britain the prime minister and his cabinet are voted into office by a majority of the members of the House of Commons and serve not only as the executive branch but as party leaders within the legislature. This working majority in a parliamentary system can be achieved either by one party clearly winning a majority in the parliament or by a group of parties allying with each other in a coalition to form a majority out of their combined strength. Though these systems extoll the value of justice under law, free from political influence, the judiciary often lacks the structural separation from the rest of the government encountered under separation of powers.

Political scientists have often felt that the executive/legislative arrangement in this particular design provides a clearer coordination of policies and actions since these two branches are controlled by people from the same party or parties, unlike in the United States where recent Republican presidents have had to deal with a Democratic-controlled

Congress. But in order to achieve this kind of smooth coordination, it is essential in parliamentary government to have a durable majority in the legislative branch, for if the "government" fails to maintain its majority, a new majority must be formed either by new elections or by the development of a new coalition. This feature has resulted in considerable instability in countries like Italy, where there has been great dependence on coalitions that have not been very durable.

It is also interesting to note how the fit among institutions affects their function. In our separation-of-powers system, constituency service functions represent an important part of the legislator's activity, yet in a parliamentary system, with its tremendous emphasis on maintaining a working majority, the legislator's role is much more strongly oriented to matters of party cohesion and party platforms than it is to his individual district.

## Authoritarian Government

This governmental design is a rather substantial departure from the previous two. Here the legislative structures are relatively weak compared to the executive—if, indeed, they are allowed to exist at all. Their most obvious function would be the symbolic legitimizing of policies and decisions shaped by the executive leadership. An even more marked characteristic is the politicization of the bureaucracy and the courts. In the Soviet Union, for example, the court system is not allowed any latitude in interpreting an independent body of law in such a way as to conflict with the political direction of the executive leadership. Even where there is the appearance of structural differentiation, the reality of governmental power tends to be concentrated in a single set of offices, causing this form of government to resemble, in some respects, more traditional governmental forms.

This lack of differentiation, though created for the purpose of achieving the ultimate in centralized direction of government, may be charged with weakening or eliminating certain kinds of functions, such as representation, public deliberation of competing political views, and the neutral adjudication of disputes between the citizen and government.

As these examples suggest, an important aspect of the study of government institutions consists of examining the overall design that is used in fitting the various components together. This matter of how they "fit" is also a key to distinguishing between ritual versus reality in the study of formal government, for the common presence of courts and legislative bodies should not hide the critical differences from one system to another in how they relate to government as a whole.

## POLITICS AND THE DESIGN OF INSTITUTIONS

Reflecting on this brief review of the machinery of government, there is one very important principle to keep in mind: the design of government is itself the creation of politics. This is to say that government is not merely the institutional setting within which politics goes on, but is also the product of political decisions and actions and the object of political conflict. A classic concern of political man through history has been the discovery of the "best form of government," and views about the proper design of government have been a major source of contention among various political doctrines.

The central reason why the design of institutions is a political question of great impact is that the *way* decisions are made and the *way* governmental duties and responsibilities are organized can have a great deal to do with *what* decisions and actions result and with *who* has political influence. The development of the modern representative legislature is a classic case in point. It was an institutional device advanced by groups in society who had no previous foothold in government; specifically it was an attempt by the new middle class, which had achieved a certain economic and social power, to translate their recently acquired social influence into governmental power. They could not do this if entry into government was controlled by heredity and accident of birth into the aristocratic class, but they could do this if entry was controlled by elections to a parliament. It was expected also that the increasing power of the legislature would result in less arbitrary and capricious actions on the part of government and greater freedom for the individual.

Political controversy surrounding the design of rules and institutions is a commonplace in political experience and can be seen in a community debating a new city charter, a national party convention quarreling over its rules, and political factions attempting to influence the manner in which legislative districts are apportioned. Governmental rules can be used as political weapons, as when the legal requirements for getting one's name on a ballot are made sufficiently difficult to discourage people from trying, thereby eliminating some political competition at the voting booth. Such conflict can appear quite petty, as in 1968, when, after the United States and North Vietnam had agreed to peace talks, diplomats wrangled for several weeks over which city the talks should be held in and even what shape table the negotiators should sit around.

One of the more dramatic instances in which institutional arrangements can affect "who gets what" in politics concerns popular election of legislators. There is a very wide variety of ways to organize these elections, but as an example we can consider two basic approaches and their effects on politics. The first method is the *single-member district method.* The population is divided into a number of districts (presumably of equal size) equivalent to the number of seats in the legislative body. If the legislature consists of one hundred seats, there would be one hundred districts with each electing one person to fill the one seat assigned to it. Each seat is filled by the candidate who receives the greatest number of votes in a popular election.

In contrast to this, there is the system of *proportional representation,* a bit more complicated. By this system, the one hundred seats would be divided, let us say, into only twenty districts, with each district having to elect five people to fill the seats allotted to it. Each party competing in the election would nominate a list of five candidates in a district and each voter would cast a single vote for one of the party lists. The number of seats won by a party would be determined by the proportion of the vote that the party receives. Thus, in the example shown in Table 3–1, Party A would win three of the five seats as a result of having attracted 60 percent of the vote in the election (for the purposes of the example the math has been made simple, though in proportional representation it can get quite complex), and parties B and C would each win one seat for their respective 20 percent of the vote. In this way, the five seats for each district are filled.

Why does it make any political difference which of these formal methods of election is used? Under the first system you can win a seat only if you attract a plurality of votes (more votes than anyone else), which would seem to discourage anyone from running for office unless he or she either had a good chance of getting that plurality or was not seriously interested in winning in the first place. As a matter of fact, if the weaker of two political parties received 45 percent of the vote in each of the one hundred districts, it would end up with electoral support from almost half of the population, despite not winning a single seat in the legislature. This system rewards only majorities. On the other hand, proportional representation results in seats being won by parties that receive neither a majority nor the greatest number of votes.

Table 3–1. Hypothetical Election Results in Which Five Seats are Filled by Proportional Representation in a Single District

| Party | Percentage of Popular Vote for Each Party | Number of Seats Won by Each Party |
|---|---|---|
| Party A | 60 | 3 |
| Party B | 20 | 1 |
| Party C | 20 | 1 |

The seats are "proportioned" to parties according to their percentage of the vote, which means that, as in our example, a party receiving only 20 percent of the vote would still receive one seat. Such an arrangement is obviously more encouraging to smaller parties that may be unlikely to achieve a majority but would still be able to be represented in government. These two electoral methods, in effect, can help determine what kinds of political parties will arise, how many of them there will be, and what political strategy they will follow. There are distinct political values at stake in the choice between these two methods, as well as advantages and disadvantages to each. Proportional representation would seem to advance the value of the representativeness of government and of making the legislature a forum for diverse political factions; the single-member system places a greater value on achieving a large consensual majority in government. The difference between the two-party system of the United States and Great Britain and the multiparty system found in many European countries has at least partially been explained by references to these differences in electoral method.

## THE BASIS OF INSTITUTIONAL AUTHORITY

These reflections on the politics at stake in the design of institutions naturally lead to the question of the basis of institutional authority. On what grounds does the formal authority of government rest, considering that government is, after all, but the creation of political man? There is a certain mystery to this question in light of the fact that government is so widely accepted in society while at the same time the justification for some particular form of government is far from obvious. There are three possible bases on which this authority may be considered to rest, each of which seldom operates totally by itself.

### Tradition

Government represents one of the traditions of a society—the way that things have always been done. Though we may not be inclined to take tradition seriously, it is nonetheless an important factor in political experience, and many societies in history have depended heavily on respect for tradition as the basis of governmental authority. An appeal to tradition means that something should be done in a particular way because that is how it has always been done, how it was done in the past.

The authority of aristocrats and monarchs is a classic instance of this principle in action. The passing on of hereditary title from one generation to another developed as a practice over centuries, becoming increasingly more accepted the more it was used. The ability to show a direct link to such ancient origins has always been a trademark of the tradition-based system. Another example of relying on the past to guide the present is the Anglo-American tradition of *common law*. Under a common-law system a judge comes to a determination in a case by making reference to the earlier decisions of judges in similar cases. In England, where this tradition of law originated, judges might go back to precedents hundreds of years old. The law thus consists of an accumulation of such precedents over time, and learning the law means quite literally reading the history of such decisions.

Perhaps because our own political system partially grew out of an attack against the traditions of monarchy, we may be tempted to dismiss the influence of tradition within what we consider a modern system of government. More correctly, we should appreciate that tradition is an important factor in any stable system over time and that our attachment to our own form of government is influenced by respect for its history. Consider your own reaction or the reaction of society at large to a proposal to replace our present separation-of-power, presidential model of government with a parliamentary arrangement. Our defensiveness or outright rejection of such a proposal hardly could be based on its unfeasibility—our British and Canadian friends have had rather good luck with it—but it could be based on the long attachment we have developed to our own institutions.

We also may be tempted to think that there is something wrong, irrational, or unjustifiable about this attachment to tradition; but, at least up to a point, respect for political tradition is a perfectly healthy and natural thing. The only way any political system can endure over time is if certain of its basic practices and principles are routinely accepted without constant question; another way of saying this is that it is useful if a political system is somewhat accepted out of habit. The political order would not be possible if every act, law, decision, rule, and public office were regularly and daily called into question by every citizen. Rationally, neither the individual nor the system as a whole could cope with such demands placed upon our judgment. For political man to function at all he needs to develop certain habits of acceptance or compliance, and the proven record of tradition is one of the things that helps him do this. If this were not present, every political dispute would lead to a challenge against the total political system. That does not happen, and it would make government impossible if it did. We do not wish to suggest that traditions and habits of compliance cannot or should not be called into question, only that there is nothing inherently wrong or irrational about them.

A final observation about tradition as the basis of institutional authority is, quite obviously, that for tradition to be relevant the political system has to be old; in other words, you have to have been around for awhile to have a tradition. In the broadest sense, all societies have some traditions but there are various ways in which their ties to tradition can be broken and their knowledge of the past lost. The two most common threats to tradition are revolution and the conquest and colonization of society by an outside power. The main victim of such violent shifts in the political destiny of a society is its ties to its own past which the new political leadership fears and attacks as a danger to their regime. The new regime is faced with depending on the complacency of the people, constructing some new basis of authority, or, as is frequently the case, resorting to a considerable use of physical force. If the new regime lasts long enough, and this probably means at least two generations, it may develop traditions of its own to strengthen its position. In any event, the use of tradition depends directly on the passage of time and the growth of a historical record of political experiences that a society can refer back to.

## Constitutional Founding

The other great modern basis of institutional authority is the principle that legitimate government is the product of a specific act of founding a state as expressed in a written constitutional document that, in one way or another, manifests the consensus of the people. Max Weber, whom we encountered in our discussion of bureaucracy, refers to this as "rational/legal" authority as opposed to traditional authority. The idea is that government represents a more or less rational system of rules and laws tied to a basic constitutional framework to which political man can appeal as the standard of justice. It is this notion of governmental authority that is described by the term *constitutional government.* The importance of this idea in the modern world can be appreciated by looking at the number of governments that have defined their structure and derived their operating authority from a constitutional document, among them the United States, Germany, Japan, France, and Canada. Indeed, the influence of this idea in the modern period is also attested to by the use of "constitutions" even in those systems that are not, properly speaking, constitutional in their actual operation; the Soviet Union, for example, has a constitution dating back to 1936.

The idea of constitutional authority brings to our attention a vital modern institution that we have not yet examined, that is, *law.* A law is simply a formal, authoritative rule made by government or accepted as the basis of government. In a very broad sense all political systems use law, but strictly speaking the idea of law is that it serves as a rule or principle that operates more or less independently from the influence of particular individuals. To quote the original draft of the Massachusetts constitution, we have "a government of laws, and not of men," which means that there are rules that cannot be obeyed, altered, or created at the unilateral discretion of some individuals. Accompanying this is the idea that all men are under the law, that is, the law itself, not the will or prerogative of individual political leaders, is the supreme expression of authority.

Of course, laws are still made by real people, and the system of law will represent the distribution of political power in society; but the purpose of law, which should still be accomplished, is to provide a constraint on the actions of powerful people and known boundaries within which they must operate. A good test of whether a particular system is really following the principle of "rule under law" is whether or not average citizens or those lacking real political power in society are able to use the law and such institutions as the courts or the legislature to redress their grievances and protect themselves from government itself. Are they, in effect, able to make legal challenges against government at all without punishment or reprisals? Usually if a government can pass this test, there is fairly good evidence that some rule of law is in force.

In constitutional government, the study of politics can lead to extensive study of the law itself, and how it is made, interpreted, and applied. That law which guides the operation of government itself is called *public* law (this is, in effect, what we call *constitutional* law), whereas *private* law is that law made by government to control individual behavior and social relationships. The latter is typically broken down into *criminal* law, which concerns actions that are considered to be against the peace and order of the community as a whole (murder, robbery), and *civil* law, which governs legal relationships among private individuals (violation of contracts). The use of law in providing legitimacy to government does not result merely from the fact that there are laws but from the fact that they derive from some constitutional source and can be changed, created, and adjudicated through known procedures that are themselves legally defined and protected. A working legal system requires appropriate institutions to go along with it and this is why we find in constitutional government the principle of nonpolitical bureaucracies and courts and a legislature with lawmaking functions.

## Ideology

Though the constitutional and traditional bases of formal authority are widespread, they do not satisfactorily account for all cases. At least one other general basis should be described, that is, *ideology*. Stated in the simplest way, ideology means an applied system of political beliefs and values that is intended to serve as a comprehensive interpretation of the political world. As the basis of public authority, the reliance on an ideology is a relatively new phenomenon in history, really appearing only in this century. It is included here because without it it would be difficult to account for such systems as present-day China and the USSR or Nazi Germany and Fascist Italy before World War II. In these political systems the justification for their form of government does not rest primarily upon tradition or constitutionalism but upon appeal to a specific ideology such as communism or fascism. It is reference to a guiding ideology that serves as an explanation for the particular design of institutions and the measure of legitimate official conduct. Thus, government is run the way it is run because "we are serving the interests of the working class in overthrowing capitalism" or "we are advancing the greatness of German culture and civilization." Ideology may play some legitimizing role in almost any modern state, but in the cases mentioned here it plays a predominant role which tends to weaken the influence of tradition and law. The fact that these types of systems happen to be totalitarian dictatorships has worried political scientists about this development.

As we mentioned, these three bases of authority seldom operate in isolation from each other but are often mixed together in political experience. How one responds to questions about the appropriateness or legitimacy of government is a good test for determining which of these principles is being invoked. For example, if asked why we should have separation of powers in our national government, it could be answered that this is the way we have always done things in this country (traditional response), or that it is dictated by the basic law of the land (constitutional/legal response), or that this principle of government protects individualism and the values of democracy (ideological response). Politically it may be important which of these justifications is employed, and it is not surprising that political systems differ according to which of these, if any, is clearly dominant.

A full grasp of any particular institution in any particular system obviously would involve a much more detailed and elaborate explanation than what has been provided here. Our immediate objective has been simply to show the kinds of things that one should look for in trying to understand the role of institutions and how these institutions tend to shape, arrange, control, and direct political action, making them a vital component of political experience.

## NOTES

[1]Arthur S. Banks, ed., *Political Handbook of the World, 1975* (New York, 1975), p. 105.

[2]R. Macridis and R. Ward, *Modern Political Systems* (Englewood Cliffs, N.J., 1963), p. 114.

[3]There have been isolated modern examples of collegial chief executives such as the Federal Council of Switzerland which consists of seven members and the presidential board system of Uruguay which went out of use in 1967.

[4]H. Gerth and C. Wright Mills, eds., *From Max Weber* (New York, 1958), pp. 196–98.

## FOR FURTHER READING

Hummel, Ralph P. *The Bureaucratic Experience.* New York: St. Martin's Press, 1977. A recent exploration of bureaucracy that is good for its treatment of the relationships between bureaucracy and politics and its stress on the human dimension of bureaucratic experience.

Jewell, Malcom E., and Samuel C. Patterson. *The Legislative Process in the United States.* New York: Random House, 1966. A basic text for pursuing the study of the American legislative process. Shows the connection between formal institutions and such considerations as roles, parties, and interest groups.

Neustadt, Richard E. *Presidential Power.* New York: New American Library, 1964. An interesting analysis of the American presidency, dealing with the relationship between institutional power and the demands of political leadership.

Pitkin, Hanna Fenichel. *The Concept of Representation.* Berkeley: University of California Press, 1972. A sophisticated and probing analysis of a central concept in the design of modern governmental institutions.

Spiro, Herbert J. *Government by Constitution.* New York: Random House, 1959. A traditional analysis of the legal and institutional structures of several major Western powers.

# 4

# Groups and the Political Process

We have approached the study of political experience from two specific perspectives so far—the individual and the governmental institutions—but if we reflect on political experience, it is apparent that it is made up of something more than just ourselves and government. It is probably rare and exceptional that we have ever been significantly involved in the business of politics as lone individuals or that the processes of government ever consist of the interplay of purely individual political actors. The missing element in this picture consists of the groups and factions that are formed by people when they engage in political activity. To round out our study of the components of the political system, we must consider (1) the variety of factions, parties, interest groups, movements, and associations that bring people together and serve to organize and direct their political action, and (2) the basic elements of the political process of which they are a part. In other words, how do people work together politically and what do they do in the political process?

The phenomenon of groups or factions is a universal element in politics. Even in monarchies and dictatorships where the mass of people are not actively involved in politics, the small ruling elite is likely to display factional differences among various members of the elite who have different objectives, ambitions, or outlooks. One of the dominant political features of the modern age is the inclusion of the mass of citizens in public affairs in one form or another and the development of large-scale political organizing to manage this involvement. In the most general sense, the role of political groups is to organize people for the purpose of achieving some political objective; groups will differ according to what these objectives are and what type of organizing is legally permitted and politically appropriate. Most significant political experience on the part of Americans has invariably led to encounters with one or more of such groups which so extensively populate our political environment—among them, the United Auto Workers, Common Cause, the American Medical Association, the National Rifle Association, the Republican party, the Democratic party, the War Resisters League, the National Association of Manufacturers. The point is that politics is something we do along with others—by its very nature it is not something that we usually do all by ourselves. To advance a political objective means, quite naturally, to seek the support of others, and politics consists not so much of a conflict among individuals but of a conflict among factions within the political system.

In studying political groups there are two basic things we want to know at the outset: (1) what different kinds of groups there are and (2) what patterns of political organization occur within different political systems. Again, as with the treatment of political behavior, there are certain general categories and distinctions that can assist us in finding our way through what would otherwise be a complex jumble of political organizations. The best starting point is to consider two general types of political groups: *political parties* and *interest groups*.

## POLITICAL PARTIES

No doubt the first type of group that we become aware of in political experience is the political party. There is much more variety among political parties in the world than we might immediately think, but they share the fact that they are organizations of people designed to seek the control of government through capturing public office. The principles and values they promote typically span the whole range of public issues, either in the form of a systematic ideology or a more loosely structured platform of policy positions. What is it that political parties do in politics? What do they do to make politics work? To varying degrees political parties can be said to perform some combination of the following functions.

### Recruitment

Political parties represent an important, if not primary, vehicle for people to get into politics and, more specifically, to get into official government. This recruitment function is most obvious in systems having elections for filling public offices in which two or more parties compete by nominating candidates. In these cases the parties serve to organize large numbers of people to vote for their candidates and to campaign on their behalf. Indeed, even though the law may allow any individual to run for any office he wants to, as long as he meets certain minimal conditions (age, citizenship), parties still dominate the electoral process. The simple reason for this is that being a candidate in a democratic election confronts the individual with the constraints of time, energy, and the necessary support of other people. The individual running independently must overcome these constraints and muster necessary resources on his own. What a political party does is provide an existing, ready-made organization of resources—money, talent, campaign workers, channels of communication—which is tapped by the candidate who is sponsored by the party. The party thus serves a very basic political function in organizing, maintaining, and distributing vital political resources essential to effective political advancement of the individual. Its control over elections and the resources necessary for winning them is one of the factors that make parties influential.

In the very task of competing in elections the party recruits into political activity hundreds or thousands of people who raise money, organize meetings, discuss positions on issues, manage campaigns. Also, the very job of getting people to go to the polls and vote serves this recruitment function; these people as well are the party's recruits into the political process. Via its influence over the electoral process, the party may also wield influence over governmental appointments. It is hardly surprising that almost all cabinet and federal judgeship appointments in the United States are of people from the president's own political party. Indeed, the creation of civil service laws governing the hiring of bureaucrats was specifically intended to remove partisan considerations from the filling of most administrative positions.

In a one-party system like that of the Soviet Union, of course, the recruitment function is not performed through competitive elections; rather, it results from the fact that advancement through the ranks of the party serves as the exclusive means of gaining entry to politics. The recruitment function is probably the most universal task of various different types of parties.

## Aggregation of Interests

Politics involves the expression of particular interests—one of the individual's orientations to politics. Trucking companies are interested in seeing highways built; hunters are opposed to gun regulation; unions want minimum-wage laws. Where certain conditions are present—a diverse, pluralistic society, governmental institutions that are responsive to special interests—the range and variety of these interests may be great. One function that political parties may serve is the *aggregation of interests* by which we mean bringing a number of interests together, creating a coalition of interests in which various views can be coordinated and allied behind a common goal (such as electing someone to office).

The party can engage in this aggregation because typically its views are not bounded by any particular area of political interest and it presumes to speak to the whole gamut of public decisions, in both domestic and foreign policy. By aggregating interests, the party builds support for the elections, and if it considers electoral success of very high value the party will be quite energetic in seeking a broad coalition of interests. In attempting to do this the party is constrained by the fact that some interests are diametrically opposed to others, and if the party takes any kind of clear stance on issues at all it will be forced to choose which interests have priority.

Interest aggregation is complicated by the fact that any individual voter may actually have several different political interests that could motivate him. In developing an effective political strategy, the party can choose which of these interests it will try to appeal to and thereby try to overcome some of the natural conflict of interests in the body politic. This is precisely what happened recently in American politics. White blue-collar workers have typically supported the Democratic party because of its greater sympathy for the special interests of the working man. Republicans have traditionally experienced difficulty in getting support from such voters because they have been more responsive to the opposing interests of employers and big business. However, under the leadership of Richard Nixon, the Republicans discovered that they could get the votes of white workers not by appealing directly to their economic interest as wage earners but by appealing to other interests. Nixon appealed to this group on the grounds that his administration would be less tolerant of campus radicals, bring law and order to riot-torn cities, and moderate the drive for racial integration in schools. As a result of the response to this approach, Nixon was able to build at least a temporary electoral majority which consisted of both business interests and working men—a good case of creative interest aggregation.

## Ideological Proselytizing

Another function of parties consists of the promotion and spreading of a particular political doctrine or set of beliefs. Ideology has already been mentioned as an element in the individual's orientation to politics and will be treated at greater length in the last chapter. One thing that parties do is attempt to convert people to their ideology. Historically, the names of political parties have frequently derived from the label of the ideology they promote; thus, around the world we find socialist parties, communist parties, liberal parties, conservative parties, democratic parties, and so on (though we have to watch out for the way in which a party's principles may change over time, even though it keeps the same label).

An important thing to understand about this function is its relationship to the aggregation of interests; to a certain extent the two are mutually exclusive. Stressing the importance of one of these two functions may inhibit a party's ability to perform the other. The reason is that if a party is strictly concerned with promoting a specific doctrine, the doctrine itself will constrain the range of interests it can effectively appeal to. If a socialist party, for example, is promoting the ideological principle that government should vigorously control and manage the economy, it will be hard-pressed to find grounds on which to attract the support of business interests. In fact, the members of such a party might positively avoid trying to get such support for fear that their ideological commitment might be watered down or compromised. The reverse of this situation is that a party seeking the broadest aggregation of diverse interests cannot afford to attach itself too narrowly to a specific ideology, and as a result, their ideological position will often be ambiguous and fuzzy. American political parties represent a classic case of this; they are not widely separated by clear ideological differences and they seek support not only from a wide array of interests but often from the same interests. This is why a foothold of both Democratic and Republican support can be found among such groups as farmers, businessmen, lawyers, and workers. The election defeats of Barry Goldwater in 1964 and George McGovern in 1972 are both attributed to the fact that both candidates campaigned on the basis of a very narrow ideological position (Goldwater, the conservative; McGovern, the "new left") which allowed the opposition party to build a broad, loose but effective alliance of interests to win the election easily.

Nonetheless, the proselytizing or promoting of an ideology is very important to many parties and may be a key reason for people joining parties. Parties serve as opportunities for citizens to ally with others of like persuasion in developing and advancing their shared system of political values.

## Political Education

Parties do an important job in educating people about what is happening in politics. A rather simple test of this is to note that people who are regularly involved in party politics, whether they are necessarily smarter or not, invariably seem to be more knowledgeable about and conversant with the prominent issues of the day and the goings on in government than those who have nothing to do with party activity. Party activity, by virtue of its central place in modern politics, is one of the main vehicles by which people learn about government and public affairs. It is often during an election campaign that the average citizen hears from the competing parties more about issues than they have heard in all the time since the last election. By the time the 1976 presidential election in the United States had gotten into full swing, many voters had become exposed to matters which normally would have been relegated to obscurity were it not for party activity—the Humphrey-Hawkins Employment Bill, our treaty relations with Panama, disarmament negotiations with the Soviet Union. Of course, whether this function is performed well or not is quite another question.

In some instances political parties take their political education function quite seriously—usually those parties that are more ideological. To do this they may develop party newspapers, public forums for discussion of issues, or formal study of issues and party positions as a regular part of party activity.

## Control of Government

This last function can be quite simply stated: by virtue of realizing success in its attempt to gain governmental power, the political party serves as an organization through which influence can be exerted over governmental policy. Quite obviously, if the Republicans are in power, the Republican party should have more influence than the Democratic party. Though in a general sense this is true and obvious, the exact extent to which the party serves this function can vary greatly depending on the type of organization it is. This can run the extremes from the American case, in which the national committees of the two major parties are rarely a decisive voice in government, to the Soviet Union, in which the Communist party is equal in power to the state itself and clearly gives direction to the state (it may come as a surprise to some that Leonid Brezhnev, until recently, did not hold the position of head of government or head of state but, rather, was the general secretary of the Communist party).

In trying to find out what a particular political party does in politics, we can refer to this set of functions for guidance. We are not suggesting that all parties perform all of these functions or that they do a good job in performing them; that depends on the specific case. Parties are political organizations and, if we know what they do, the next question is what kinds of organizational differences we find among parties. Parties are not all organized in the same way and, as with the formal organization of governments, the thing to look for is some connection between how a party is organized and what it does. How is the organization suited to the task?

As a suggested way of categorizing different kinds of parties we will consider three types of party organization.[1]

## The Caucus Party

The *caucus* form of party organization is one in which the party's business is primarily run by small groups or committees of party leaders. Though the caucus is a closed leadership group, the various caucuses which operate at various levels in the political system are not centralized at the top and may not even be tightly coordinated.

American parties represent the purest case of caucus parties. Party membership is very loosely defined, and the permanent organization of the party is relatively small and, in between elections, somewhat inactive. Formal membership, through payment of dues or possession of a membership card, if it exists at all, is fairly small and most people consider themselves "members" only by virtue of regularly voting for the party's candidates and sympathizing with its political views. Party committees will exist at various levels from the local to the national and will usually be organized to conform to the boundaries of important electoral units such as the county, ward, congressional district, and state. The smallest such organizational unit in the United States is the precinct, which is a neighborhood-size unit of people who all vote in the same location.

The caucus party is mainly designed to win elections and broadly aggregate interests. Its organization is tailored to turn people out on election day and to get the largest number of them to vote for the party's candidates. This explains why their permanent organization is quite small, party activity in between elections is scaled down, and official party position or "platform" on the issues lacks ideological definition. This pattern of operation means that the party really consists of a small core of professionals and loyalists whose job it is to whip up enthusiasm during campaigns and then recede into the woodwork the morning after the election.

One consequence of this organizational looseness and lack of ideological clarity is that such parties do not display a great deal of "party discipline." Party members or, more importantly, public officials elected by the party, are not expected to show consistent agreement on public issues; in other words, loyalty to a "party position" is at best only one of the forces determining the position a politician takes. The members of the same party in the legislature need not vote together all the time and the individual legislator will be quite independent in deciding whether he should respond more to the pressure of his own party, the pressure of his constituents back home, or his own conscience. This lack of party discipline is encouraged in the United States not only by caucus parties but by separation of powers in which, unlike in a parliamentary system, the president does not require a majority in the Congress in order to continue in office. This also shows how party functions fit with the functions of formal government, for the caucus party tends to make the legislator more dependent on the voters in his district than on the party organization at large. For this reason, the American legislator can spend much of his resources performing the constituency service functions described earlier, supporting the favorite American maxim of "voting for the man, not the party."

## The Branch Party

In this type of structure the various local units of the party are connected in a formal, centralized way and are seen as "branches" of the larger national party organization. The branch-type party differs from the caucus party in having more formal membership, in being active at other than election times, and in attempting to achieve a more permanent mobilization of large numbers of people. These organizational features better suit the objectives of ideological promotion and political education, though not necessarily to the detriment of effective electoral recruitment or of interest aggregation.

Organizationally, the idea of the branch is that it is an arm or extension of the party as a whole, unlike the caucus, which operates as a more autonomous unit of the party. The branch party is thereby more centralized and also has more of the features of a formal and permanent organization at its various levels, including a division of labor among hierarchically arranged party offices. Unlike the caucus party, in which effective membership is limited to party elites, the branch party explicitly aims at mass membership and involvement. Branch party organization is seen as a device for increasing the more or less permanent following of the party over time; thus the lower-level membership of the party will be more systematically drawn into party affairs and activities even when no election is going on. Outside election time the party will convene to consider its policy positions and at various levels in the organization there are regular meetings for the membership.

This type of party organization, which characterizes many European parties (particularly socialist parties), has its own consequences for the way in which politics is carried on. For one thing, the individual official is more likely to be motivated in his conduct by party loyalty. In this connection we can examine the cumulative effects of a number of circumstances. Thus, if we imagine a parliamentary legislature in which party discipline is required for maintaining a government (the prime minister and his cabinet), combined with a system of proportional representation in which the voter votes for a party list (where a prospective candidate must have a record as a strong "party man" to acquire a favorable position on the list), further combined with a branch type of party organization, we can see that the cumulative result of these various factors will tend to produce strong party discipline and generally increase the influence of the party as an organization within politics. Thus, the nature of organizations and institutions plays a very distinct role in shaping political roles and political behavior.

## The Cell or Militia Party

The first two types of parties are primarily designed to operate within a competitive, democratic political system and should be distinguished from those types of parties designed for revolutionary objectives or for totalitarian, single-party forms of rule (which are considered below). The cell type of organization was developed originally by the Russian Communist party. One of its distinctive features is that the basic organizational unit, the cell, is small, restricted in membership, and organized not on a geographical basis but at the place where people work. The overall organization is extremely hierarchical from top to bottom and is designed not so much as a mechanism for reflecting the opinions of the members as for coordinating and directing their political activities. In its purest form, this type of party serves the functions of spreading an ideology and educating its members with the intention of gaining power through revolution. It is designed as an effective subversive organization. Thus, the Communist party that gained power in Russia in 1917 under the leadership of V.I. Lenin displayed this type of structure. Over the years communist parties that have operated within constitutional democracies with party competition have altered this strict cell structure, run candidates in popular elections, and adopted some of the features of a branch party.

The militia party refers to the type of structure used by Fascist regimes, the term deriving from the fact that such parties were organized along military lines and virtually developed as private armies. When Adolph Hitler developed the Nazi party in Germany in the 1920s, the party structure was dominated by the "SA," which consisted of a military unit with uniforms, ranks, officers, and military-style discipline. In this form, the party becomes both a weapon in achieving the forceful takeover of governmental power and a tool for dictatorial government after such a takeover. What cell and militia parties reveal is that the phenomenon of the political party is not exclusively associated with the growth of democracy but is a result of the much broader modern development which makes the political support of the masses, in one form or another, an important if not vital ingredient in achieving and maintaining political power. The political party is now a fixture of modern politics and is found in virtually all systems, except possibly those that are still based on the power of a traditional elite (such as the rule of the Shah of Iran). Almost all of the various newly independent states of Africa and Asia organized their opposition to their colonial masters and have ruled their ultimately independent governments through the means of party organization of one sort or another.

Since we have been talking about types of parties, a brief comment should be made about certain small, marginal political groupings that call themselves parties and seem to behave like parties (they might run candidates for election) but do not really appear to be parties in the sense described here. Examples on the American scene include such groups as the Vegetarian party and the Prohibition party. In effect, these are more like interest groups that use the identity of a party as a device for advancing their cause. While they may be exceptions to the rule of normal party behavior, they do not contradict it.

Political analysis is concerned with the party as an organization and with its functions as important tasks in the political process, but another concern in studying parties is with *party systems*. The term refers simply to the number and type of parties and the relationship among them within a political system; in other words, when the political system is seen as a whole, we can describe and explain the pattern of party politics that is going on. Indeed, one of the things the political scientist wants to look for is the way in which the function and organization of parties are connected to the kind of party system. The most common way of distinguishing among different party systems is by the number of major parties that exist; that is, we can speak of one-party, two-party, and multiparty systems.

## One-Party Systems

In trying to determine why some political systems operate with only one party, there are two possible explanations: (1) either other parties are explicitly illegal or suppressed or (2) other parties are unable to establish a sufficiently large following to be significant. The first reason is always worth investigating initially because it is, by far, the more common. The classic type of one-party system in the world today is a dictatorship that does not permit organized opposition or may not even have popular elections in which the strength of opposition could be tested. In such a system the function of the party is to provide political direction to the government, though in many cases the party may be almost indistinguishable from the government itself, with party leaders and governmental officials often the same people. Though the single-party dictatorship provides direction and ideological justification for government, it is not effective in mirroring or representing public opinion and may not serve to aggregate interests. The cell or militia-type structure is typical in such one-party regimes and therefore the function of the party is really the same as the function of the one-party system—to extend the political control of the ruling elite. It is almost as if the party actually supplements many of the functions of government itself by being an exclusive avenue for people to get into government, supporting compliance with the regime, and generating basic public policy.

Though the second reason for the single-party system is rarer, it is not unheard of. One of the classic examples of it has occurred in the southern United States, where the Democratic party has almost exclusively dominated for the hundred years or more since the Civil War. There is no legal obstacle in Mississippi, Alabama, or Georgia to having a Republican party, and indeed they each have one, but these have been nonetheless one-party systems. In this particular example, the explanation for this pattern has to do with the peculiar historical circumstances following the Civil War. Since this situation occurs within a political system that is open and democratic, political opposition and competition still exist but they take place within the single dominant party rather than between two or more different parties. In the American South, the Democratic candidate has traditionally won in the general election; it has been in the primary elections, where voters have been able to choose the Democratic candidate, that the real electoral choice occurs among several candidates. Despite the existence of such competition, democratic thinkers have usually argued that the single-party arrangement is not a particularly desirable situation.

There are other cases, somewhat difficult to classify, where an assortment of different parties exists even though one party consistently comes out on top. In India the Congress party governed continuously for the thirty years of Indian independence from Great Britain, despite electoral challenges from a number of other parties. This may show that the difference between party systems is a matter of degree rather than a clear-cut distinction.

## Two-Party Systems

Beyond the one-party system, politics involves real political competition between two or more parties. The two-party system is one in which this competition is dominated by two major parties which, over time, typically swap power back and forth. The United States and Great Britain have been held up as classic instances of two-party politics, the Democrats and the Republicans in the former and the Conservative and Labor parties in the latter. There is usually no simple reason why there are only two parties, though a good place to begin seeking an explanation is in the institutions and rules of government. The use of single-member districts, described in the previous chapter, tends to favor the development of two parties since there are so few political rewards under such a system for the small minor party. Laws making it difficult to get on the ballot may discourage the formation of new parties. In the United States, federalism makes it difficult to start a new national party since election laws are controlled mainly by the fifty states. A new party would thus have to comply with fifty different election laws to get on the ballot nationwide. When George Wallace founded his American Independence party as a means for him to run for the presidency, it required a substantial team of lawyers and campaign workers who devoted themselves exclusively to getting on the ballot in as many states as possible.

But it is not only the machinery of the system which may support two-party politics. We can also look to tradition, voting habits, and the political culture. How often have we heard someone say that he or she is not going to vote for a party because it does not have any chance to win? The primacy of winning an election is such a strong element in our own political culture that it is often difficult for people to imagine why anyone would bother to organize a party and run candidates if they could not realistically win. The recruitment function of parties is seen as much more important than ideological or educative functions, and the prevalence of this attitude among the voting population does much to strengthen the hold of the two dominant parties.

The likelihood of achieving a clear majority by one party in an election is thought of as one of the virtues of a two-party system. For two-party politics to work almost invariably means that each party places high priority on interest aggregation and winning elections, and the caucus type of party has been particularly successful in doing both of these things in the United States. It is unlikely that the two parties will be divided by sharp ideological differences. The result of these common patterns is that while a clear electoral majority can be won the governing party may still contain conflict among a number of internal divisions and factions that probably cannot be permanently resolved. Political leaders will govern with one eye constantly on trying to maintain the alliance of interests in their party that got them elected in the first place. Though this type of politics is an effective way for electing leaders it does not always produce a clear, distinct direction to public decisions.

## Multiparty Systems

The third type of party system is one in which there are more than two significant parties competing in the political arena. This type of party system, traditionally characteristic of European countries, such as France, Germany, and Italy, confronts us with an array of different parties and often a great deal of shifting and movement in the balance of party strength. Again, we can look both to institutional as well as cultural explanations for this pattern. Proportional representation rewards the efforts of smaller parties, thereby encouraging their formation. In many European countries, deep historical divisions between different social classes or between the church and the state tended to produce a variety of distinct parties with the advent of democratic politics.

The most urgent political problem in a multiparty system is achieving a majority that is capable of governing. If there are too many parties of roughly equal strength, this can be done only by forming a coalition among several parties which collectively add up to a majority after an election. After the 1973 election France was governed by a legislative majority consisting of three parties with the elaborate names Union of Democrats for the Republic, National Federation of Independent Republicans, and Democratic and Progressive Center. Here we encounter the classic difficulty of keeping the coalition together; this difficulty increases with the number of parties in the coalition and is aggravated by the fact that multiparty systems more frequently tend to occur where parties have distinctive ideological positions. Because multiparty systems are prone to these difficulties, they have tended to produce excessive political instability with the frequent need for elections and frequent change in governments brought about by fragile coalitions. Coalition government need not always be the case, however; it may be possible for one party to be considerably stronger than all others, producing a pattern of a single dominant broad-based party surrounded by numerous smaller parties. This has been the case in Italy for much of the time since World War II with the predominance of the Christian Democrats.

Multiparty politics is not only encouraged by such things as electoral laws, but it also reflects the intensely ideological character of party politics. A proliferation of parties means that each is making a fairly narrow, discrete appeal to the citizens, and it is not surprising in such systems to find parties that are more concerned with ideology and political education. Indeed, elections themselves may not accomplish much aggregation of interests at all; this function is often left to coalition-building and actually governing.

An understanding of possible party functions and of the types of parties and party systems that exist in modern politics can serve as an initial road map in studying the role of parties in political experience. As with governmental institutions we can watch out for how the party system operates as a constraint and an opportunity for the individual in politics, and for how people's orientations to politics contribute to the kind of party politics that goes on. Parties will not be able to fill every variety of political need and will be confronted with a choice of purposes and functions. The choice they make will determine the way in which the party is useful to the individual political actor. Antiwar protest against our involvement in Vietnam was greatly frustrated by the experience of trying to work through the Democratic party, which operates as a broad and shifting aggregate of interests and not as a strictly ideological party. Rightly or wrongly, the objective of the protesters was effectively to change the character of the party, not to use it as it stood. This frustration resulted in serious splits within the party, the attempt to create wholly new "third parties," and the organization of the antiwar movement outside party politics altogether. In this example the party and, in fact, the whole party system operated as a political resource specifically tailored to do certain things well and not to do other things at all. In a multiparty system, on the contrary, the antiwar movement might very well have organized itself in the form of a distinctly pacifist political party or found an existing party with an ideological point of view that carefully fit its own. What the party system can do for the individual in politics and what it cannot do will vary, and this is one of the first things the effective political actor must appreciate.

It is also the case that we bring to our experience with political parties certain orientations, certain beliefs and expectations about what they should be doing and about how they can be of use to us. Do we feel that the political party should recognize our special interest, should take a clear ideological stand, should win elections? The dispute among these different orientations is itself an important kind of political conflict. In the 1976 U.S. presidential elections we found the two men contesting the Republican nomination, Ronald Reagan and Gerald Ford, engaged in a debate about what kind of party the Republican party should be. Should it be, as Reagan contended, an ideologically strict and pure conservative party or, as Ford contended, a conservative-oriented party ready to adjust itself pragmatically according to the prevailing mood of the electorate in general? To somewhat oversimplify this dispute, it was a question of whether the party should be *right* or whether it should *win*. As noted earlier, Americans typically approach party politics with the notion in mind that the purpose of parties is to win and that parties that have no chance of doing this are a waste of time. Such a widespread attitude among the electorate can represent a real political force shaping the party system.

## INTEREST GROUPS

Political parties are by no means the only way in which people organize themselves to engage in politics. The other common type of political organization is the *interest group,* an association of people concerned with protecting and promoting shared values through the use of the political process. The characteristic function, which really describes the role of such groups in politics, is *interest articulation.* Interest groups perform tasks such as consolidating and distributing information about the group's shared interest, encouraging support for this common interest among members, organizing the resources of such members (their dues, special skills, voting power) to achieve these goals, and using the power of the organization to influence public decisions that could affect their ability to achieve their common interest. Such groups are all around us as unions, professional associations, consumer groups, religious groups. And in the United States they consist of such organizations as the United Steel Workers, the American Medical Association, the National Association of Manufacturers, the National Rifle Association, the Sierra Club, Common Cause, the American Bar Association, the International Ladies' Garment Workers Union, the National Organization of Women, the National Association for the Advancement of Colored People, and literally hundreds more.

In order to see what interest groups do in politics, let us look at a single interest group in the United States which many people have likely never heard of—the Experimental Aircraft Association (EAA). The EAA is an organization consisting of people who share an interest in designing and/or building their own airplanes. To serve the interests of the members, the EAA publishes a monthly magazine, *Sport Aviation,* which disseminates technical information of use to the homebuilder, reports on the activities of various homebuilders around the country, advertises materials, parts, plans, and kits, and keeps the members abreast of recent developments in the field. The EAA also runs an aircraft museum, sponsors courses and workshops around the country, has an annual meeting in which members put their aircraft on display, and creates local chapters which meet regularly and may even own facilities for aircraft construction. None of these activities, of course, is directly political in nature, but there are various aspects of aviation that the federal government has taken an interest in regulating or controlling. The government licenses aircraft, issues Airworthiness Certificates, licenses the airfields they fly in and out of, and in each case government authorization requires that certain conditions are met before an aircraft can be flown or an airfield used commercially. All of these activities are of material interest to the members of the EAA. What decisions government makes can determine how difficult, expensive, safe, or enjoyable it will be to take part in their hobby. The government may be able to determine whether they can engage in their hobby at all and, indeed, in the early days of aviation the government would not certify home-built aircraft and only later allowed such planes to be certified as "experimental." As a result of governmental concern with the implications of private aviation activity for the public, organizations such as the EAA must regularly concern themselves with what government should do, might do, or is doing by way of regulation. Thus, in addition to the other activities of EAA, the organization has a representative in Washington who regularly deals with such agencies as the Federal Aviation Administration (FAA). What the organization does through this representative might be called interest articulation by the political scientist; put less technically, the EAA watches out for new proposals for regulating aviation that come up within the FAA, provides the FAA with information about the activities and needs of EAA members, communicates FAA proposals and decisions to members and explains what they mean, and proposes changes in federal regulation to the FAA or to Congress. In regard to these activities, the EAA is not merely an association of people interested in experimental aviation. It can also be treated as a political interest group, a group which attempts to influence government and is actively concerned with what government does as one of the means necessary to protect and promote that which it commonly values—private, experimental aviation.

As with political parties, it is useful to observe that there are different types of interest groups; for our purposes we can distinguish two general kinds. Many interest groups, like the EAA, are not primarily or exclusively organized for political purposes but become active in politics as a necessary way of meeting the organizations' objectives. Political activity represents only part of their overall function, and it will vary in its importance as issues important to the groups come and go. Organizations of this type would include the Chamber of Commerce, the

National Council of Churches, and the American Farm Bureau Federation. They will come and go in politics, sometimes being quite active, sometimes not. At times their interest, like that of a labor union, will necessarily involve them in almost continuous political activity; but they enter politics as the needs of the group demand it. Groups such as this represent an important part of political experience for the average individual and a likely source of his information and impressions about politics.

Distinct from this type of interest group are those groups that organize for primarily or exclusively political purposes. This would include such organizations as the American Civil Liberties Union, Young Americans for Freedom, or Common Cause. By definition, the shared interest that binds them together is an interest in exerting influence over government—an interest in protecting civil liberties, promoting the ideals of individualism and free enterprise, or reforming the institutions of government. Though their interest is broadly political, and may be identifiably ideological, they are different from political parties in not formally competing for governmental offices and in not necessarily offering a comprehensive platform addressing the whole range of public questions.

How do interest groups get done what they want to get done in politics? How do they accomplish their goals? As we will see shortly, the full answer to such questions requires that we take into account the nature of the political system as a whole. The initial answer to the questions, however, is that they attempt to use political resources available to them to sway public officials. What resources might groups have?

## Numbers

If the interest group has a large enough membership, it may find that it can use its numbers to political advantage, although the size of the organization will not be much advantage unless the membership can be encouraged to take concerted action when it is necessary. If this is possible, then the organization can endorse candidates in elections who are sympathetic to its cause or encourage candidates to be sympathetic by getting its members to vote as a bloc, that is, to vote their special interest. In an attempt to encourage the passage of the Equal Rights Amendment (ERA), women's groups in several states during the 1976 elections systematically identified those candidates committed to vote for ERA and, with some success, encouraged their members and voters at large to vote for those candidates. This was an obvious strategy, considering that the interest they were advancing could materially advantage such a huge chunk of the population. Aside from electoral strength, the large size of an organization may help in mobilizing people to communicate with government officials and register complaints or support in impressive numbers.

## Wealth

Money is, of course, a tremendous political resource, and as such, it can be of great use to an interest group. If an organization is sufficiently wealthy, its financial resources can outweigh the disadvantages of small size. Thus, the American Medical Association is not necessarily that large, but it is an association of well-to-do professionals—medical doctors—and that is one of the reasons it wields considerable influence in American politics. What does money do? With it you can maintain an expensive professional "lobbying" office in Washington, hire the best legal advice to handle court cases, lavishly wine and dine public officials, maintain a large staff to manage the organization's affairs, finance sophisticated advertising to get your message across to the public at large, and make critical contributions to candidates and political parties. Indirectly, the very fact of having a well-to-do membership is a factor in elections, since middle- and upper-class individuals are more likely to vote and more likely to be able to influence others in whom to vote for.

We also cannot ignore the illegal and unethical use of money in politics, in other words, bribery. Economic interests—oil producers, milk producers, for example—who have such substantial economic stakes in what government does, have been accused in recent years of seeking influence through illegal donations of money to politicians whose support they were effectively attempting to "buy."

## Control of Information

The very factor that gives bureaucrats influence also applies to interest groups; they are one of the main sources of information about the special area of public policy that they are concerned with. Another way of putting this is that the specialization of the interest group makes it influential. Using our earlier example, if a congressman is trying to decide how to vote on a new aviation regulation, he may likely have to turn to an organization like the EAA to get concrete, organized, useful information about what the impact of the new law might be. It is true the information might not be the most objective but it may be the best available. The interest group will actively feed studies, reports, and data to policy makers in government and attempt to advance itself as the most knowledgeable voice on a particular topic.

## Importance of Their Interest

An interest group will be in a more advantageous position politically if the interest it represents is of central importance to its members. An individual may be affiliated with a number of interest groups of varying importance to him, and he will be more likely to expend his resources to support those that are the most important. Thus, the EAA may have a fairly large membership and healthy financial resources, but it is probably unlikely that many of its members would vote in an election on the basis of EAA-type issues. These people are also businessmen, union members, and professionals, and their economic and occupational interests are much more likely to determine their political behavior. This is one of the reasons that the more powerful and politically significant interest groups tend to be unions, corporations, and professional associations; in these instances it is people's livelihood that is at stake. This also helps explain one of the reasons why consumer groups have often experienced difficulty, for though they may have a large membership and even wider appeal, the issues they are fighting may be relatively less important for each of their members and supporters than other issues. We may be very sympathetic to those who would like to see certain food preservatives banned because of their health danger, but it is unlikely that our concern with this issue will be of great weight in voting for a president or even a congressman, compared with our concern for taxes, inflation, national defense, or welfare.

This represents only a sampling of the complex array of factors that can help explain the relative power of interest groups, but as we indicated above, there is a more basic issue involved in examining the role and influence of interest groups: the type of political system. For an initial understanding of the idea of interest groups, we have been talking exclusively about interests in American politics. But one of the ways in which political systems differ is in the role, organization, and function of special interests. A useful way to analyze these differences from one system to another is to think of them as differences in degree relative to two extreme types—"strong interest groups" and "weak interest groups" (see Figure 4–1). The United States probably comes as close as any modern system to having strong interest groups in politics. The main indication of this is the extent to which such groups organize themselves and function in a free and unrestricted manner. The strong interest group model assumes few, if any, legal barriers to voluntary association and the independence of such associations from governments and political parties. Typically, these conditions will produce a wide diversity of active and specialized interests.

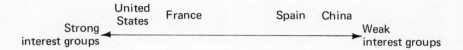

Figure 4-1  Degree of Interest Group Strength

The strong interest-group model will be reinforced by institutional designs that enhance the opportunities for such interests unilaterally to influence government. The relative independence of legislators from strong party discipline in the United States makes the individual legislator susceptible to influence from major organized interests in his constituency. Thus, congressmen from states like Virginia and Kentucky can be depended upon to be strong advocates of the interests of tobacco growers because of the importance of that crop to the economy of their states. Similarly, we find ties between Texas politicians and oil interests and California politicians and the aircraft industry. In a broader sense, the general institutional fragmentation of government—through separation of powers and federalism—increases the number and kind of opportunities available to special interests. They can pick and choose which avenue may be most productive. The civil rights movement experienced considerable difficulty in using legislative means of promoting its cause, which it compensated for by turning to the courts, where most of its early victories were won. Interest groups can both survive and succeed as independent political forces by having available a variety of opportunities for gaining access to government.

At the opposite extreme are those systems in which interest groups are very weak. Groups are not allowed to exist as independent, autonomous political forces that people may voluntarily organize and join. If organized interests exist at all, they exist only as appendages of government or the ruling party, but when organized in this way their purpose is not interest articulation but the extension of the government's control over various social and economic activities. Thus, the state sponsors organizations of scientists, doctors, writers, farmers, for the purpose of exerting control over such groups. In 1932 in the Soviet Union, for example, existing literary organizations were replaced by the Union of Soviet Writers, which was a creature of the Communist party.[2] The perfect cases of such a system of weak interest groups are totalitarian political systems such as the Soviet Union or Nazi Germany. This is not to say that competition among different political interests does not take place at all in these systems, but to the extent it does take place it appears as competition among members of the governing elite and occurs within the strict boundaries of the prevailing ideology. In this sense, the role of special interests is a universal feature of modern politics, but the strength, autonomy, and role of organized interests vary considerably. Between the two extreme cases described here we may find a number of political systems that can be compared according to which model they most closely resemble. An authoritarian regime such as Spain is closer to the position of weak interest groups, but unlike a totalitarian regime may not attempt to directly sponsor or control all interests as long as they are not subversive. Toward the other side of the scale, a multiparty democracy such as France would be much closer to the strong interest-group model, except that the wide array of specialized parties with greater party discipline may tend to foreclose certain opportunities for the extensive activity of special interests.

As with the other components of the political system we have examined, interest-group activity represents another set of constraints and orientations acting on the individual citizen and an important source of political controversy as well. Though we may pride ourselves on the political freedom that makes interest groups possible and be pleased at their usefulness to us in articulating our own interests, we also frequently complain that one of the faults of American politics is the extensive power that certain interests are able to wield. As we discover so often in political experience, constraints and opportunities are mixed together in the same institution, principle, or aspect of the system; rarely do we encounter a part of our political experience that is an unmixed blessing.

## POLITICAL MOVEMENTS

In considering the ways in which man organizes his political efforts, a word should be said about forms of collective action that do not fit into the broad categories of parties and interest groups. Not all forms of collective action are as stable and established as those we have just looked at; these other forms can be grouped under the heading *political movements*. This term refers to loosely organized political efforts on the part of usually a large number of people who share a general political objective. Thus, reference is made to the "peace movement," or the "civil rights movement." By their very nature such movements tend to be temporary and to form around dramatic and prominent public issues or concerns. They may supplement already organized interests or, if they endure for any length of time and gain a certain permanence, they will likely transform themselves into an interest group or a party. There are several antiwar groups in the United States, such as the Fellowship of Reconciliation, which existed well before and continues to exist well after the flourishing of the peace movement of the 1960s in reaction to the Vietnam war. So also the NAACP, which was founded in the early part of this century and still functions as an important organized interest, both preceded and outlived the feverish civil rights movement of ten to fifteen years ago.

Though movements tend to be short-lived and relatively unorganized phenomena, they are not without their political importance and may serve as effective ways for people to express their political views. A serious political question is why they arise at all or why the job of parties and interest groups is not adequate to meet the needs they fill. One reason is that the movement provides an immediate way of filling people's need to engage in direct action on a public question and in a broader array of activities for popular participation. Though many of us belong to parties and interest groups, our membership in them may involve us only as spectators; we show ourselves as part of a movement precisely by virtue of the action we engage in. The "consumer movement" draws its supporters into the political arena not by membership but by boycotting products, picketing stores, and passing petitions calling for regulation of manufacturers. The civil rights movement mobilized thousands of people to integrate lunch counters by using "sit-ins," to participate in public marches, and to run voter registration drives.

The growth of movements can also result from outright frustration with existing political organizations and their failure to function as responsive popular organizations. The movement may represent the inability of existing groups to handle new political demands and forces. Sometimes it is the case that no political group is dealing with a suddenly important new issue. In this way the "ecology movement" sprung up quickly a few years ago and now has spawned an assortment of more permanent political groups. In any event the political movement should be included in any study of the ways in which people attempt to act together for political purposes.

## THE POLITICAL PROCESS

To this point our approach to the study of politics has involved descriptions and explanations of certain major components of the political system: roles, influence relationships, institutions, parties, and groups. But these components, examined individually and in isolation from each other, do not *tell* us what politics is all about; they merely provide us with a foundation of information that we can use to *study* what politics is all about. The real trick in understanding political experience is the ability to grasp how these particular features of political life connect and how these connections produce distinct political systems and political events and place public affairs in the condition they are. A few years ago, the United States government decided against putting money into the development of a supersonic transport plane (SST) similar to the British-French Concorde. How do we account for this political decision? Our analysis of such a specific event would have to build on a familiarity with a number of components of the political system: the role of Congress in decision making, the attitude and power of certain interest groups, the condition of the economy, and the outlook of the president and his advisors. But ultimately our understanding of such an event has to hinge on an explanation of the activities and processes that occur among different actors and groups in and out of formal institutional settings, of how they influence each other, and of how the decision was a product of their interaction.

Another way of putting this—to hark back to our discussion in the first chapter—is that we have to look at politics as a system. The central idea conveyed by the notion of a "system" is easy to state but sometimes intricate and difficult to apply: a system is a set of interactions among distinct parts. In this way the life sciences speak of the human body as a "biological system." The human body functions as a living organism by virtue of the complex of relationships among heart, lung, nerves, muscle tissues, blood vessels, and so on. It is difficult to understand any one of these parts of the anatomy without some reference to the system as a whole, and it is the interaction of these parts with each other that distinguishes or marks the boundaries between one biological system and another, that is, my body and your body do not form a common biological system because your ulcer does not make me sick; in the same way, Britain and France do not form a common political system because a law passed by the House of Commons is not enforced in Paris. Biology also reveals how systems interact with their environment through taking in food and sunlight and discharging waste, which shows that although systems have distinct boundaries (our skin, for example), they are not totally self-contained or self-sufficient. If the human body lacks food, it will starve to death.

In recent years political scientists have widely promoted the concept of the "system" as a way of understanding the complex relationships in politics.[3] Figure 4-2 shows a very simple conception of the political system in diagram form. What the diagram indicates is that the political process consists of transforming certain "inputs"—demands, protests, interests, values, personal ambitions, patriotic feelings, ideologies—into certain "outputs"—decisions, policies, actions, judgments. Thus, this simplest of relationships shows that what government does is somehow related to the forces acting upon it. There is a connection between

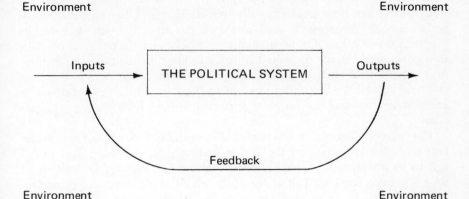

Figure 4-2  Model of the Political System

inputs and outputs at least to the extent that we can look for the ways in which different inputs lead to different outputs. This is what we have been observing in pointing out, for example, that the need for leadership felt by the people tends to produce the model of the single, dominant head of government, or that a multiparty system can tend to produce instability and shifts in governmental direction, or that the demands of individual constituents where there is weak party discipline in the legislature produce governmental decisions more responsive to special interests.

The transformation of inputs into outputs consists of the governmental process; in more familiar terms it consists of the use of authority, coercion, bargaining, deliberation, advice, and compromise. As the diagram also indicates, there is a step in the process called *feedback*, which indicates simply that the outputs of government can influence and shape inputs. The government decides to develop the use of nuclear energy, leading to objections from citizens concerned about the safety of nuclear facilities in their communities; laws are passed regulating political contributions, and candidates and parties reorganize their activities accordingly; Medicaid programs are instituted and abuses in the use of these funds create a new political problem needing solution.

It must be appreciated that this is a very abstract model and any part of it could be elaborated in fine and extensive detail, but it does help show that the component parts of politics interact in some systematic way; that how people behave in politics, who plays significant roles, what function parties perform, what kinds of institutions exist with what kind of authority are mutually interrelated considerations by which we learn how politics really works. The inability to completely isolate any single aspect of such a system has already been revealed in our treatment of parties, institutions, and behavior. In order to explain two-party politics, we have had to refer to laws, institutional practices, and the political culture. In order to account for what people become political actors, we have had to refer to the distribution of wealth, the social structure, and the range of opportunities for legitimate participation.

The idea of "system" is also useful in keeping before our attention the fact that politics is an activity. Roles, institutions, attitudes, groups, all tell us in a static or descriptive sense about the setting or context in which people act; they tell us about the kinds of patterns and organization that characterize politics, and they help direct our attention through what would otherwise be an incomprehensible mass of events, like a child looking at the inside of a television. But when all is said and done, the purpose for studying these things is to find out what people do in politics, why they do it, and with what effect. A modest analogy which might help is to imagine yourself encountering the game of football for the first time. You might think it a rather bizarre game, every one running every which way, periodically stopping and starting over, sometimes kicking, sometimes throwing, and sometimes running around with the ball. If you were to ask someone what this game on television is all about, it would not help you very much to be told that the Pittsburgh Steelers are trying to establish a running attack in order to ease the pressure on the quarterback so he can begin throwing some passes. Your likely response might be: What is a quarterback? In order even to begin understanding the game, you have to know how the field is laid out, how many men there are on a team, how a score is made, what the rules are for the offense and the defense, and what the different positions are. This kind of information allows you to make sense of what is going on; you can discern the operation of rules and the presence of certain patterns and, on a basic level, enjoy the game. This is about where our treatment of politics is at the moment but, as with the game, there is another level of understanding that is necessary in order to "know about football." What strategy is used, how do you play the game effectively, and how do you make the choice to run or throw the ball? In order to understand football, it is not sufficient merely to know what the rules are. You must know how and why people do what they do to win the game. So also in studying politics, knowledge of roles, institutions, groups, and laws helps us find our way around in politics but this knowledge is valuable because it lays the necessary groundwork for confronting the more central issue of what people do in politics.

Many political scientists have developed and used the concept of the political system by elaborating in formal detail the various steps of the process, such as the various kinds of inputs and outputs. Our purpose in introducing the concept of the system here is not to describe it in all its technical operation but to convey the idea of politics as a type of human activity among individuals which, when looked at as a whole, reveals these activities as interconnected and as forming a discernible process by which the control of public affairs takes place. Therefore, what we wish to explore further is the variety of political activity—what people do in politics—with an eye to the part these activities play in the total mission of politics.

## RAISING POLITICAL ISSUES

Politics is an activity through which people achieve control and regulation of their common affairs. What control and how it should be exerted is a source of conflict among people in politics. When this conflict arises we have a *political issue.* We can begin examining the political process by asking, What constitutes a political issue and why does it arise in the first place?

Much of what is done in government on a day-to-day basis is not a source of political concern or dispute, though all of it potentially may be. Even as this is said, thousands of bureaucrats busily work away at the public's business as unnoticed as plumbers and dentists, though they are paid by our taxes and perform tasks that were politically defined at one time or another. But regularly the question of what government is doing or should be doing in one or another area becomes an issue, that is, it becomes a matter that has to be decided in some way and about which there are different points of view. It is at this juncture that politics replaces the mere routines of "governing" and "administering." Should convicted murderers be executed? Should industrial pollution of the air be controlled? Should unemployed people be given financial support by the government? Should we sign a disarmament agreement with the Soviet Union? Should low-cost housing be subsidized?

How does a political issue become an issue? The answer can be sorted out by considering an analogy with how a personal issue becomes an issue. The issue of what house I should buy could come up either because I would like to live in a nicer house or because my present house has just burned to the ground. In other words, the "house issue" can come up either because I make it an issue or because circumstances impose the issue on me by altering my routines. These two causes can also be and frequently will be connected. If a new highway is built right next to my house and I would prefer not to live so close to the traffic and noise, external circumstances and my own desires interact to raise the issue.

It is much the same in politics. Political issues come up because *people raise them* or because *events impose them* in such a way that they must be confronted and, like personal issues, we can expect there will be a connection between these two factors. As for the former, civil rights for blacks has been made an issue by people concerned with the unequal and unjust treatment of black citizens; legalization of marijuana has been made an issue by people who feel its use is not harmful and its prohibition unjust; the abolition of capital punishment has been made an issue by people who consider it an excessive form of punishment. As for the latter, the imposition of events, our entry into World War II was made an issue by the outbreak of the war in Europe and the attack on Pearl Harbor; the question of government regulation of the economy was made an issue by the Great Depression; the meaning and application of the principle of free speech were made an issue by the development of the new technology of television which put a major form of communication in the hands of a few large corporations.

People raise political issues when they feel their values or interests are being threatened. They also raise issues in politics when they undergo changes in their attitudes and values. We have always had capital punishment for major crimes. Why is its abolition now a significant issue? The answer is that people's values have changed; there is now a smaller proportion of people in society who feel that this type of criminal punishment is ethical or civilized. When such a change in values occurs, a gap develops between what government is doing and what many people think it should be doing. People also raise issues because their values have not been recognized in public decisions and, when an occasion arises, they will express their political differences. Thus, patterns and changes in the general culture—in beliefs, values, and attitudes—gain political importance.

Events impose political issues by raising new dilemmas that must be confronted, such as changes in economics, social relationships, and technology. In a more ordinary way, the specific need to carry out certain governmental responsibilities provides regular political issues. Every year the Congress of the United States must approve a new budget for the federal government, so every year the details of that budget constitute a political issue. There is a constant interplay between these events and people's values, such that it is frequently difficult to say that one or the other is clearly the cause of an issue. Has concern for ecology become an important political issue because people are more sensitive about environmental pollution or because there has been increased damage to the environment? Probably both.

The important thing to understand about the appearance of a political issue is that the very way in which this happens is something that people in politics will try to control. Another way of putting this is that the ability to control which issues are taken up and handled is an important exercise of political power. For an individual or group of individuals to raise an issue requires the use of political resources and available opportunities, and these resources and opportunities may be susceptible to control by other people who may not want to see the issue raised at all or may want to control who raises issues. The appropriate resources and opportunities will, in turn, be a function of the prevailing institutions and organizations in the political system. To begin with, raising an issue means being heard and being heard by the right people. Let us say you and some of your neighbors hear of plans by city officials to build a sewage treatment plant near your neighborhood. You feel the issue of the effects of this proposal on your neighborhood should be considered; that is, you do not want the plant and you want to "make an issue" out of it. Effectively raising the issue means getting it taken up by those who will have something to say about the decision or getting yourself and your friends into the decision-making process. Various political resources now begin to play a role. Are you sufficiently knowledgeable about city government to know which officials or political leaders should be approached? Do you have the free time to organize your neighbors to support the cause? Do you have the personal self-confidence and skill to organize a meeting, pass a petition, and confront public officials with your complaint? Do you have powerful friends among your social group who could make it easier for you to speak with appropriate officials? Whether the issue will be raised or not depends on such factors as these, and thus we may find a significant difference between a wealthy, upper-class, well-educated neighborhood and a poor, lower-class, poorly educated neighborhood.

Assuming all of these conditions can be handled, in order to draw attention to the issue you try to get a meeting with officials in the appropriate government office, but they are difficult to reach and they delay making an appointment with you. You finally get through to a lower-level official in the department who listens to your complaint and says he will take it up with his superiors. He delays doing this, and when he finally gets back to you he says only that your position is being considered. You try to get the local newspaper to cover a neighborhood meeting at which the complaints over the sewage plant will be aired. The paper does not cover the story or innocuously buries it in the last section because the editor does not want to embarrass his friends, the mayor or the contractor who is anxious to get the contract for the job. Finally, you approach your city councilman, who is sympathetic to mentioning your problem at a meeting but who has agreed to the sewage plant as part of a deal with another councilman to support one of his pet projects and your complaint interferes with this kind of dealing. Regardless of the disposition of this issue, the point is that the raising of an issue is itself a political issue which entangles one in conflict and power relationships. This is just as true of an open, democratic system as any other. There are critical values at stake in whether an issue gets raised or not. In our example, the contractor has a job and profits at stake; the newspaper editor has his association with and access to powerful people at stake; the councilman has his complex arrangements with other councilmen at stake; and you have your neighborhood at stake.

This is but one isolated and specific example of something which occurs throughout political experience. Every political system offers certain means as well as certain distinct limitations to the way issues can be raised, and the use of these is part of the political process. In nondemocratic systems, issue raising is a function systematically limited to a very small elite. In a traditional aristocracy it is a matter of being a member of the aristocratic class or gaining the attention of the king. In a Communist system, it is a question of gaining power within the party sufficient to allow you to raise a fresh issue without damaging your political career. In democratic systems it is a question of mastering political techniques and acquiring personal resources. Certain institutions facilitate the raising of issues more than others: a multiparty system is better at this than a single-party system; strong interest groups are better than no interest groups; and a competitively elected, professional legislature is better than a merely ritualistic legislature.

What are some of the implications of these different arrangements for the operation of the political system? If the system allows for the raising of issues with ease, as a result of the wide distribution of political resources and the openness of institutions, it will have to confront at a later point a substantial task of aggregating or managing an intricate assortment of demands. It will also have to deal with the expectation that if issues are so easy to raise they must be responded to. If, on the other hand, the raising of issues is strictly and narrowly limited, the bulk of the people must be prepared to accept the notion that politics is not an activity for them. In either case circumstances may arise where frustration in raising an issue combined with the expectation that one ought to be able to can bring about political action outside the normal channels of politics and government and perhaps beyond the bounds of law. Rioting, burning draft cards, occupying public buildings, or, indeed, revolution itself are examples of such action. There is real danger when the desire of people to be heard in politics outstrips the ability and willingness of the political system to listen; the result is political conflict of the most basic sort.

Quite a different set of problems is encountered with those issues imposed by events. We cannot completely control the rise of new technology (nuclear weapons), the economic decisions of other countries (the Arab oil boycott), or the collapse of our own economy (the Depression). But since the general function of politics is to exert control over public affairs, we might say that we are always in the business of trying to remove the historical surprises that are around the corner and anticipate consequences of present actions and decisions. The political system that lacks any ability to do this will find its effectiveness and stability endangered.

## GOAL SETTING

An important activity that is going on throughout politics is goal setting, that is, the definition of political ends and purposes by individuals and groups. Those goals which help direct people's action can be divided into three types, depending on whether the goal is oriented to the acquisition of power, the protection of particular interests, or the promotion of the public interest as a whole. These three types of goals are expressed respectively as ambition, special interest, and ideology; they are not mutually exclusive and are often found operating together. In order to advance himself personally, a politician may need to serve as the spokesman for a particular interest; and for success in advancing an ideological cause, personal power must be acquired.

An important effect of goal setting on the political system is that the predominance of certain types of goals will determine the nature of political conflict and the capacity of the political system to resolve such conflict. Where political conflict is dominated by two or more distinctly different ideologies or views about the basis of political authority, severe strain may be placed on the political process which could ultimately lead to internal war or revolution in the most extreme case. Thus, the conflict between the Viet Cong and the Western-oriented regime in South Vietnam during the 1950s and 1960s was a dispute between two movements that held fundamentally different conceptions of what kind of society Vietnam should be. On the contrary, at many levels in American politics it would seem that conflict over personal power is much more important than such ideological disputes, which has the advantage of being less socially divisive. Yet this may produce problems of its own; it has been cited as the source of that widespread cynicism that Americans have about politicians, and a connection has also been drawn between politics based on personal ambition and the amount of petty corruption that tends to develop.[4]

Conflict also appears among people with different types of goals over the question of what type is most important or legitimate. People who enter politics to promote an ideology often condemn others as being in politics only for the power and the professional career it provides them. Finally, as we saw in our examination of political parties, the types of goals that are set determine what type of political organization people will employ and how they will behave in politics. If you ignore these differences in goals, you can be easily misled about why people do what they do in politics. For example, in 1964 Lyndon Johnson beat Barry Goldwater in the presidential election by a huge margin. To the average observer, who assumed that winning elections and gaining public office are what this kind of politics is all about, it appeared that Goldwater and the Conservative movement for which he stood had been utterly defeated and humiliated. Curiously enough, Goldwater himself did not speak like a beaten man and at times even seemed to see the election as a useful and effective exercise. He argued that the main objective was to advance the cause of conservative thinking and principles in American politics, to steer public debate toward a reconsideration of conservative values. These goals, he felt, had really been accomplished as shown by the fact that Johnson himself had adopted many policies which Goldwater had proposed, particularly in American foreign policy, that Richard Nixon had run in 1968 as a more distinctly conservative candidate stressing law and order and American strength in the world, and that in 1976 we found the Republican nomination being contested by two candidates each trying to prove that they represented true conservatism. The point of this example is that the measure of success in politics is directly related to the goals that people have, and one person's failure may be another person's success.


## ACHIEVING SUPPORT

Both for raising an issue and successfully advancing your own point of view on an issue, it is necessary to gain the support of other people. Who are these other people? Generally, they are any other people who are in a position to help your cause; specifically, the power relationships, institutions, and groups in the political system will determine who those other people are. Political support must be tailored to the circumstances. Getting the support of public opinion may be neither easy nor useful in a dictatorship, and achieving the support of the chief executive may not be as important as it might seem in a system of separation of powers where the executive's hands can be tied by the legislature. The decision as to what kind of support is appropriate is an important tactical question in politics, one to which there may not be a single answer.

Identifying useful support is essentially a question of determining who will be influential. If the cause you are pushing is getting yourself elected to office, you may need the support of political party leaders, of people wealthy enough to finance a campaign, and ultimately of the voters themselves. If your cause is getting appointed to office, you will need the support of the person who makes the appointment, his advisors, or those organized interests that influence him. If your cause is getting your property tax assessment lowered, you will need the support of the tax assessor's office, or you might find the support of your city councilman useful.

Two factors can complicate the judgment about whose support is needed. First, there may be more than one way to push your cause and therefore different groups of supporters depending on which method you use. To the extent that the civil rights movement tried to achieve its purposes through the courts, it was necessary to get the support of federal judges, donors who could contribute financial resources for lengthy court fights and appeals, and those who made appointments of judges. However, to the extent that it used legislative means to achieve its purposes, it needed the support of political parties and of the voters at large. Second, this judgment is also complicated by the fact that the support of some people is needed to get the support of others. A candidate may need the support of financial backers before he can get the support of voters; the president may feel that the support of public opinion can be used to get him the support of Congress to pass a law.

Though you want the support of those who can do your cause some good, practical politics requires the ability to make good use of that support which is easiest to achieve, that is, those who are already predisposed to back your position. Tactics must be adjusted to the available support. Because of this there are obvious advantages to a political system which provides a choice of tactics and a greater variety of ways of influencing decisions. It should also be pointed out that a good deal of political support is organized on a more or less permanent basis. Interest groups and political parties constitute ongoing forms of support, and their ability to grant or withhold their endorsement for a cause or an individual is an important element in their influence. The task of mobilizing support is thus not usually a question of starting from scratch but of dealing with existing factions and groups that already populate the political landscape.

Finally, it should be stressed that gaining political support is an essential part of politics at all levels and at various points in the system. It is as much of a concern for a prime minister or a president as it is for the average citizen; it is a problem that every political actor has to solve. It is as important in advancing a new issue or cause as it is in assuring compliance with decisions and laws already passed.

## ACQUISITION AND USE OF POLITICAL RESOURCES

Again, this activity occurs at all levels in the political system; as we noted earlier the acquisition and use of resources are essential elements in exerting influence. Because resources are so fundamental to the political process, their distribution and control are a paramount consideration. The ability to raise issues and gain political support can be limited to a very few people in society by explicit government restrictions on political activity (the persecution and harassment of dissidents in the Soviet Union and the outlawing of political parties) but, even where this does not occur, activity can be limited through control of resources. An important link between politics and the distribution of resources is the fact that much of what government does in regulating the public's business either directly or indirectly touches the distribution of such resources. If governments put money into schools or put conditions on admitting people to school (such as the requirement of equal opportunity or, in the reverse direction, the requirement that a person be white), they are determining the availability of educational opportunities. When government passes a tax law or a welfare program, it is partially determining the distribution of wealth. In licensing television and radio stations, government is determining the availability of means of communication.

The acquisition and use of resources are important when trying to influence government, but also at the point of trying to enforce what government has decided to do. For the latter purpose government is provided with certain resources that are essential to its successful operation—a treasury, organized bureaucracies, soldiers, weapons, jails. For all these impressive means of exercising power, governments may still fail because of a lack of resources. Taxes are a limited resource if the economy of the society provides little wealth to tax, and widespread lawlessness can strain the most efficient police system. Also, the power of government is sufficiently imposing that in democratic societies explicit steps are taken to limit the exercise of this power; it was for this reason that our forefathers were so suspicious of standing armies which they felt were easily open to abuse in infringing on the rights of the people.

Because of the importance of resources in shaping political life, a major element in studying a political system is the nature of the social and economic environment. The degrees of economic inequality, rigidity of class divisions, general level of literacy and education, and presence of powerful economic interests provide us with valuable clues as to the kind of politics that may be going on and the kind of politics that is possible.

## POLICY MAKING

Very much the heart of the political process is the way in which diverse inputs are transformed into public policies and decisions, or outputs. We have already explored two ways this process of transformation occurs: through the exercise of influence and through the formal institutional rules of decision making a political society creates. The immediate process is one in which influence operates within the confines of norms, rules, and institutions to produce policy. Though policy making is at the very center of the political process—and effectively engaging in it defines who the political elites are—it is still an activity that is shaped and constrained by the other steps in the system. Even where a prime minister or parliament possesses the immediate responsibility and power to set policy for the public, they cannot exercise their will unilaterally or autonomously. As a matter of fact, they have probably gained and nurtured their power over policy because of their sensitivity to the constraints of the system. Their activity as policy makers must take account of the issues that get raised, the legitimacy that decisions are likely to have, the factions that have formed, the influence impinging on their institution or public office. This reality is captured in the often-heard expression that "politics is the art of the possible."

The critical element in policy making is that the system must include a known or recognized way in which debate, bargaining, deliberation, and pressure culminate in a decision. This happens when a legislature votes, when a jury hands down a verdict, when a general gives an order, and when the president signs a bill into law. Controlling policy means either being the policy maker or being able to influence the policy maker. In highly centralized systems the number of policy makers will be greatly limited, and much policy will ultimately reside in the hands of a very few people. In less centralized, democratic systems decision making is dispersed and a single decision may require the coordination of different officials; two houses of the legislature may be required to pass a bill and the signature of the chief executive to make it law. This dispersal of decision making also allows certain officials to overrule others, creating a complex process in which policy is not so much made at a specific moment but evolves out of a series of reviews. In the United States a mayor could announce a policy, the city council could then pass a statute amending the policy, and a court could then come along and declare the new statute unconstitutional. This is the essence of that proud American tradition of checks and balances. Though policy in this system is less definite and constantly susceptible to change, this process has the advantage of allowing greater access to policy making by more people.

Policy making is an activity which by its very nature is engaged in by only a small elite in society; voting is as close as the average man on the street comes to the experience. Democratic societies have coped with this fact not so much by including citizens in policy making, though that has often been tried, but by placing in the hands of the people the means of controlling the constraints on policy makers, that is, the ability to define issues, organize support publicly, criticize the government, and change their elected officials. One way of putting this is that the democratic citizen may not be a formal part of the government, but he is part of the political system and it is from that fact that he derives his influence and role.

## THE CONTROL OF PUBLIC AFFAIRS

The ultimate purpose of politics is the management of the public's business, exerting control over those matters which society has come to recognize as shared interests and concerns. This means first that the political system must maintain order and second that it must maintain a particular kind of order; the former objective is shared by all systems, the latter is what makes one different from another. Not any kind of order will do, and whether or not government should deal with the health or education of its citizens, or means of transportation, or traveling to the moon and how it should do any of these things is what the political process is all about.

Aside from the exact subjects calling for governmental attention, there is an important political choice in selecting the means by which government will control public affairs. These may be thought of as "types of policy" of which the following three are significant.

## Regulative

Government can control public affairs by regulating people's behavior, that is, by setting down conditions under which certain behavior can be engaged in or by prohibiting certain forms of conduct altogether. Speed limits, control of sales of certain drugs, safety standards for the manufacturing of airplanes, codes specifying standards for the construction of homes, the prohibition of prostitution, theft, and assault, are all examples of regulative policies. One advantage of regulative forms of policy is that regulation is a matter of degree, and it may be carefully tailored to the exact needs of the situation. Countries like the United States, which believe in free enterprise and limited government, will often turn to regulation where other countries might employ more strenuous means of control since regulation may preserve a degree of freedom along with control.

## Distributive

A distributive policy is one which allocates values over which government has control. The classic example of a distributive policy is taxation, through which government decides how much money each citizen is to provide to the state and in the process affects the distribution of wealth in the society. Welfare programs, social security, and the distribution of funds for public projects like highways or housing are other examples of this type of policy.

## Direct Control

There are certain aspects of the public's business which government manages through complete, direct, and sometimes exclusive control. This typically includes maintenance of armed forces for the military defense of the country, printing of money, mail delivery, road building, and may also include operation of utilities and basic industries, schools, and the means of mass communication. The extent of this direct control is an important measure of the differences among various political systems, with "free enterprise" sharply limiting the direct control of government and "socialism" calling for public ownership and control of important segments of the economy.

The choice among these different types of policies is an important political question, and it will reflect the prevailing conception of justice, freedom, equality, and public purpose in the society.

## CONFLICT MANAGEMENT

One way to think of politics is as a type of controlled conflict. Conflict is inherent in political life, but if it is totally out of control politics itself has broken down. At every point in the political system, but particularly at the point of transforming inputs into outputs, conflicting demands into decisions, we find various kinds of conflict management going on.

One method of managing conflict is to attempt to keep conflicting factions from arising in the first place. The most direct way to do this is for the government to simply prohibit certain kinds of political activity. The creation of a particular political party, vocal opposition to the government's policies, the publishing of newspapers independent of government supervision and control, may all be deemed illegal activities. In this way, using the terminology of the political system, the inputs to the system are being explicitly controlled by the outputs of government. There is a direct feedback.

Though this method has appealed to numerous political elites throughout history by virtue of its attractiveness and seeming simplicity, it poses many difficulties for the performance of the system. To begin with, it places heavy demands on the ability of government to enforce the array of restrictive laws that is required to suppress dissenting views and thereby necessitates the expansion of the government's power. Indeed, it is because of this that only recently in history have governments been able to exert such control over large nation-states by virtue of the modern technological improvements in communications, transportation, and weaponry (which also reveals the effect of technological changes on the forms of government that are possible). Tremendous numbers of police, investigators, and bureaucrats are needed to monitor the activity of a large population of people and to enforce restrictive laws when necessary.

Another difficulty with this method is that it tends to breed political frustration among those inclined to criticize the existing regime. When dissent does surface or when the government's grip is loosened at all, political violence and instability result. When it is expected that such a method of conflict management will be employed, it drastically raises the values that are at stake in politics, for winning or losing in a political struggle then becomes not only a matter of how much power you will have or whether your special interest is protected, but a matter of personal freedom and safety. As in some of the less stable countries of Latin America, we see a self-destructive cycle of violence and repression, the one feeding on the other. The difficulty with repression is that the problems it brings when it does not work well can be as bad as the problems it brings when it works all too well.

Since the stifling of conflict is opposed to the value of political freedom, it is fortunate that there are other methods by which political conflict can be managed. The political culture of a society is an important harness on conflict. This can occur where there is widespread acceptance in society of fundamental political values or of nondestructive means for handling conflict. The notion of aristocratic privilege was unchallenged in European society for hundreds of years not so much because of explicit repression but because of a class structure which was perceived as legitimate by the various levels in society. Highly homogeneous, tradition-based societies are often able to cope with political conflict through the force of their shared values and beliefs, since conflict is, after all, a product of the diversity and variety of interests and values. Totalitarian regimes, impressed by this fact, turn their efforts toward creating a new and uniform political culture through propaganda, control of education, and massive campaigns of public indoctrination.

Even where diversity and the resulting conflict are present, political culture may be a stabilizing force if it includes the widespread acceptance of certain means by which differences may be expressed and conflicts resolved. Such a culture is required in open, democratic societies which, for the most part, abandon the attempt at trying to manage conflict by prohibiting political differences from arising. Democratic systems are designed to confront the problem of dealing with political conflict where such conflict is left free to arise in the first place. In contrast to repressive systems, democratic systems are aided by the fact that the stakes of politics are lowered as if by mutual consent. Losing an election means being out of power until the next election; it presumably does not mean being harassed or jailed. The expectation is reinforced that the effects of conflict will not be pushed to the limit by any political faction. This is supplemented by democratic methods themselves which allow for diverse views to be advanced within the political process and within the government itself, with parties, interest groups, and representative legislatures being the main vehicles by which the array of conflicts arising in society is to be mirrored in the political process. Though this has the advantages of recognizing political freedom and eliminating a fair amount of frustration, it places a substantial new task on the political process: how to handle, resolve, and ameliorate incessant friction among different political factions and at the same time provide government with the leadership and sense of direction which represent an equally important political need. Some have argued that the balancing and managing of the conflict it permits has become such an absorbing task of the democratic state and such a hindrance to decisive leadership that in periods of crisis—particularly in the area of foreign policy and war—some openness and looseness should be sacrificed. The expansion of presidential power in the United States has resulted in great part from the powers we have granted presidents during war time emergencies. Yet some of the most blatant infringements on civil liberties have occurred during such foreign emergencies or in the name of national security, such as McCarthyism in the 1950s.

It should also be pointed out that in the early development of modern democratic ideas a rather clever approach to conflict management was introduced in the form of the principle of toleration. At that time religious differences constituted one of the major sources of political discord, including war. Early democratic thinkers suggested that the best way to cope with this type of conflict was for government to simply get out of the business of trying to regulate religious beliefs and to only take upon itself the role of protector of everyone's religious freedom. We might describe this as coping with conflict by "depoliticizing" it; certain kinds of conflict are simply made private affairs. The ability to do this can be of tremendous value to the political system but again requires a supportive political culture.


## PERFORMANCE


In speaking of the performance of the political system we are referring to ways in which we can evaluate the feedback effect of what government does on society and on subsequent political events. There are two general measures of performance. *Effectiveness* is a measure of the extent to which the goals of the system are achieved, in other words, the extent to which the government is able to do what it is supposed to do. *Legitimacy* is a measure of the extent to which the actions of government are accepted as rightful. The legitimacy and effectiveness of the political system may be both high or both low, but it is also possible that an effective system may lack legitimacy, and vice versa. Even a system that is perceived as legitimate may lack the means to defend the nation in war, improve the conditions of life in society, or cope with economic crises. By the same token, an extremely efficient and effective regime may operate in such a way that its rule is not generally supported by the people. In a colonial government where a country finds itself ruled by another country, such as British rule over

India or French rule over Indochina until after World War II, there is often noticeably more effectiveness than legitimacy.

If people perceive the decisions and actions of government as legitimate this will translate into support for leaders and such support, as well as demands and conflicting interests, is one of the inputs to the system, and a vital one at that. The lack of such support will mean that the government will not be able to depend on the backing of the people, which is especially important at times of crisis, or that it will have to use repressive means to insure that this lack of support does not become active opposition. The ineffectiveness of government raises the prospect that the system will be faced with continued pressure and demands to solve problems that are not being dealt with, though the government may possess sufficient legitimacy to be able to weather this pressure. Though legitimacy and effectiveness are separate standards of performance, it should not be surprising that there is a certain interplay between the two. A regime which initially lacks legitimacy may be able to gain it by a long-term record of effective performance. The long line of British monarchs who constituted the essence of public authority in England can trace their ancestry back to William the Conqueror who established his rule through forceful conquest. In contemporary totalitarian systems the effective use of governmental power is used to confront the legitimacy problem through political education and propaganda, in effect creating a new generation trained and oriented to support the system. Also, a problem of effectiveness may tend to weaken the legitimacy of government over time. In this way the deeply rooted sympathy of the Russian people for the czar was eroded by the inability of the monarchy to deal effectively with the most basic problems of national security and domestic welfare.

In evaluating the performance of a political system, we should realize it is not just a question of how competent the government is or of what type of government it is, but is also a question of the severity of the problems and crises it must confront. Immediately after the American Revolution the thirteen colonies had to confront the problem of establishing a new government and building legitimacy for a federal arrangement. The ability to do this was aided during the first couple of generations of the nation's existence by the lack of foreign or domestic crises forced upon it all at once, its distance from the international quarrels of Europe, and a favorable environment for economic growth and individual opportunity. The same institutions have not fared well under the strained conditions of civil strife, war, or poverty, as seen in the unsuccessful attempt of South Vietnam to adopt an American-style constitution.

## SUMMARY

Raising issues, wielding influence, making decisions, enforcing rules, creating and managing conflict, are what people do in politics; they are the activities and the processes that take place within the system we have described. They go on in a dictatorship as well as in a democracy, in a neighborhood meeting as well as in a national government, but by different people in different ways. They are the constant and perpetual stuff of political experience. When the political scientist studies politics, it is these activities that he wants to systematically relate, that he wants to use to explain why political systems operate as they do, some succeeding, others failing; some stable, some unstable; some arbitrary and repressive, others not.

The job of the political scientist in all of this is to act as an investigator or map reader, tracing down through the intricate wiring, switches, and currents of the system the causes of a certain political result or performance, always with an eye to the intricate possibilities of the system, always suspicious of the type of explanation which tends to ignore the fact that there is a system at all. Why is it that so many Americans do not vote compared to citizens in other modern democracies? Apathy? Is that the answer? But what *is* apathy? A mysterious contagion to which Americans show some special susceptibility? The political scientist cannot be satisfied with this. He looks at the American voter as an individual within the political system in which there are laws regulating voting and registering to vote, there are particular kinds of choices he faces on the ballot, particular kinds of socialization that are going on that form attitudes about life and the role of politics in it. He will want to trace these larger patterns on the assumption that the phenomenon of nonvoting, like other political behavior and political events, is not a random or accidental event but a reflection of the political processes and experiences in which the citizen finds himself.

The analysis of politics as a system reveals two interrelated sides of our experience. These consist of what we may call the *constitution* and the *processes* of the political system. Here constitution is not used in the narrow sense to refer to a written document of basic law but in the broadest sense to indicate all of the outward forms of the system: public offices, institutions, laws, traditions, symbols of authority, formal organizations. Processes refers to such actual activities as we have just reviewed: the use of power and influence, mobilization of support, communication of views, the raising of conflict. In the study of politics we cannot exclude one of these sides of experience from the other. The constitution of the body politic channels, orders, and defines the processes that occur while those very processes maintain, alter, or give birth to constitutional forms. One cannot study politics merely by reading laws and organization charts nor by merely observing peoples' attitudes, values, and interpersonal relationships; rather, politics involves a mixture of these two sides of experience, the formal and the informal. When the political system was described as controlled conflict it was in reference to this relationship between a system's constitution and processes, the former the steadying and ordering force, the latter the dynamic force in the relationship.

The use of the system idea also requires identification of the central organizing principle that every system possesses. In the biological system this principle is the maintenance of life; in the "football system" it is winning a game. In politics the corresponding principle is society's mastery and control of its common affairs, and from that principle all of the important questions about politics derive: Who governs? How do they govern? What is governed? What do people disagree about and why? How is this disagreement expressed? How is it handled and kept from destroying society? Why does it sometimes destroy society? How are institutions created? How do they assist in the governing of public affairs? In answering these questions, the political system appears as a changing, adapting, pulsating network of human relationships affecting the basic values of human life—security, freedom, order, justice—a constant, ceaseless process of human conflict and order, stability and change. What we need to turn to now is an examination of the various ways this system has been designed.

## NOTES

[1]Maurice Duverger, *Political Parties* (New York, 1963), pp. 17–36.

[2]Carl J. Friedrich and Zbigniew Brzezinski, *Totalitarian Dictatorship and Autocracy* (New York, 1966), p. 330.

[3]David Easton, *A Framework for Political Analysis* (Englewood Cliffs, N.J., 1965).

[4]Seymour Martin Lipset, *The First New Nation* (New York, 1967).

## FOR FURTHER READING

Duverger, Maurice. *Political Parties.* New York: John Wiley, 1963. A classic study of Western political parties, covering their historical development, the types of parties, and party systems.

Easton, David. *A Framework for Political Analysis.* Englewood Cliffs, N.J.: Prentice-Hall, 1965. A formal statement of systems theory and its adaptation to the study of politics.

Lipset, Seymour Martin. *Political Man.* Garden City, N.Y.: Doubleday, 1963.
A comparative examination of groups, factions, and the dynamic effect of
social and economic forces on politics.

Sorauf, Frank J. *Political Parties in the American System.* Boston: Little, Brown,
1964. A good standard treatment of the American party system, covering
various aspects of party structure, personnel, issues, and tactics.

Truman, David. *The Government Process.* New York: Alfred A. Knopf, 1965. An
extensive and detailed analysis of the dynamic role of interest groups in
American politics. A basic work that did much to define "group theory" as
an approach to the study of politics.

# 5

# Comparing
# Political Systems

The study of politics cannot be limited merely to the study of our own immediate political experiences or to a single political system; it would be like studying biology by looking exclusively at monkeys. Recall that the term *political experience* has been used here because of its double connotation: the study of politics should help us both in understanding our own experience as well as in expanding our knowledge of political experience in general.

Thus, from the earliest period of formal political thinking in Western history, the comparison of different types of political systems has been a matter of continuing interest. Historically, this fascination with comparing and categorizing political systems has produced the terms we often rely upon to characterize some of the different forms of politics we see around us: dictatorship, democracy, totalitarianism, monarchy, constitutionalism. Such terms are ways of summing up and identifying the overall character of the political process discussed in the previous chapter. Why have political thinkers been so absorbed with this comparison and categorization? The most obvious reason is that different societies have settled upon different ways of managing public affairs, and a full understanding of politics requires an appreciation of these differences—in institutions, laws, means of distributing power, forms of political organization—all presumably leading to different performance and different results.

However, there is another good reason for taking an interest in comparing political systems. Political institutions and relationships are something that man has made for himself, and different political systems may be viewed as different options or alternatives that have developed historically as solutions to the basic dilemma of controlling public affairs. Though these options are not a matter of completely free choice for a society, they are not beyond the means of political man to alter. The comparison of political systems thus provides us with a basis for evaluating as well as understanding alternative political solutions and for measuring the performance of various systems.

Comparison solves an important problem for the social scientist and for political man. The natural scientist can test an idea under controlled conditions in a laboratory without tampering with the real world, but in the study of society the "laboratory" is usually the real world itself. In politics it is rather difficult merely to experiment, because the trial run is itself a public decision with public consequences. Citizens complain, quite justifiably, when they are used as guinea pigs to test someone's new theory or idea. Thus, in social and political decisions we are called upon to know as much as we can about the consequences and implications of a new idea *before* we can actually test it. The traditional way of compensating for this problem is to base the development and growth of new political knowledge, as much as possible, on the study of various different kinds of actual societies. This does not mean that such study gives us conclusive, laboratory-type answers, but it does indicate the type of knowledge we must necessarily rely upon. What are the consequences of socialized medicine, of military leaders unchecked by civilian authority, of multiparty competition, of a different tax structure? We cannot answer these questions definitively by looking at other countries and their histories, but other countries do represent a source of information and experience that is otherwise lacking and would be difficult to replicate in any other way.

One of the intriguing aspects of the study of comparative politics is the way in which it causes us to question our own political perceptions and values. Most people would find it difficult to imagine how their own political system could operate any differently and how other kinds of systems are capable of operating at all. An amusing example of this is how American students are typically bewildered, in being initially exposed to British politics, by the fact that the prime minister does not have a defined term of office dictated by a written constitution. Though tradition dictates elections at least every five years, what prevents the prime minister from simply staying in office and not calling elections? What prevents the monarch from rejecting the majority party's choice of prime minister? How can the prime minister govern effectively if he can be removed from office upon merely losing a vote in Parliament (we ask as we think back to the number of vetoes used by President Ford)?

Other societies, of course, may be equally bewildered by us. In some of the less stable systems of Latin America, one can imagine the astonishment at the extent to which Americans accept the results of elections and the forced resignation of a president without resort to violence. Other Western democracies find it curious that we allow a body like the Supreme Court to declare laws unconstitutional and thereby seem to make policy.

These varying perceptions, of course, reveal that people tend to be prejudiced in favor of their own experiences but they also reveal something very basic to politics itself. Particular political systems work the way they do in part because of the perceptions, attitudes, and values that prevail within the society. We might say that the reason the workings of British institutions seem a bit bewildering is because we do not think exactly like the British, and the reason our institutions seem so natural is because we think like Americans. The British place greater confidence in the ability of custom and tradition to restrict the abuse of power, whereas Americans are more comfortable when resorting to explicit legal controls on such abuse. The point is that our differing perceptions may contain the very reason why one type of institution will work for the British and another for the Americans. This is why the study of comparative politics calls upon us not only to gather information about different political systems but to try to put ourselves in their place.

Another way of looking at this problem is to keep in mind that we are comparing *systems*, and while one aspect of the system may seem odd and incomprehensible, it is but one of several interrelated factors. In many of the newly independent nations of Africa and Asia we see a preponderance of nationalistic leaders or dictators and few successful cases of representative legislatures and competitive parties. This phenomenon may be misread and misunderstood unless we put it in historical context, unless we look at the nature of their political experience. In these countries the need to achieve political independence through force, the achievement of national identity after independence in the face of a culturally and linguistically diverse population, the lack of constitutional traditions, the friction between the forces of tradition and the forces of change, represent some of the considerations that may help explain the particular political forms that arise. A more rigorous analysis of this sort is what is needed to avoid the inclination to dismiss contrary political systems as oddities and aberrations resulting from incompetence. Other systems tend to share one basic trait with our own, in that they all represent attempts, good or bad, successful or unsuccessful, to deal with the problems of political control and order in light of their unique experience.

# WHAT DO WE WANT TO COMPARE?

The first and most important issue that is confronted in comparison is the choice of a standard of comparison or criteria. If you want to compare various individuals, you have to decide what it is about them you want to compare. Do you want to compare them according to their height, intelligence, personality, religious beliefs, or some other criterion? The results you come up with will be determined by the criteria you use, thus it is important to keep the criteria in mind and to question the relevance of the criteria. If you are organizing a basketball team, you should be interested in height; if you are awarding a scholarship, you should be interested in intelligence. We encounter much the same issue in comparing political systems; we have to choose criteria and suit the criteria to what our interests or purposes are. Do we want to compare systems according to the basis of authority, the amount of political freedom, the kinds of institutions, or the distribution of political power?

Another decision in drawing comparisons between things as complex as political systems is whether we are interested in comparing the system as a whole—a *comprehensive* comparison—or comparing some aspect of it—a *particular* comparison. A comprehensive comparison is very difficult because it requires capturing in a single abstract category —like democracy or aristocracy—a very complex set of patterns and relationships (which is why such labels are difficult to define briefly). When the average layman looks at other political systems, he typically is trying to grasp the significance of the systems in comprehensive terms. Political scientists are frequently interested in particular as well as comprehensive comparisons, and for this purpose, they may focus their attention on any number of aspects of a system. They may compare styles of local government, bureaucracy, parties, law, political beliefs, legislatures. It is important not to confuse particular and comprehensive comparisons and to keep in mind that particular comparisons may be limited in what they tell you about systems as a whole. The Soviet Union and the state of Alabama may both be one-party systems, but that does not mean they are the same in other significant respects; both Great Britain and Iran have a monarch but there the similarity ends.

One additional thought in approaching the comparative study of politics is that comparison means looking for both similarities and differences. It may be true that in fine detail each political system can be said to be unique, but by the same token the broadly defined political task of man is common to all systems. It is easy to exaggerate either differences or similarities; what we should be prepared to find is a mixture of both. This is what allows the political scientist to compare political systems not by examining a hundred national systems individually but

by developing types or categories of systems. It is these types of categories that guide the formal study of comparative politics.

## PARTICULAR COMPARISONS

We have already used particular comparisons of different systems in
our earlier discussion of institutions and political groups. Thus, different
party systems were delineated—single-party, two-party, and multiparty—as a means of comparing the different ways in which political
activity is organized and studying the various implications of such organization. We also compared different ways in which institutional components could fit together—separation of powers, parliamentary
government, and authoritarian centralization. Numerous aspects of the
political system are susceptible to this type of comparison. We can add
to these earlier comparisons the following examples of other aspects
that the political scientist might be interested in isolating for examination.

### The Basis of Authority

Earlier we described formal authority as deriving from tradition, rule
of law, or ideology. To these can be added another important source of
political authority which is noninstitutional, what Max Weber calls *charisma.* Charisma refers to various characteristics attributed to the single
ruler or dictator who governs through the force of his own personal
authority; these characteristics may include such attributes as vision,
insight, virtue, eloquence, leadership. We find at times the appearance
of a leader—an Adolph Hitler, a Gandhi—whose purely personal authority outweighs and may even tend to destroy the authority of law,
tradition, and ideology. The basis of public authority is one particular
aspect of the political system which can be used as grounds for comparison. Where one of these bases is predominant, the comparison can be
quite significant.

### The Role of Government in Society

The performance of government is specific grounds for comparison,
and an important criterion in this regard is the range of control that
government exercises in society. The role of government may be defined in very limited terms and it may be understood that most social,
cultural, economic, or religious activities should be free from governmental regulation. Government regulates social conflict and maintains
order but does not dictate all values for people in society. At the other

extreme are systems in which government takes an active interest in virtually every aspect of social and even personal life; it directs the educational process, tells people what kind of art is good and what kind is decadent, controls the price of commodities and sets explicit production goals for the economy, declares an official state religion or bans religion altogether. Needless to say there are varying degrees of governmental control between these two extremes. If we have any doubts about whether there are real material differences between one political system and another, the comparison of government's performance and the way it touches people's lives should be enough to dispel such doubts.

## The Distribution of Resources and Roles

From what has been said already it should be easy to see why roles and resources can be treated together; if the political elite is going to consist of a wide and diverse group, it is essential that the necessary political resources be more broadly distributed and, conversely, a broader distribution of resources can affect the composition of the elite. We can compare political systems according to how diverse and numerous the opportunities are for being a political actor or a member of the political elite. Again this is a matter of degree involving a number of factors which we can analyze by looking at the extreme polar cases. On the one hand is the society in which there are minimum legal restrictions on political activity, the class structure allows for movement from one class to another (social mobility), and such basic political resources as money and educational opportunity are fairly equally distributed as indicated by a fairly large middle class. Though we still find a distinction between elite and followers in such a system, there is greater openness and fluidity in the acquisition of significant political roles. The opposite of this would be a form of politics in which political activity is explicitly restricted (opposition political parties might be illegal or open criticism of the government suppressed), and in which one would find few avenues open for political advancement, very little social mobility, and basic resources distributed in a highly unequal way. Between these somewhat extreme models we are likely to find political systems which display varying degrees of resource and role distribution.

## Political Culture

An important ingredient in the political process is the pattern of political attitudes, values, and beliefs that are prevalent in society— what we have simply called the political culture. Comparing political cultures is not nearly as easy as comparing institutions or political groups, but it may be as vital to understanding the differences among systems. When we characterize the United States as a highly individual-istic society, we are effectively describing a key element of our political culture. This means that Americans are inclined to believe that govern-ment should not interfere with their personal lives, that their quality of life is primarily a result of their own independent effort and achieve-ment, that they should look to their own conscience and rational abili-ties in making decisions, and that they are primarily responsible for themselves and cannot assume that others will assume responsibility for them. Such attitudes affect many aspects of people's lives, and among these is their relationship to government. The "individualistic" culture can be contrasted to a "traditional" culture in which the individual perceives himself as a bearer of society's traditions and customs. There is a feeling of mutual interdependence and responsibility, and the indi-vidual is as much a product of his social position as of his personal efforts. In the modern period some have spoken of an "authoritarian" personal-ity or culture in which the individual seeks out and depends upon the guidance of an authority figure, whether it be a father or a political leader, and has a strong need for a sense of order that is provided by such attachments.

In many political systems it may not be possible to use a single charac-terization of the political culture, and splits or divisions may be discov-ered. It has been observed that in many of the developing nations of Africa and Asia there is often a split or conflict between the traditional elements of the culture and the modern elements, those introduced by pressures from economic development and from political elites who, educated in Europe or America, have come to adopt the principles and values of a modern, secular society. In any event, the study of political culture is quite a complex subject in its own right and these remarks are intended merely to identify it as a relevant area of comparative analysis.

Table 5–1 shows how these various particular grounds for comparing systems might be assembled and applied to various specific political systems. It is very important to keep in mind that what is presented here is a general example of what particular comparisons might pro-duce. We have not exhausted all of the particular grounds for compari-son or even all of the possible criteria within each of these. Within the limited terms described here our comparison has necessarily involved some sweeping generalizations which leave great room for refinement. But this analysis is useful for what it tells us about the study of compara-tive politics. We will notice that there is no absolute connection be-tween one of these features of the system and all the rest; indeed, if we were to elaborate this comparison in even finer detail, we could make

TABLE 5-1. Comparison of Selected Features of the Political System

| Features of the System | United States | USSR | Nazi Germany | Italy | India |
|---|---|---|---|---|---|
| Type of Party System | Two-party | One-party | One-party | Multiparty | Multiparty |
| Institutional Patterns | Separation of powers | Centralized | Centralized | Parliamentary | Parliamentary |
| Basis of Authority | Law | Ideology | Charisma | Law | Law |
| Role of Government | Limited | Extensive | Extensive | Mixed | Mixed |
| Distribution of Roles and Resources | Broad | Narrow | Narrow | Restricted | Restricted |
| Political Culture | Individualistic | Authoritarian | Authoritarian | Traditional individualistic | Traditional individualistic |

each political system look unique. These aspects we have looked at assist us in comparing the main features of different systems but should not be confused with an exact and full description.

To appreciate this point better, imagine how we might compare ourselves to a group of a hundred different people. If the group was evenly divided between Catholics and Protestants, as Catholics we could say we have something in common with 50 percent of the group. Let us say that the group is also divided into those who live in urban areas and those who live in rural areas and it turns out that half the Catholics live in urban areas. As a Catholic living in Chicago, I have two characteristics in common with 25 of the 100 people. If the whole group is further subdivided along lines of race and sex, I may find that there are 10 of the original 100 who, like me, are white, male, urban Catholics. If I carried this far enough I could probably define a set of characteristics which finally would apply only to me alone of all the 100 people—that is, I would be the only white, male, urban, Catholic lawyer with five children. If I were writing my autobiography or describing myself to a stranger, this detailed uniqueness would come out, but to a social scientist studying the above group, I might be just one of the Catholics or one of the males. For the social scientist these are grounds for comparison and analysis of the group. He does not intend (or should not intend) that they serve to describe me adequately as an individual.

Much the same thing is encountered in comparative politics. Saying that the United States is a two-party system means that this is something it has in common with some other systems and does not have in common with others, while at the same time we can say that as a total system, there is no other country in the world that is governed exactly like ours. To compare means to generalize and categorize.

There is something else we should notice about the collection of characteristics in the table. Even though two political systems that share one thing in common need not share other features, not just any combination of features is possible. A multiparty system does not fit with highly centralized dictatorship; effective limits on government do not fit with the presence of charismatic or ideological grounds for authority. In other words, we can discern certain patterns or "clusters" of characteristics, such as the link between individualism, a wide distribution of political resources, and limits on the extent of government control. The practical value of these clusters is that when we move from a particular comparison of political systems to a comprehensive comparison they can be used to help determine general types of political systems. In fact, it is very important for the political scientist who is focusing on a single feature for comparison to keep in mind the cluster of characteristics it may be a part of. All of this naturally leads us to the other level of comparative study, the comparison of systems as a whole.

## COMPREHENSIVE COMPARISONS

Though the analysis of particular comparisons can serve many useful purposes, the ultimate purpose behind comparative politics has been to discover a workable and useful categorization of political systems as a whole. When the ordinary layman contrasts the United States with the Soviet Union, he would likely not express this in terms of party systems, political culture, or the distribution of resources but rather by calling one system "democratic" and the other "communist." Creating an adequate scheme of comparison for all systems—*a typology*—is very difficult and represents a fairly high degree of abstraction.

The ancient Greek philosopher Aristotle developed a typology of political systems which is interesting to look back to as an example of a basic and early scheme of comparison.[1] Aristotle felt that political systems could be compared according to two criteria. The first criterion was the number of people who ruled, according to which there could be government of one person, of the few, or of the many. The second criterion was whether or not those who ruled did so in their own interest (the bad form) or in the interest of the community at large (the good form). Combining these two criteria, he produced a typology like that in Table 5–2. Thus, *kingship* was a form of one-man rule in which the ruler governed on behalf of the common good; *tyranny* was also one-man rule but the tyrant's self-interest guided decisions; *aristocracy* was the rule of an elite group in the interest of the whole community. Of the six types of systems which Aristotle's typology produced, the *polity* is the one term that is unfamiliar today, though it bears a general resemblance to the type of "mixed" constitutional structure of the United States. Aristotle felt that *polity* represented the best practical form of government, for while it included the mass of people in politics it included some of the virtues of kingship and aristocracy. A similar notion of mixing the elements of various simple types of government into a complex type influenced the arrangement of our own constitution. Our founding fathers thought of the popularly elected House of Representatives, with its short two-year term of office, as the "voice of

TABLE 5–2.  Aristotle's Typology of Political Systems

| Number of Rulers | Importance of the Common Good | |
|---|---|---|
| | Good Forms | Bad Forms |
| One | Kingship | Tyranny |
| Few | Aristocracy | Oligarchy |
| Many | Polity | Democracy |

the people" in government. The influence of the people would be balanced by the Senate and president, neither of which was directly elected under the original constitution. It is interesting to notice that popular government in its purest (unmixed) form was called *democracy* by Aristotle, and this was considered one of the bad forms of government.

Though typologies like Aristotle's were used frequently up to the modern age, and though they tell us something about the traditional meaning of terms such as *oligarchy* and *democracy*, contemporary political scientists would not be very likely to compare systems in this way. Today the distinction between "good and bad forms" measured according to whether the public interest is being served is not considered a very useful or objective criterion. The very meaning of the public interest, how it should be defined and if it is even definable, is too controversial and intricate a question. The other criterion, the number of people who rule, still has some relevance today, though Aristotle's distinction of the one, the few, and the many is too much of an oversimplification. As we indicated, for example, in our discussion of executive power, it is very difficult to conceive of literal one-man rule, for even the modern totalitarian dictator maintains power on the basis of an organized party or class or group. The dictator creates an oligarchy, in effect, through which he is able to govern and without which he is powerless.

## A MODERN TYPOLOGY

In attempting to capture the diversity of modern politics, several political scientists have offered basic typologies for use in comparative study. What we will describe here is one of the more popular schemes that we can test against what we have already learned about politics.[2]

This typology first breaks down all systems into two groups according to whether they are basically democratic or oligarchic, the former characterized by the possible inclusion of the bulk of adult citizens into the political process in some significant, independent manner, and the latter characterized by the power of an exclusive, defined elite to which access is formally controlled. Within such broad categories there are certain sub-types, that is, certain types of democracy and certain types of oligarchy. Including these variations, this scheme consists of five types of political systems: political democracy; tutelary democracy; totalitarian oligarchy; traditional oligarchy; modernizing oligarchy.

These five types should be useful in telling us about the differences among systems in the way that institutions are designed, political action is organized, power is distributed, and roles are played. In describing each type we want to look for how such features hang together or "cluster" in such a way as to form an identifiable type of political system.

## Political Democracy

In identifying democracy it is most important to look for the means by which citizens can achieve access to and representation in government and for the presence of personal and political liberties. Typical institutional components consist of a popularly elected legislature with a significant role in lawmaking; a directly or indirectly elected chief executive responsible to a party, legislative majority, or public opinion; and a bureaucracy and court system free from arbitrary political influence. The principle of rule of law, with or without a formal written constitution, provides the basic source and framework of public authority. The governing relationships within and among these institutions are not solely characterized by hierarchical commands but just as prominently include bargaining, deliberation, advising, review, and investigation.

Since one of the most characteristic features of a democracy is the tolerance of open, public opposition to the government, democracy typically brings with it the proliferation of parties and interest groups that openly compete for influence. Such "loyal opposition" will not be sufficient unles it is buttressed by a distribution of political resources that makes it possible for opposing views to engage in politics effectively and independently. The right to oppose the government must correspond with the ability to achieve access to government. Breadth of access is achieved by providing opportunity to influence public policy at several institutional points or levels, which results from not having institutional power concentrated in any one office or branch of government (a prominent feature of American federalism and separation of powers). Access is also achieved by widening the role of "political actor" through increasing the availability of political resources.

An appropriate political culture is of considerable importance to the functioning of democracy. Self-reliance in the exercise of political freedoms must be balanced by toleration of opposing views and a commitment to democratic processes. As with any system, socialization serves a vital political function in maintaining relevant skills and attitudes among the people, that is, conveying a sense of "citizenship."

We should be careful to note the "fit" among the components of the democratic system. Competitive parties and interest groups and a variety of independent bases of power within governmental institutions all require a refined ability of the system to ameliorate and manage conflict. Institutional rules of decision making (such as rule by majority vote) are not enough; it is also critical to have the support of the population at large for the kind of open, competitive politics that is allowed and a widely accepted understanding of the processes of compromise and deliberation. These supportive attitudes among the people must in turn be based on a social, cultural, and economic environment that allows people to deal with each other in the political realm on a more or less equal basis. The degree of democracy that occurs and the success and stability of the democratic approach to politics will depend on the kind of fit that develops among social environment, behavior, and institutions.

This characterization of political democracy is intended as a descriptive way of distinguishing certain political systems from others, not as a definitive theoretical statement about what democracy is. American politics is frequently criticized for not being democratic enough, for unnecessarily restricting people's access to government, or not guaranteeing equality before the law. These are important issues in their own right, deriving from the very values that a democracy promotes. But the validity of these criticisms does not deny that one system is different from another and that one can be called democratic. Actually, our description of political democracy probably applies to no more than two dozen nation-states in the world today. Among these are countries such as the United States, Great Britain, Canada, Australia, France, Germany, Sweden, and Japan.

## Tutelary Democracy

There are some political systems that appear democratic in regard to their institutional forms or the hopes and aspirations of their leaders, despite the absence of true democratic politics. These types of systems, in which the elite nurtures the development of democratic politics, may be called tutelary democracies. The lack of a democratic tradition, a suitable political culture, and a supportive social and economic environment are the typical factors keeping such systems from the full development of political democracy. They rely on an adjustment and compromise of democratic principles for the purposes of maintaining political stability.

Many of the trappings of Western-style democracy will be found in these systems. Popular elections will be held, to some extent rule of law will prevail, two or more political parties will compete for power, and a semi-functioning legislature will be used. Yet unrestricted political activity and broad access of people to the political process are lacking either because resources are so unequally distributed or because the political elite feels a need to keep a harness on the forces of democracy. A system such as this is almost inherently unstable, and it is not surprising if some fail to mature into fully democratic states and slide easily into a form of oligarchy. The ability to maintain democratic forms is easily threatened by foreign or domestic crises to which the elite feels a need to respond through the exercise of central authority. Freedom of the press and of political association and the right to form an opposition party are not assured.

Certain Latin American countries—being neither fully democratic nor explicitly oligarchical—would seem to fit this category, and two countries, Indonesia and Turkey, have been good examples of the type at certain points in their history. In Turkey, a parliamentary republic was formed by Kemal Ataturk in 1923 and was subsequently nurtured and developed by Ataturk himself, who unilaterally removed bans on opposition parties. In Indonesia, President Sukarno coined the phrase "guided democracy" to characterize his attempts at permitting more open political competition, attempts which ultimately led to disastrous conflicts between the Indonesian military and the Indonesian Communist party (PKI) in the mid-1960s. The Turkish and Indonesian examples reveal what may at first seem to be a paradox about tutelary democracy: though democracy is a form of "popular rule," its introduction into such unfavorable circumstances is the result of initiatives from the political elite. Tutelary democracy requires the skill and commitment of political leaders and often the inspiration of an almost charismatic figure at the head of state. Not unlike American fondness for George Washington, many Turks look upon Kemal Ataturk as a founder of modern Turkish government, and long after his death reference was made to "Kemalism" as a political movement and set of principles.

In effect, we are talking about elite-created democracy, a phenomenon which is much more natural than it sounds. Democratic politics can come about only through political means and, lacking a revolution which itself is likely to be led by a small elite, democracy will have to be the creation of those who are part of the ruling class. The elite may turn to democracy in response to popular pressures it senses or anticipates, but it also serves to initiate democratic values as an independent force for whatever personal or political reasons. Strangely enough, the prospects for democracy in such systems will depend greatly on the care and wisdom with which the elite uses its power to minimize the resort to coercion and tolerate opposition, yet govern with a firm and steady hand.

## Traditional Oligarchy

Oligarchic political systems are distinct from democratic forms in that political power is in the hands of an identifiable ruling group and there is the lack of any normal, legitimate means of challenging or contesting this power or of participating in the political process on the part of people who are not members of the elite. In a traditional form of oligarchy, the power of the ruling class is maintained on the basis of political values and principles which receive their legitimacy from long-held customs and practices of the past. The classic institutional expression of traditional oligarchy in the West has taken the form of kingship and aristocracy, which both serve to sort out rulers and nonrulers in society according to birth and inherited rights and privileges. The ruler maintains power by appealing to the traditional values of the society which have a strong attraction to the people themselves.

Unlike other forms of oligarchy which may use certain modern institutions such as parties and legislatures at least as a facade, traditional systems, by virtue of being distinctly antimodern, will have less use for such devices. Administration is in the hands of those with sufficient personal loyalty to the rulers and suitable class position, and policies and laws are made by decree. The political processes we described earlier do not occur through a diverse assortment of institutions and organizations but take place as the activities of a tightly defined elite group governing the political system more like a household. The average man in such a society relates to political experience as a subject, supporting government through his own attachment to the cultural traditions on which it is based, yet wary of it as an alien force of which he is not a part. In traditional oligarchy, the political realm, in effect, shrinks to include only a small segment of society.

For its stability and continuance, such a system requires the preservation of broadly accepted and deeply respected customs and traditions and is extremely vulnerable to the threat of cultural and social pluralism. Thus, tradition-based regimes are not well equipped to confront the forces of modernization, the need for rationally guided economic development, and the breakdown of cultural isolation that is so much a part of the contemporary world. By its very character such a system requires continuity and permanence, while so many of the countries of Asia and Africa where traditional oligarchies have been strong are confronted with the challenge of rapid development. Not surprisingly, strictly traditional oligarchy is steadily disappearing in the modern world.

## Totalitarian Oligarchy

Totalitarian regimes involve the rule of an organized elite free of the constraints of political opposition, which is explicitly and forcefully prohibited, and of legal principles, which are thoroughly lacking. But totalitarianism carries oligarchy a step further by attempting to dominate every sphere of social, cultural, and economic life and destroy all independent associations and bases of authority in society. This form of rule is more than just closed and arbitrary, it is total.

Totalitarian politics replaces tradition with an ideology that serves as the basis of political legitimacy by presuming to provide a coherent, exclusive, and singular interpretation of society. The ideology is militantly proselytized by a tightly disciplined, hierarchically organized elite. The elite forms itself as a party organization which, in practice, is almost indistinguishable from the state itself and governs through the vehicle of a large centralized bureaucracy. Courts, legislative assemblies, and constitutional documents are primarily cosmetic, though they still have the practical function of symbolically legitimizing the regime. Though active and elite political roles are closed off, totalitarian systems draw the mass of people into politics through a continuous demand for expressions of popular support. Systematic propaganda and political education are important means of control, particularly as they are aimed against the threat of traditional elites, the forces of cultural pluralism, and associations and loyalties independent of the state (such as religion). The appearance of a single charismatic leader is common but not essential, and we typically associate totalitarianism with the rise of leaders like Hitler, Mussolini, and Stalin.

One of the more prominent features of totalitarianism is the strident use of coercion and violence to maintain control as seen in the persecution, jailing, and killing of political opponents. Since the greatest danger to the totalitarian state is a serious division among the ruling group, and since institutionalized processes for resolving such splits are often not available, the purge of one elite faction by another is a frequent outcome of such elite confrontations. The intolerance of opposition and the constant use of repression lead to the continued necessity and justification of force to insure order. Though tyranny is nothing new in history, totalitarianism may be considered a truly modern phenomenon in which pervasive political control within the large nation-state is made possible through the centralized control and use of contemporary technology in the areas of communication and transportation and techniques of bureaucratic organization. This ability to organize and extend physical control over sprawling countries like the Soviet Union or China makes the twentieth-century dictator incredibly more powerful than the absolute monarchs of Europe a few hundred years ago. The need to maintain such centralized and complete control of society requires the swelling of government bureaucracy and the massive mobilization of resources.

The unique feature of totalitarianism is its attempt to use the centralized power of the state to transform society. Though they may seem similar on the surface, traditional oligarchy is concerned with preserving the past—though it may take on some of the traits of totalitarianism when internally threatened (as in the case of Iran)—whereas totalitarianism has mainly been a tool for crushing tradition and altering the fabric of social life.

The most prominent examples of modern totalitarianism have been the fascist regimes in Germany and Italy prior to World War II and the major communist regimes of the Soviet Union and China.

## Modernizing Oligarchy

The simplest characterization of this type is that it is a system which turns to oligarchy as a means of achieving rapid, orderly progress and development. Like other forms of oligarchy, it excludes political opposition and open competition, reduces democratic institutions, such as a representative legislature, to at best a symbolic role of ratification and support for the elite, and weakens those institutions that could threaten the effectiveness of the elite, such as an independent judiciary. The modernizing elite, occupied with the task of development, is particularly concerned with controlling the forces of tradition which it perceives as reactionary and against which it makes a populist appeal to the common man.

The controlling principle in such regimes is the country's need for modernization, "catching up" with more advanced industrialized societies. The modernization task may be specifically defined in terms of the need for economic growth, adoption of contemporary techniques of agricultural and industrial production, and the proliferation of technical skills and rational principles of social organization. The elite will attempt to recruit and will need the support of that segment of society with the knowledge and talent relevant to modernization. This helps to explain the central political role played by the military in many developing nations, for the military often represents the one disciplined, relatively modernized institution in society and an important avenue for social advancement. In contrast to European experience, where the military often functions in politics as a conservative force, military elites in developing nations often see themselves as a progressive element in society. Whether military or civilian, however, the modernizing oligarchy often assumes the image of a benevolent leadership made necessary by the impossibility of democratic methods combined with the need for directed and managed change. The elite is not so much guided by an all-encompassing total ideology as by the practical exigencies of effective growth.

Pakistan, Egypt, and many African systems represent examples of modernizing oligarchy, though such systems are susceptible to instability and the modernizing elite may find itself in and out of power through the forceful takeover of government.

The above typology considers political differences among sovereign nation-states, but there is one form of political rule, colonial government, in which one country takes over the government of another country, thereby effectively destroying its existence as a sovereign political unit. This phenomenon is known generally as *imperialism,* and in the nineteenth century in particular imperialism was widespread. France governed in such places as Algeria and Indochina, the Dutch governed Indonesia, and the British governed in India, West Africa, and the Caribbean and possessed such far-flung territories that it was said at the time that the sun never set on the British Empire. Though this great age of imperialism has for the most part died out, only in recent years have we seen Portugal finally give up its African territories of Angola and Mozambique.

We could categorize colonial government as a kind of oligarchy, but certainly a rather special kind. The political elite consists of the representatives of a foreign nation governing the colony in the interests of the mother country. The elite achieves power through forceful takeover and proceeds to govern on the basis of alien principles, values, and institutions. Even when the colonial period is over and political independence is achieved, the experience of colonization still has an impact on politics through the language, political boundaries, institutions, and cultural patterns left behind by the colonizers. Indeed, it is often the influence of this colonial heritage on a segment of the native populations that supports the rise of the modernizing oligarchy.

## USING A COMPARATIVE TYPOLOGY

In trying to categorize systems, as we have just done, it is important to understand exactly what a typology can do and what it cannot do. As we have said, it cannot describe or explain in detail the workings of a specific political system. To do this we have to treat each one individually. What it can do is serve as a guide in comparing particular systems on the assumption that a number of particular systems will have enough features in common to speak of them as a type and that, as a type, they display certain features that distinguish them from other types. Each type of system is therefore an abstraction consisting of a general description that applies to each of the systems that make up that type. This is roughly analogous to other kinds of comparison; we might break down the differences among automobiles by talking about compacts, station wagons, sports cars, luxury cars, and so on. Not all sports cars are the same, obviously, but they can be distinguished as a class from other types of cars. The consideration of basic types is an important first step in comparative analysis. If you are comparing two systems that are of different types, say the United States and the Soviet Union, you should expect to find quite basic differences between them; if, on the contrary, you are comparing the United States and Great Britain you should find different versions of political democracy. For these purposes the number of types need not be very large and, indeed, the scheme described here reduces them to only five; more than ten or twelve types would begin to destroy the usefulness of the typology.

There is no such thing as a single accurate typology, but only typologies that are more or less useful. In using such categories we should be wary of the fact that the political world is changing and that the subtleties and complexities of the real world of politics often resist our best efforts at making such abstractions. It is interesting to note that at least two or three of the categories mentioned here refer to political forms that have only really appeared in this century. Perhaps the violent methods of pervasive social control in totalitarianism are most prominent at one stage of development and become moderated at other stages. Such things as typologies are meant as useful tools to direct our investigation, not as definitive statements of what we will find when we are through; in other words, we should remember Marshall McLuhan's advice and avoid the disease of "hardening of the categories."


## DO DIFFERENCES MAKE A DIFFERENCE?

The business of comparative analysis itself raises a political dispute over whether or not the political scientist is exaggerating or minimizing the differences among political systems. What we may call the "conventional" view holds that the differences among systems are profound, simple, and fundamentally consequential as captured in President Kennedy's remark that the world is "half slave, half free." The political scientist may seem to minimize these differences by pointing to the universality of certain basic political processes and functions and to certain common elements of political structure. What we may call the contrary "cynical" view questions whether any of the technical differences that are enumerated really are very significant and whether the political scientist is artificially distinguishing between forms of rule that are all, in the final analysis, similar in the way that the few rule over the many. This has been a favorite argument of many twentieth-century political theorists such as Robert Michels, who observed, "Organization implies the tendency to oligarchy. In every organization . . . the aristocratic tendency manifests itself very clearly."[3] Ortega y Gasset argued, "Human society is always, whether it will or no, aristocratic by its very essence."[4] An even stronger argument along these lines has come from anarchists who see government in any form as arbitrary and unrelieved repression.

The reason these opposing views are at all credible is that political systems reveal a mixture of similiarities and differences, and to move to some resolution of the dispute we must return to this admonition: the importance of a distinction depends on what you are looking for, on what you consider important. If it is important whether or not you can openly and publicly criticize the government without being punished for it or whether you can compete in free elections for public office (setting aside your chances of winning), then there are some marked differences among political systems. If, on the other hand, what is important is whether a political system provides equal influence to all people in the political process or allows one to engage in private business completely free of governmental regulation, the variety of political systems in the world may appear less distinct and their similarities in the unequal distribution of political resources and insistent regulation of economic activities may stand out. Thus, comprehensive comparison assumes a certain perspective on politics, not in the form of an objective, scientific point of view, but rather a subjective interest in certain criteria.

There is a certain surface similarity of political systems, which is the only thing that has allowed us to generalize about them. All political systems contain formal institutions, organized means of enforcing policy (police, armies), collections of resources for the maintenance of government (taxes), unequal distribution of political influence, and a defined and recognized public authority. But the typology presented here suggests important criteria for distinguishing the character and performance of different political systems. These include, for example, the breadth of access to public decision making, the degree of freedom to oppose government, the conditions on the use of violence and force by government, and the relative importance of institutional over purely personal authority. These criteria represent important grounds for distinguishing among political systems.

Finally, we distinguish among political systems not merely for the purpose of better understanding politics, but for the purpose of evaluating and passing judgment on the alternative ways that man has organized political experience. It is precisely because political systems are man-made and artificial that the classic question of the "best form of government" is of continuing significance. We are concerned with the differences among political systems because as political actors and citizens we are concerned with how things can be done differently and better. Much of politics consist of conflict and dispute over the very character of the system, its institutions, and its use of power and authority. On one level politics is a matter of exerting control over the business of government, but on another, more fundamental level it is a matter of attempting to alter and change the very way in which the public's business gets conducted. Revolution, internal war, illegal protest, are the result of the system itself having become the object of political action on the assumption that there is a different way of doing things. Comparative politics thus becomes a matter not only of academic interest but of direct political interest as well.

## THREE CASES FOR ANALYSIS

To this point we have shown that we can compare different political systems descriptively according to particular characteristics (institutions, party system) and in regard to a comprehensive typology. Though these approaches serve the political scientist in providing a basis for comparative analysis, the further step they lead to is the explanation of the differences in the performance of various systems. In other words, how do they work differently? To ask such a basic question is to open the floodgates of the study of comparative politics, but within the bounds of the present discussion we can identify certain key elements of the political system that we have already talked about and use them as examples in comparing the operations of the political systems in our typology. To show how this analysis might proceed we will look at three such elements as cases for comparative study: socialization, interest aggregation, and the distribution of political resources.

### Socialization in Comparative Perspective

Recall that socialization refers to the process by which people become oriented to a political culture, adopt political roles, and generally learn and absorb the values and expectations of the political system. Recall also that because of the importance of socialization to politics generally—it affects people's beliefs, behavior, and political roles—political actors, as well as government itself, may be interested in controlling how people are socialized.

It is fair to say that no political system is indifferent to the way people are politically socialized, but systems will vary according to how much they wish to hold on to or surrender the means of controlling socialization or the rigor with which they will employ these means. Totalitarian systems are the most ambitious and systematic in their use of governmental power to control socialization. The political beliefs and values behind totalitarian states justify and demand such tactics, and this is reinforced by the fact that such regimes typically find themselves in the position of directing fundamental social change and stamping out elements of traditional culture. Their efforts along these lines will include the monopolization of education by the state, explicit political indoctrination in formal schooling, imposition of political criteria and standards for artistic and literary activity, massive public propaganda through state-controlled media, and insistence on public adulation of political leaders. The most dramatic version of this has occurred over the last ten or twenty years in China, where the development of commitment and loyalty to a national communist government has employed pervasive state-directed programs of socialization. In doing this, political leaders are mobilizing the resources of government to shape the inputs to the system, that is, generating uniform, reliable, and widespread support for the system while at the same time eliminating the possibility of divergent, widespread interests being expressed as demands on the system. One of our own founding fathers James Madison stated, "There are two methods of curing the mischief of factions: the one, by removing its causes; the other, by controlling its effects."[5] China represents a case of managing the inevitable conflicts and factions of political life by trying to remove their causes. Madison goes on to explain that the causes of factions can be removed by destroying liberty and by "giving to every citizen the same opinions, the same passions, and the same interests,"[6] which is precisely the objective of totalitarian regimes.

All oligarchies tend to be designed with the capacity for such organized and directed socialization, but their need or willingness to use this will vary. A traditional oligarchy need not rely on coerced conformity as long as it is not threatened from attacks on traditional values; a highly supportive socialization process may go on without any conscious political supervision. One way to see how this happens is to look at life in small, stable communities in the rural United States. The small New England town, for example (or at least the customary picture of it in our imagination), consisted of a very tightly knit group of families who lived in the area for some time and shared similar occupations, religious beliefs, and social and political attitudes. People born and raised in the

town would be socialized into these patterns which were so consensu-
ally accepted. Some individuals exposed to this situation might consider
the culture and social structure of the town confining, lacking in diversity, and unsupportive of expressions of individuality that run counter
to prevailing customs. This may all be true, but it is not the result of
totalitarianism but a result of the continuity and uniformity of their
historical heritage; the town elders hardly need rallies, indoctrination
sessions, and constant public worship to maintain their political influence and social standing. However, when a traditional oligarchy perceives its values to be under attack and sees the bonds of tradition
weakening (through the challenge of a modernizing elite), it may respond by resorting to political coercion and the adoption of almost
totalitarian techniques, not for the purpose of creating a new society
but for the purpose of maintaining the old one. In effect, customs and
values once taken for granted now become an object of political dispute
and preservation of the "old ways," a political task. The introduction of
outsiders and dissenters into the community, for example, may bring
out a greater political consciousness of the importance of patriotism and
"Americanism," expressed as a concern for what is being taught in
schools and for the political views and loyalties of neighbors.

In democratic societies socialization is also politically important in
maintaining a viable system, but there are some vital differences. One
very basic way in which democratic societies limit the control of socialization as a political task is simply by stripping certain kinds of behavior,
values, and beliefs of any kind of political significance. It divorces these
aspects of personal and social life from the realm of governmental
action and thereby makes them private and voluntary. Using religious
belief as an example, the totalitarian system will feel a need to stamp
it out as a threat to its political beliefs, the traditional system may
associate its survival with the preservation of a shared religious faith,
but democracy proclaims that religion is a private concern of no consequence to government and of no essential importance in maintaining
support for democratic politics. Thus, the socialization of people into
particular religious beliefs is not a matter over which government need
exert control not because political socialization is not important but
because religion is separate from the critical political beliefs and expectations characteristic of democracy. The technical term for this is that
these realms of life are "depoliticized" and in a democracy this applies
not only to religion but to science, personal life style, literary and artistic expression, choice of occupation. Government may experience the
results of socialization—because the individual's orientation to politics
will still be affected—but it will not attempt the centralized, state-
directed control of the socialization process. Of course, the ability to

depoliticize these areas is itself an important means of control over political conflict in a democracy and it replaces oligarchy's reliance on the coercion of beliefs and values.

Depoliticization does not answer the whole problem in a democracy, for the political system still requires adequate support based on widely held democratic beliefs that people acquire in one way or another. Democracy can hardly ignore the danger that would result if belief in the democratic method is not sustained. Thus, the teaching of good citizenship will be officially recognized as an objective in public schools. And numerous civic organizations, from the Boy Scouts to the League of Women Voters, will effectively spread and promote civic virtues characteristic of democratic citizenship. As in other systems, when values are perceived to be under threat in a democracy, a militant concern with socialization may arise which, itself, may appear inconsistent with democratic values of free speech and the right to oppose government. Thus, during the polarization and conflict of the 1960s, many officials at various levels of government attempted to use their public office to suppress the spread of dissenting or radical ideas in schools and on college campuses. This included withdrawing state scholarships from student protestors, taking actions against so-called underground newspapers, and challenging the employment of teachers on the basis of their political views. These were explicit attempts to monitor and control the political expression of people and thereby influence the processes of socialization. Even in a political democracy like the United States, what is taught in schools from the earliest years of a child's education frequently becomes a matter of political import and controversy.

Democracy is caught in a real paradox in regard to the problem of socialization. Like any political system it requires a supportive political culture, the beliefs and values of which are passed on through effective socialization. Yet at the same time democracy seems to surrender control over the means of socialization by defending freedom of choice, free speech, and academic freedom in the classroom. Classical democratic thinkers like Thomas Jefferson in the United States and John Stuart Mill in England argued that the solution to this is, briefly stated, that if all ideas and points of view are allowed to compete freely with each other, sound ideas will receive the strongest acceptance and incorrect or false ideas will be the least able to withstand the scrutiny of public debate and exposure. This optimistic view concludes that the best way to produce democratic results is through democratic methods, though the experience of tutelary democracies reveals the practical difficulties of this approach. The attempt of the elite to systematically loosen authoritarian constraints on political action, as is now beginning to happen in Spain since the death of Franco, is by no means guaranteed to produce the tolerant, gentle, and understanding spirit of democratic politics. This paradox still haunts practical democratic politics, and it would seem that the principle of liberty operates only where socialization has prepared the conditions for it to work. On the positive side, what the principle of liberty does show is that democracy should tend to reinforce itself in such a way that as it develops it requires less and less resort to politically directed socialization.

As these remarks indicate, socialization is a general process important to the functioning of any political system, but how it is carried out and the form that it takes differ according to the type of political system in question.

## Interest Aggregation in Comparative Perspective

Interest aggregation has been defined as "the function of converting demands into general policy alternatives."[7] The demands consist of people's expressions about what they want from government, and policy alternatives encompass proposed solutions for responding to an assortment of specific and seemingly contradictory demands. We can look at the legislative committee process in the United States as one of the more familiar examples of interest aggregation. The committee will hold hearings relating to some particular concern requiring governmental attention. Various individuals and groups will use the hearings to voice their demands or express their special interest in the issues at stake. The committee in turn will generate proposed laws to be presented to the Congress for passage, thus, in effect, proposing what it sees to be the most suitable policy in light of the demands that have been presented. Policy alternatives such as party platforms, legislative bills, and bureaucratic planning documents are all the product of interest aggregation.

Because aggregation is a particular function within the larger processes of the political system, the difficulties it entails and the means by which it takes place are somewhat the result of other aspects of the system. For example, the problem of interest aggregation is a function of the diversity of interests within society and the degree of control that is exerted over people's ability to express political demands. If society is relatively homogeneous in respect to such things as life style, culture, and occupations, as is typically the case with traditional social systems, there will be a corresponding narrowness in the range and variety of political demands. This, in turn, will lessen the strain on the political system as it confronts the task of transforming demands into policy alternatives. Also, oligarchies in general restrict, to varying degrees, the ability to express interests. On the other hand, systems that are both socially and culturally pluralistic as well as democratic legitimize and encourage the use of politics as a platform for expressing self-interest and thereby place greater burdens on the process of aggregation.

Interests and demands, once given expression, can be aggregated by discovering policies that accommodate or reconcile the differences among divergent demands. The pure case of this is bargaining as seen, for example, in the negotiation of a contract between a labor union and the management of a corporation. A tax law may balance the political pressure of numerous interests by its intricate combination of deductions, credits, exemptions, and exceptions. Bargaining is an explicit attempt to deal with the conflict of political interests by at least partially satisfying a variety of interests, by giving various parties some of what they want. More specifically, this may take the form of compromise, as when a labor agreement specifies wages that are somewhere between the original demands of labor and management. Or, it may take the form of "trade-offs" in which support for one demand at one time is simply balanced off against support for some other demand at another time, as when a congressional leader says to the president that he can get support for the president's tax proposals if the president does not push his idea of closing down certain government projects.

This type of interest aggregation is characteristic of democracies; in oligarchies, bargaining is not absent but it frequently is displaced by a type of aggregation in which comprehensive political doctrines, defined by ideology or tradition, are imposed on political demands. In a communist state, for example, demands will be evaluated and interpreted in light of already established ideological values, such as the principle of guiding economic development through the direct control of the government. In this type of system the values that are imposed definitely limit the possibilities for accommodating a wide variety of interests, but some aggregation is going on in making difficult choices between, say, emphasizing industrial development or agricultural development, or stressing consumer goods over military technology. Such a process is confronted with the prospect of demands that will not be met or recognized and thereby become the source of political discontent. How do these more elitist and authoritarian means of aggregating interests deal with the dangers inherent in such a situation? The answer must be found in other attributes of the system which reinforce this process: (1) as mentioned above, restrictions on political activity (opposition parties or voluntary groups) which limit the diversity of demands and the kinds of people who will be in a sufficiently influential position to make them; (2) the previous socialization of people, and the elite in particular, into an acceptance of the ruling doctrines of the state and

the use of such acceptance and loyalty as important criteria for individual political advancement (thus the emphasis, in tradition-based systems, on the leadership role of the "elders" who most embody the
society's customs, and the need, in totalitarian states, for regular demonstrations of ideological enthusiasm on the part of younger members
of the elite); (3) the direct political attacks made on demands that simply
cannot be reconciled with the prevailing political dogma, as in the
attack by traditional elites on the corruption and decadence of modern
society or the communists' attack on "reactionary capitalist" elements
in society. Features such as these are important in understanding the
operation of this less pragmatic form of aggregation.

While oligarchies do not abandon bargaining, though they narrow
the range of bargainers and close off the activity, by the same token
democratic politics is not always capable of solely relying upon it. The
open accommodation of competing demands also has certain requirements attached to it, such as (1) an acceptance, again through socialization, of the values of compromise and accommodation and a tolerance
of political differences and (2) the existence of demands that are susceptible to being aggregated through some sort of bargaining. The second
point is particularly problematic, for one of the difficulties in accommodating interests pragmatically is that some demands by their very
nature are not amenable to such a tactic. If a demand is for peace in
Vietnam, it is not clear what it would mean to compromise so that we
would be partially at peace, nor is this the type of demand that would
be susceptible to being traded off. It means little to continue the war
but agree to protect the environment instead. The result of such a
demand is that society tends to become polarized. The established
democratic elite will be heard to complain about dissenters who make
nonnegotiable demands and possess an uncompromising attitude which
threatens the democratic process. There are limits to the ability to
create policy alternatives through the process of free-wheeling give-
and-take.

Just as there are different styles of interest aggregation, there are
varying structures as well involved in performing this function. Political
parties and representative legislatures immediately come to mind as
important mechanisms for this in democracies. The American–British-
style two-party system is particularly effective, less so the multiparty
system in which the process of coalition building within the legislature
may have to be relied upon. These examples also provide us with insight
into the concept of "structural specialization" as a characteristic of a
modern political system in which each structure is designed to perform
only certain functions or, conversely, different important political functions are performed by different structures. Thus, while the American

political party serves to aggregate interests well, there are other structures assuming the job of articulating demands (interest groups) and
making policy decisions (executive and legislative branches of government). Where this specialization of structures is lacking we find a single
structure assuming a wide variety of tasks. Imagine a very traditional
system with a monarch governing in conjunction with a small assembly
of aristocrats or elders; this single structure may assume the exclusive
burden of articulating demands and interests, aggregating them in
some fashion, making policy, determining the means of its enforcement, and interpreting the law. Oligarchies generally have less specialized structures, and aggregation may be performed by quite different
institutions than in a democracy. The bureaucracy, for example, might
become important in this process as the main institution with direct
exposure to the impact of public policies on society, combined with its
role in formulating and planning policies.

Every system, therefore, must deal with the problems of creating
general policy for the public out of divergent demands. Exactly how
they carry out this central political task is one of the grounds for comparing various systems, one of the more important differences being the
relative weight that is given to pragmatic/bargaining forms as opposed
to ideological/authoritarian forms of aggregation.

## The Distribution of Resources in Comparative Perspective

We have already emphasized the importance of political resources
for maintaining political activity and achieving influence. Differences
in the distribution of such resources as literacy, higher education,
health, leisure time, social standing, and wealth among people in society are a critical way of distinguishing the systems in our typology. The
general issue of resources actually involves two questions, both of political importance: (1) What resources are considered politically important? and (2) How are these resources distributed? The first question
considers what factors are or ought to be the basis for the achievement
of political influence. The attack of democratic thinkers on the traditional power of the aristocracy in European states was based on the
contention that inheritance of wealth and social position should not be
a source of political power. They argued that this should be replaced by
the principle of majority vote in which all people enjoying full citizenship would have an equal voice in electing leaders. The point is that
elites may exert control over politics by limiting people's access to
resources and also by basing power on those resources that most serve
their own interest and are least susceptible to wide distribution. The

political system may be designed in different ways to place emphasis on different types of resources.

The idea behind democratic politics is to make political power available through the use of political resources that are not necessarily or inherently controlled by a few people in society, thus rewarding personal effort and talent and giving weight to individual opinion. This is partially achieved through institutional devices—majority rule, equality before the law—but these principles are not sufficient in themselves and need the support of actual equalization of resources. One of the classic problems of tutelary democracy is the attempt to institute forms of democratic politics even while substantial inequalities of resources still exist. Using wealth as an example, in relation to the two questions above we can see that democracy is enhanced both by equalizing wealth and by putting controls on the influence of money in politics and government. It has been commonly observed that political democracy works best where there is a fairly large middle class rather than an economic gap between a small wealthy class and a large number of poorer people. Where such a middle class does not result from the forces of free enterprise, the argument has been made that explicit attempts at equalizing wealth should be used to enhance the prospect of democracy, an argument associated with "democratic socialism." But a general equalization of wealth cannot remove the effects of unequal wealth completely; therefore, democratic systems may also take steps to limit the influence of wealth in politics generally. Recent enthusiasm in the United States for campaign-reform laws has led to restrictions on the amount of money an individual can contribute to a candidate and has led to a program of partial government support for campaigns as a means of cutting back a candidate's dependence on wealthy donors. The same principle has led to the requirement that courts appoint lawyers for defendants unable to afford a lawyer themselves. The idea behind such practices is to decrease the possibility that someone will have influence in politics or receive special treatment from government merely because he has more money than someone else.

Money is not the only consideration. Universal, legally required education has been looked upon as a democratic value in providing everyone with at least the minimal educational requirements for the performance of his responsibilities as a citizen. Civil service laws were created on the grounds that they provided people the opportunity to work in government jobs based on merit and skill rather than personal friendship with politicians. But all of these attempts to equalize the availability of political resources or to minimize the influence of resources that should not be allowed to intrude on politics do not mean

that the importance of unequal resources has been thoroughly eliminated in democracies.

In oligarchies we will find more rigid distinctions of wealth, education, and social class serving to maintain the rule of the elite. Oligarchies
more strictly define those resources that are the critical basis of political
power and historically they sometimes have been distinguished accordingly (the term *plutocracy,* for example, referred to an oligarchy in
which the elite based its power on wealth). Traditional oligarchies stress
the importance of inherited social class position over individual merit
or even over money. Modernizing oligarchies place great value on the
acquisition of secular, westernized education and skills. Communist
systems are an interesting case in their own right, for they claim that
their purpose is to tear down all forms of social and economic differences in order to establish the rule of the working class or proletariat,
yet they have for the most part ended up creating a new kind of elite
having its power based in the bureaucracy of the state and the party,
with the resources of such instititional power being sharply limited.[8] In
the case of oligarchy, the limits and controls over the distribution of
resources are meant not only to maintain elite power but also to inhibit
the possibility of rebellion or revolution against the elite. In such societies we will usually find large economic gaps between rich and poor,
significant differences in the level of education, rigid social class distinctions, and politically significant differences among racial and ethnic
subgroups.

Because of the importance of the distribution of resources to political
life, a central part of the study of politics is the analysis of the social and
economic differences among people in society. Generally, it can be said
that where these differences are great, it will be difficult for democratic
institutions to nullify their impact on politics and that where oligarchy
is sustained as a form of rule, it rests on a fairly stable foundation of such
inequality. The difference between one society and another in regard
to resource distribution may be thought of as purely a matter of degree
and, since all societies contain inequality, this has led to suspicions about
exactly how significant these differences may be. Another way of con-
ceiving of these differences is to distinguish between *cumulative* and
*noncumulative* kinds of inequality. Cumulative inequality refers to a
situation in which people who are unequal in one respect tend to be
unequal in all other respects. Thus, where inequalities are cumulative
those who possess most of the wealth in society are the same people who
are the best educated, of high social class, and in control of government.
Noncumulative inequalities represent a reverse situation in which inequality in one respect does not necessarily mean inequality in other

respects. Accordingly, if inequalities are noncumulative, those who are the best educated in society are not necessarily the wealthiest and those born into the upper class may not necessarily be the richest or the best educated in society. If differences in the distribution of resources are important in comparing political systems, the difference between cumulative and noncumulative inequalities may be a more accurate way of comparing oligarchies and democracies. But the basic point is still this: fundamental inequality of resources is common to all political systems and basic to an understanding of how they operate. A key component of political analysis consists of an appreciation of the basic differences among people discovered through the study of the social, economic, and cultural environment of the political system.

In reviewing the comparative study of politics, a very basic question may come to mind: Why is there so much variety within political experience? Why have not some forms of rule proven themselves and become generally accepted? These questions are basic and their answers necessarily involved, but without trying to answer them here, we should keep in mind that the differences among political systems are deeply rooted in the history and culture of the society, in the peculiar political dilemmas the country has been faced with, and in the variety of human values that are turned to in order to confront these dilemmas. Although we may evaluate different systems as just or unjust, desirable or undesirable, we must try to understand them in relation to their own historical circumstances, not because these circumstances totally determine or justify the shape of politics but because they shape the political environment and define the task of governing for each society.

## NOTES

[1] Aristotle, *Politics,* ed. and trans. Ernest Barker (New York, 1962), Book IV.
[2] H. V. Wiseman, *Political Systems: Some Sociological Approaches* (New York, 1966), pp. 70–86.
[3] Robert Michels, *Political Parties* (New York, 1959), p. 32.
[4] Ortega y Gasset, *The Revolt of the Masses* (New York, 1932), p. 20.
[5] James Madison et al., *The Federalist Papers* (New York, 1960), pp. 54–55.
[6] Ibid. p. 55.
[7] Gabriel Almond and G. Bingham Powell, Jr. *Comparative Politics: A Developmental Approach* (Boston, 1966), p. 98.
[8] Milovan Djilas, *The New Class* (New York, 1957).

# FOR FURTHER READING

Almond, Gabriel A., and G. Bingham Powell, Jr. *Comparative Politics: A Developmental Approach.* Boston: Little, Brown, 1966. A discussion of the elements of a functionalist framework for comparing political systems.

Cantori, Louis J., ed. *Comparative Political Systems.* Boston: Holbrook Press, 1974. A collection of articles by major political scientists dealing comparatively with particular aspects of the political system—parties, interest groups, and bureaucracy.

Groth, Alexander J. *Comparative Politics.* New York: Macmillan, 1971. Compares various systems primarily in terms of public policies and the delivery of goods and services.

Wiseman, H. V. *Political Systems.* New York: Praeger Publishers, 1966. A convenient overview of the development of various comparative theories and approaches in modern political science.

# 6

# Political Change

It is useful and natural enough to study political phenomena as if our subject matter were standing still for our examination. We have discussed such things as party systems, law, bureaucracy, and socialization as if these were stable and unchanging parts of our experience. For much political analysis this impression of the political world as unchanging may be suitable, but at the heart of the study of politics is the study of change. The relationship between order and stability on the one hand and alteration and change on the other is central to the very nature of politics. Political man confronts a world of people with different aspirations, hopes, interests, and values, and also with the same needs for food, health, shelter, and security that are not or cannot be met to the same degree for all. He constructs and fabricates in this world structures of public authority which bring a certain order and predictability to his life with others in society. Though one of the greatest virtues of such structures is their ability to survive and to justify our reliance on and belief in them, they are still man-made and still artificial. There is no natural and universal guide to the making of the state; the formation of the good political order is not a result of discovery but of creation. The design of these man-made structures, as we have seen, is fundamentally at issue in politics, the subject of different and competing views of justice, freedom, and authority. In fact, from the point of view of many in society it is the government itself which becomes the source of fear and insecurity in their lives, a force to be opposed, removed, and overthrown. These political structures of human creation are limited by their own partial justice, and their own tendency to become one of the sides in political struggle.

The very nature of political experience in human history reveals the constant interplay between the forces of stability and change and the succession of one political form after another. Any particular political form, we may say, represents a tentative order which is never definitively settled or resolved, which may work well or poorly, justly or unjustly, which may rise under certain historical conditions and fall under others. One indication of the tremendous dynamics that are at work in politics is the great extent to which violence appears in political life, including assassination, riots, governmental terror, coups d'etat, revolutions, and wars. Politics has never been one of the safer activities of life, and Harold Lasswell reports that "31.9 percent of a series of 423 monarchs of different countries and different periods died by violence. Forty percent of the presidents of the Republic of Bolivia came to a violent end."[1] Even in the United States, which has been presumably freer of political violence, we have had three assassinations of major political figures (John Kennedy, Robert Kennedy, and Martin Luther King Jr.,) and one attempted assassination (George Wallace) within recent memory. Lasswell also reports that, although the amount of time major European countries spend engaging in war has decreased (while the conduct of war has become more vigorous and destructive), these countries were at war 25 percent of the time in the nineteenth century, 50 percent in the eighteenth century, and 75 percent in the century before that.[2] Other research has shown that in France, for the twenty-year period from 1830 to 1850, there were 551 incidents of collective violence in which 50 or more people engaged in attacks on property or person and in the decade of the 1950s there were 302 such incidents with an estimated participation of over 600,000 people.[3] It is curious to note that despite the cynicism of the common man about politics and politicians in general, his discomfort at the demands and restrictions of government, and his feeling of a lack of immediacy of public affairs in his own life, the form of government is one of the main things that he will give his life to change and give his life to protect from the forces of change.

In turning our attention to the question of change, not only does the tumult and violence that surrounds politics become more apparent, but we also gain a much better sense of historical time. Particularly in a system like the United States, which has experienced relative stability, there is the temptation to think and act as if the shape of our political experience were immutable, as if it always has been this way and always will be. A broader historical perspective reveals the tremendous historical changes that have actually taken place and the relative newness of our own experience. The American Democratic party is fond of calling itself the oldest political party in the world; if this claim is substantially true it means that political parties as we know them today are only about two hundred years old. This period of time is only one-fifth of the period that historians define as the Middle Ages and less than 10 percent of the span of recorded Western history. The centralized nation-state with a distinct national boundary and population is equally new and, indeed, many of the political practices and principles we are familiar with today, including constitutionalism, representative government, popular elections, as well as totalitarianism, were unknown only a few hundred years ago. Finally, we might point out that scores of nation-states that exist today on the Asian and African continents did not exist as sovereign systems until after World War II, and this includes such prominent countries as India, Indonesia, Algeria, Israel, Congo, Nigeria, and the Philippines among a host of others. We have witnessed in only the past generation a veritable explosion in the creation of new nation-states. We are thus caught in a whirlwind of major political changes despite our feeling of political permanence not unlike the sensation of leisurely progress in an airplane racing at hundreds of miles an hour.

What all of this ought to suggest is that our present political experience is the product of relatively recent forces and events and that a reflection on the past gives us every reason to believe that the future will not be a continuation of the present. Those who weave visions of an alternative future may be thought of as soft-headed and lacking in seriousness, but at least their exercises are based on the quite realistic assumption that over the long run things will be very different than they are today. In this connection Americans have a disturbing way of referring to the nations of Asia, Africa, and Latin America as "developing" nations with the implication that the United States and the industrialized democracies of the West are, therefore, "developed" nations. But the concept of developed nations implies that some terminus has been reached, that progress has arrived at a resting point, an end. The thoroughly presumptuous notion that the pinnacle of civilization has been reached is one of the distinctive hazards of rich and powerful societies throughout history and would hardly seem to equip society to confront the inexorable forces of change. Thus, there is some merit in the suggestion that the industrialized West look upon itself as enmeshed in the process of development, though the task of development may be defined differently than in other areas of the world. The importance of this outlook results from the fact that not only have we not yet fully resolved the mysteries and paradoxes of political freedom, equality, order, and justice, but also the technological, cultural, economic, and social forces that we are trying to govern are themselves ceaselessly presenting new and unexpected challenges.

Thus, it is to the study of the dynamics of political experience that we now turn to seek guidance in approaching the host of questions surrounding the causes, forms, and results of political change.

## TYPES OF CHANGE

Any element of the political system is susceptible to change, and a first step in the analysis of change is to consider what it is that is changing. The appointment of a new government official, the passage of a new law, the victory of a new political party over an incumbent party, the government-directed redistribution of land, and the creation of a wholly new form of government, all constitute political changes in the literal sense of the word. In this very literal sense all political systems constantly undergo change, but normally when we speak of political change we mean to distinguish between those ordinary activities of politics that bring new faces and new issues on the political scene as a matter of course and those changes of a more substantial sort that alter the bases of public authority, the institutional design of government, and the fundamental distribution of power. The target or object of change serves as an initial means of identifying what type of change is going on, and in this connection, we can identify four situations or conditions that the political system can find itself in.

### The Static Condition

The static political system is one which, we might say, is frozen in time and experiences changes of the most limited and natural sort—the death of a king or chief and the succession of his heir. These traditional, indeed primitive, societies do not include within their form of rule accepted, institutionalized means of adapting to forces of change that impinge from without or of altering their time-honored way of doing things. In a truly static situation a visitor could return to such a society a generation or more later and find things essentially as he or she left them. Needless to say, such a static condition requires a very special set of circumstances for its maintenance. A deep cultural homogeneity and an insulation from other contrasting cultures are essential and if present may allow the society to remain in its static form for some time. Since static societies survive not so much by any ability to cope with change, but mainly through their ability to remain immune to the initial causes of change, it is often the case that once exposed to such causes, these societies reveal themselves to be very fragile. This fragility, however, can also result from the superior power and physical force of the cultures that threatens them.

What immediately comes to mind is the situation of indigenous populations in such areas as Africa and North America and their encounters with European colonization. Here societies with tradition-based forms of rule, which remained essentially the same for some time and would likely have continued to if uninterrupted, found themselves face to face with an alien culture bent on settling their lands, exploiting their resources, taking their labor, or some combination of these. In this situation, such societies may try to preserve themselves or will be destroyed by the alien culture—much like the American Indian—but there are few social or political resources available to absorb the shock and dominate its effects, even if the physical means might be available to them. The American Indian's inability to understand or cope with the cynicism, alien economic motivations, and concept of property of the white man finally led to disaster.

The Middle Ages in Europe represent a somewhat similar situation. Held together by the universal faith and institutions of a single Christianity and with an authority that had become deeply rooted in tradition, medieval Europe could also be characterized as politically static. The leadership of the feudal aristocracy, the church, and monarchical authority were fatally threatened by a host of forces that arose one on the heels of the other: the Crusades, which exposed Europeans to other cultures; the invention of printing, which broke apart the social control over knowledge and information; the Protestant Reformation, which instigated religious pluralism. Though it may be incorrect to say that medieval culture was exactly fragile, it nonetheless by its very nature could not survive the consequences of these new forces.

Not surprisingly, the prospect of such static societies surviving for long periods has decreased in the modern world, for the tremendous sophistication of modern mass communications and transportation and the effects of European imperialism have greatly diminished the possibility of the cultural homogeneity and isolation required for such a static state of affairs. Yet we still observe with fascination the observations of Alex Haley who, in researching his widely acclaimed book *Roots*, returns to an African village astonishingly similar to what it must have been like when his ancestors were presumably taken from there to become American slaves.

## The Homeostatic Condition

What we mean by the rather technical term *homeostatic* is a system capable of adjusting itself to changes in its environment without abruptly altering its basic structure. Similar to a static condition, the general framework of authority and power remains intact, but it is different in that stability is achieved not as a result of being immune to the forces of change but as a result of the capacity to absorb the impact of these forces while at the same time maintaining continuity in political order. Though the fundamentals of the system will not change under this condition, considerable change may occur over time in laws, public policies, the distribution of access to political influence, the types and ranges of competing political factions, and the actual role of government in society.

The political history of the United States represents a good example of this homeostatic condition. For almost two centuries we have governed with the same constitutional document, have had an uninterrupted series of popular elections, a substantially unchanged party system, and an orderly evolution of political traditions and values. The system was successfully designed to allow change to occur and thereby to reduce the prospect of new forces as threats upon the very system itself. What is intriguing about the American experience is not merely the continuity of our governmental arrangements but the fact of that continuity in the face of fundamental social, cultural, and economic changes. In the same two hundred years we moved from thirteen loosely organized states to one of the largest nations in the world; from a slave society to one in which basic political rights have been achieved for all racial groups; from a rural, agricultural to an urbanized, industrial society; from a minor, neutralist actor in world affairs to a military and economic superpower. Each of these changes stressed and strained the capacities of government; they required a shift in the balance of power from some groups and interests to others; and a society more rigid and static could have been easily broken by them.

We do not mean to suggest that our homeostatic system is thoroughly malleable nor that the mechanisms of change are always sedate and orderly. Rather, we mean that it has coped with the inevitable dynamics of politics by trying to harness and institutionalize them.

## The Revolutionary Condition

A political system experiencing changes of a revolutionary sort has gone beyond the parade of new issues and political personalities and even beyond the mere regrouping of political factions to changes that are aimed at the very transformation of the system itself from one type to another. Revolution is commonly associated with the use of violence and disruption in politics and this may give the term a wider application than is appropriate. The distinctive traits of revolution are the changes

it brings; as the term itself suggests, the basic structure of public authority and the processes of government are altered. The French Revolution of 1789 and the Russian Revolution of 1917 come to mind as classic
instances.

Revolutionary change by its very nature has convulsive effects on
society, and by virtue of replacing normal politics with new norms, it
violently disrupts and ultimately destroys the old order. Although revolution is typically associated with the specific act of overthrowing the
old form of government and deposing the old rulers, the revolutionary
process is really of longer duration. Preceding the main act, a set of
circumstances and forces sets the stage for revolutionary change and,
some would say, makes it inevitable. And following this, the new revolutionary leadership must consolidate its power and establish the principles of the new order. The process of creating the new order after the
overthrow is very much the essence of the revolution and it can easily
take a generation or more. Because revolution constitutes such a profound change in the political system, it is not fulfilled by a single act of
violence but represents an extended series of clashes. The Russian Revolution of October 1917 was preceded by the revolt of 1904 and the
overthrow of the czar in the spring of 1917 and was followed by internal
war between the Bolsheviks and their political opponents into the
1920s.

Since the aim of revolution is to destroy existing authority that defines
the bounds of legitimate political conduct, the revolutionary must provide an alternative conception of authority to justify both his illegal acts
and the new regime. Thus, revolution is guided by a revolutionary
ideology or vision which serves to condemn the old and paint a picture
of a more just future. It is misleading to think of revolution as merely
a struggle for power that has got out of hand; what makes a revolution
is the much more fundamental struggle over public authority, in which
power is used as the means of carrying out a dispute between opposing
political forces that share no common ground of political right and
justice. By striking at such basic issues, revolutions are also pervasive in
their effects on the political community and will seek to implant themselves through altering the way people think and relate to each other.
During the French Revolution the designation "citizen" was used to
refer to someone as a way of symbolizing the democratic equality and
fraternity that had replaced the artificial titles of rank and nobility in
the old regime, not unlike the use of "comrade" in post-revolutionary
Russia. Similarly, the Communist Chinese revolution was followed by
an intensive campaign designed to build allegiance to the new regime
and stamp out the remnants of "bourgeois, reactionary" thinking. Revolution tends to infuse all aspects of life with political significance and to
divide a society in such a way that political neutrality or indifference

cannot exist. In considering political change, clearly the phenomenon of revolution more than the ordinary and routine adjustments of political life is a matter of central attention.

## The Unstable Condition

In order to provide a reasonably comprehensive set of categories for the kinds of change experienced in a political system, we may add to the above types an unstable condition of political life in which many facets of politics are subjected to change in a disjointed, disruptive, often violent fashion without any underlying change in the power relationships in society. We might think of this condition as standing somewhere between homeostatic change and revolution. It is not revolutionary, for though it interjects violence, it fails to produce revolutionary results. Indeed, as the people themselves begin to notice, each new power group seems to resemble the previous one. At the same time, this cannot be confused with homeostatic change, for the very reliance on forceful acquisition of power and widespread and regular violent challenges to public authority results from the inability to discover the mechanisms for absorbing change in a more orderly way.

In certain Latin American countries it is not uncommon to find a political history checkered with military takeovers, new constitutions, constitutions dissolved and then replaced, popular elections voided by the losers who take to the streets, and so on. The frequent resort to violent methods, combined with the lack of any significant change over time, creates the impression that violence has become almost institutionalized and customary. This represents an odd situation in which the change of constitutions, dissolving of legislatures, and voiding of elections, rather than being symptomatic of revolutionary developments, have become the tools of more ordinary, less innovative political struggle.

The purpose of identifying these four conditions—static, homeostatic, revolutionary, and unstable—is to describe the kinds of change that we may find occurring within the political system. As with any such abstractions, the actual difference between one of these conditions and another may be a matter of degree; there may be a bit of a blurred line, for example, between a static and a homeostatic system or, perhaps more likely, between a homeostatic system and an unstable system. But the usefulness of these distinctions is to show that it is important in speaking of political change to clarify what kind of change is being considered and what it is in the political system that is undergoing change. They also allow us to make a general distinction between political changes that ordinarily occur within the law and those changes that go beyond the bounds of existing public authority, whether with revolutionary results or not. It is mainly the latter type of change we are interested in here, change that operates outside politics as usual, that testifies to the failure of the political system to achieve one of its fundamental objectives—order and security—and that creates political instability and revolution.

## THE SOURCES OF CHANGE

In a general sense, to ask about the sources of extralegal political change is to ask about the very motive forces of politics itself. Where a certain amount of movement derives from the regular rhythm of political conflict and orderly resolution, there are times when the system experiences severe strains, calling into question its ability to maintain itself. Ultimately, these strains take the form of a dispute over public authority, which is what revolutionary conflict is all about. Who should govern, and why? What form of government—monarchy, dictatorship, democracy? Should there be free enterprise or state control of the economy? Should people be free? How free? Should they be treated equally? What powers should government have? What rights should the people have? On what principles should wealth be distributed?

One way to imagine the source of these strains is to think of politics in terms of a relationship between the material environment of the society and its values, between reality and ideals, if you like. Hypothetically, in a perfectly static situation we can imagine a kind of "fit" or coordination that exists between the kinds of values and ideals the society lives by and the actual social and economic environment, the material condition of life. If one or both of these sides of the social equation undergoes change, however, this "fit" may be lost. Since the function of politics is the control of public affairs based on standard, institutionalized values of the community, this lack of fit naturally affects the performance of government by challenging its effectiveness and legitimacy.

We can begin by looking at changes that occur in the environment. The communications theorist Marshall McLuhan has advanced the argument that the invention of the printing press was a critical factor in the demise of medieval society. Prior to this development, books were in short supply and they were produced by hand in a most laborious and expensive manner. Both of these circumstances meant that people's access to books and the very proliferation of literacy were institutionally controlled by the church and the university, which served the elite in society. The Bible, for example, would be chained to the wall of the church where one would go to read it, if one could read, and scholarly books were held in libraries where their availability was both limited and controlled. The invention of printing created the possibility of producing large volumes of books relatively cheaply, thereby making literature suddenly available to a much wider audience. But it was not merely a question of more people being able to get books; printing also had the effect of freeing the individual from the influence of those institutions which had traditionally controlled the dissemination of ideas. Inevitably it was asked why the authority of the church should stand against the authority of one's own reason and knowledge acquired in an individual way.

Without evaluating McLuhan's singular explanation of history, the example is instructive in showing how environmental changes can challenge the suitability of existing values and ideas. Interestingly enough, our own society is confronting a version of the same problem, also in the area of communications. The United States grew up with the tradition of free speech and a free press. Though these freedoms had to be fought for and defended, there was no fundamental ambiguity about what they meant—government should not control or interfere with the expression of ideas. It should not, for example, censor newspapers. Free expression, in its original formulation, fit rather well with a society in which the means for disseminating ideas were relatively varied and accessible. There were thousands of small newspapers, oratory to local crowds was still a political art, and the inexpensive political pamphlet was a common vehicle for propagating diverse opinions. However, in this century and particularly in the past few decades, we have witnessed a profound change in the media of public communication. Daily newspapers are dying out and the bulk of information people receive about national and international affairs is acquired through the mass media of radio and television—specifically the latter, which is organized along the lines of three major networks. This new situation poses a dilemma regarding the meaning of freedom. Should the large commercial networks be thoroughly unrestricted by government, thus raising the prospect that diverse and challenging points of view may not have the opportunity to be expressed at all through such a powerful medium, or should government require that "equal time" be provided for alternative political views, thereby limiting the freedom of the network and putting the government somewhat in the position of telling the television industry what will be aired. The point of these examples is not to show that the development of mass media carries the seeds of political revolution, but simply that when traditional political values and ideas confront wholly new circumstances in the environment the dynamics of political change are set in motion.

The range of environmental changes that may provide the conditions for political change is very broad and may include new technology, scientific discoveries, economic collapse, discovery of new territories for settlement, invasion by a foreign power, alterations in life styles. Certainly the inability of traditional elites in many developing nations to adjust to many of the innovations of the colonial powers assists in explaining their political weakness in the period of independence. Such changes pose the prospect of some political adjustment, though they do not by themselves directly explain or trigger revolution and reform.

The other side of the equation consists of changes in people's values, beliefs, and perceptions of the world. These may come from exposure to other cultures, which causes people to call into question their own values, or these changes may take the form of philosophical or religious innovations such as the Protestant Reformation and the growth of empirical science in the early modern period. The conflict between the early astronomer Galileo and the Catholic church represented a classic struggle pitting the authority of the revealed truth of the Bible against the authority of modern science.

It should be apparent that there is a mutual interaction between value change and environmental change, and it may not always be easy to distinguish one of them clearly as the cause of the other. How such rudimentary changes in the social system begin in the first place is itself somewhat complex and even mysterious. How do particular new inventions and theories arise, and why does people's thinking change? Among an assortment of historical explanations, it would seem that some room must be left for human creativity and for unpredictable innovations. However, our interest is not with how these sources of change immediately occur but with the effect they have on the performance of the political system.

The lack of fit resulting from these circumstances consists of an imbalance, or what political scientists sometimes call a *disequilibrium*. This metaphor is used to suggest that the political system tends to seek a state of equilibrium, and when it is not in this state forces are set in motion to move toward equilibrium. Thus, the existence of a variety of Protestant sects after the Reformation created a disequilibrium in a political system which allowed for and was based on the political power of a single church. This led to religious wars and conflicts, which were only ultimately avoided by the adoption of the principle of the separation of church and state. At the time of the French Revolution, the new middle class which based its wealth on commerce, trade, and industry confronted the privileged aristocracy which based its wealth on land and upheld social and political institutions which maintained an unfavorable climate for the growth of capitalism. Also, with the rise of the industrial revolution in Europe the new class of factory workers lived under free enterprise which defended a system of production and distribution of wealth based on the individual initiative of relatively equal individuals differentiated only by their degree of ambition, cleverness, and personal enterprise. Yet the factory worker's real situation seemed more the result of an accident of birth into the wrong social class and the tremendous social and economic barriers to self-improvement rather than the result of laziness and lack of initiative; this perception of things called into question the justice and validity of the free market mechanism. Consider also the experience of American blacks, freed from slavery, contributing their labor to the American economy and their lives to American wars. It became ever increasingly apparent that the legal and extralegal forms of discrimination against them were incongruous and evil in light of the presumed civil rights and political equality that they ought to have enjoyed according to the explicit law of the land and the larger tradition of American political ideals. Finally, consider the revolutionary witnessing the growth of the sovereign nation-states of the world and insisting on the injustice of his own homeland's being submissively ruled as a colony of another country.

In each of these examples, the principles and values of the existing political system are in some conflict with the real state of affairs, resulting, in a general sense, from some alteration in the conditions of life in society or in accepted values and ideals. Notice that the reformer or the revolutionary, the one who leads the movement for political change, becomes the spokesman for some new concept of political authority and justice which would create a new order. Thus, as the basic sources of change begin to affect the political sphere, they assume the form of a dispute over public authority, over the values that ought to guide the organization of political life. But they ultimately assume this form only when it appears that a fundamental change in the political order is essential to create some adequate new equilibrium. These political pressures may become the basis for reform (homeostatic change) or instability, or a certain amount of instability may bring about reform. The ability to find a reformist solution assumes that the pressures for change can be met without resorting to revolutionary change in the total system. In the above examples, the protection of the civil rights of blacks and the vigorous legal assurance of equal opportunity and the recognition of the worker's right to organize and collectively bargain with his employer, combined with a variety of favorable historical circumstances in which these changes have taken place, have forestalled

if not eliminated challenges to the basic political and economic structure of the country. Yet where homeostatic solutions are not possible,
where the dispute is seriously divisive, the conditions for revolution set
in.

## THE DYNAMICS OF REVOLUTION

Exactly how and why revolutions occur is one of the more intriguing
subjects of political science. The above discussion of the sources of
change indicates the elements that make up the dynamics of politics
generally, but revolutions are a special case in point and the circumstances that go into their creation are not easily unraveled.

One theory, based on the kind of analysis we have already been using,
employs the idea of "relative deprivation" as a way of explaining revolutionary dynamics. According to this view, the key consideration inclining people to revolt against government is not their actual standard of
living, what they are getting out of life in society (their real or objective
deprivation), but the relationship between what they are getting and
what they think they ought to be getting (relative deprivation). James
Davies has explained this idea in the following way:

> ... revolution is most likely to take place when a prolonged period of
> rising expectations and rising gratifications is followed by a short period
> of sharp reversal, during which the gap between expectations and gratifi-
> cations quickly widens and becomes intolerable. The frustration that de-
> velops, when it is intense and widespread in the society, seeks outlets in
> violent action. . . .This is an assertion about the state of mind of individual
> people in a society who are likely to revolt. It says their state of mind, their
> mood, is one of high tension and rather generalized hostility, derived
> from the widening of the gap between what they want and what they get.
> They fear not just that things will no longer continue to get better but—
> even more crucially—that ground will be lost that they have already
> gained.[4]

The sequence of events according to this view (as seen in Figure 6–1)
begins when what people want and what people get both increase at
about the same rate; that is, people's demands and expectations of social
and economic benefits are going up but they are being met at about the
same rate. Then the gap that Davies speaks about between expectations
and satisfactions widens as a result of a reversal or decrease in the
amount of satisfaction which occurs even while people's expectations
continue to rise. The result at this point is that people think of themselves as more deprived because of this widening gap, even though

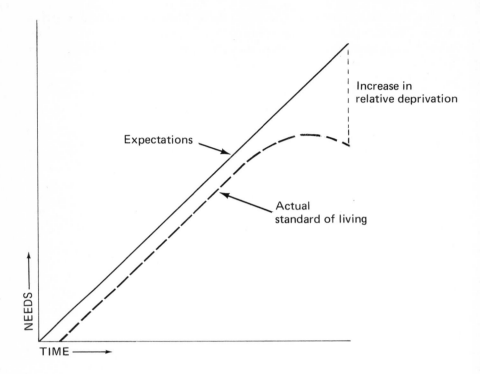

**Figure 6-1  Model of Relative Deprivation**

their actual condition of life is much improved from some earlier point in time.

To appreciate the idea of relative deprivation we might use an example drawn from an individual situation. Imagine your income increasing at a rather steady pace from about age twenty to age forty. In the early years you are not making that much money, but recognizing your youth and your lack of job experience you do not expect that you should be making much more than you are making. In the later years your expectations have increased—you think you ought to be able to buy a house, and a new car every few years, and take pleasant vacations—and your income has also risen to allow you to meet these additional expectations. Throughout this twenty-year period there has always been a gap between what you wanted or felt you should have and your actual level of satisfaction, but while both of these factors were on the increase, the gap between them remained about the same. Let us say that at age forty there is a serious economic recession and the industry you work in is particularly affected. Your employer tells you that in order to keep you he must give you another position with a cut in salary and little chance of any significant raises in the immediate future because of the economic difficulties the company is experiencing. At this point there is no reason why your expectations and wants would not normally rise—up to the time of the recession you may have been anticipating how comfortable things would be with another promotion in a few years—but a sudden reversal has occurred in the degree of satisfaction you are receiving. At this juncture you will likely experience a feeling of deprivation greater than you ever have before even though your actual standard of living is still greater than it was when you were younger. Thus, you are so disturbed and depressed because of the *relative* deprivation to which you find yourself victim.

Davies' explanation raises an example of this sort to the level of general expectations and satisfactions in the society at large. The theory of relative deprivations offers some valuable insights into the phenomenon of revolution. For one thing it explains why revolutions are not restricted to the poorest and most backward societies, for revolutions are not a function of a low standard of living or a high standard but a function of the patterns of change that are occurring. When American blacks were militantly voicing political demands in the United States, the argument was sometimes heard that their demands were unreasonable because they were benefiting from living in one of the richest nations in the world. Yet for the American black the relevant criterion was not how his standard of living compared to that of the average black African or of his own slave ancestors in America, but how it compared with other Americans', particularly white Americans', in a society which publicly upheld the values of equal opportunity and nondiscrimination. Being deprived in the midst of wealth presents a more volatile situation than being deprived in the midst of poverty where your own situation does not look like an unjust exception but a part of the inevitable.

There is another curious situation relating to relative deprivation. The pattern of rising expectations that creates relative deprivation is often set into motion by reforms or exposure to new ideas and alternative cultures (the Castro revolution in Cuba, for example, affected the expectations of leftist movements throughout Latin America). Thus, it appears that reform may function not only as an alternative to revolution, but also as a prelude to it. Reforms may raise expectations beyond the ability of the political system to ultimately satisfy them. Thus, it is tempting for the elite holding power to resist even modest reform not because the reforms themselves are so unacceptable but because they are afraid of setting into motion the dynamic processes described above. To turn around the old trite expression, if you do not give them an inch they will not expect a mile. Remember that the process of relative deprivation describes a downturn in satisfactions which is *preceded* by a general period of improvement. In this respect it is interesting to note that the Russian Revolution was preceded by modest attempts a decade earlier to establish a degree of representative government. This may also explain why the white rulers in South Africa so strongly resist attempts at reform for fear that they will set into motion political forces that will easily go beyond their ability to control.

Relative deprivation may be experienced in relation to a number of values; we may feel deprived of the material benefits of society, of freedom, of power, or of respect. But in each case the focal point of political revolution is the question of injustice. The question is not merely how my condition of life is compared to the next person's but whether our comparative situation in society is a just one. The medieval serf's ability to accept the prevailing values of society and not see an earthly injustice in the differences between his station in life and that of the landed aristocracy made him an unlikely recruit for revolutionary action.

The theory of relative deprivation is in part derived from the theories of Karl Marx in the nineteenth century which provided the philosophical foundation for modern communism, perhaps the most influential revolutionary doctrine of the contemporary period. Marx's analysis centered on the condition of the factory worker in such newly industrialized capitalist systems as England. He believed that initially the worker's values and orientation to his place in the social system merely reflected the values of the capitalist class even though it was the actual operation of capitalist economics that put the worker in the position he was in. But as the economic system developed and tension grew between the interests of the capitalists and the interests of the working man, the worker would begin to appreciate that justice for him required a thoroughly different form of political and economic relationships. In other words, the worker was poor not because he was an unsuccessful capitalist but because capitalism itself demanded the existence of a class of poor workers. This change in the outlook of the worker is described as the achievement of "class consciousness," or the movement from "false" consciousness to "true" consciousness. The worker's adoption of true consciousness was, for Marx, the prelude to revolution and the creation of a new order of things. It is interesting to note that the idea of "consciousness" still appears, perhaps in a diluted form, in the politics of contemporary dissent. American blacks talk about "black consciousness" and the movement for women's liberation uses the technique of "consciousness raising" as a means for women to reevaluate their traditional position in society.

Thus, the view of radical political change that is taken here is that certain disequilibrium in society at large, under certain conditions, leads to a sense of relative deprivation which takes the explicitly political form of a dispute over questions of justice and authority. According to this view, dissenting or revolutionary politics is more than a mere struggle for power. It is not a matter of ordinary politics merely getting out of hand and being pushed to the use of extreme tactics; rather it consists of a fundamental challenge to the prevailing principles and values dominating the existing political order.

## AGENTS OF CHANGE

Political change is not made by abstract forces; it is made by people. The study of change requires an understanding of the people who push for it, demand it, bring it about. Who are the agents of political change? It is an understandable assumption that reformers and revolutionaries in history are those who are downtrodden, repressed, and excluded from the existing political establishment. This assumption is misleading and only partially true. It is true that the agent of change inevitably is someone who is, to some degree or another, at odds with the existing political system, out of step with its values, and critical of its direction. But such persons are by no means from the lowest class in society, nor are they typically the most economically deprived or uneducated. Indeed, the leadership of radical movements is often in the hands of relatively educated people from the middle or upper classes. Fidel Castro, like Mahatma Gandhi, had been trained in the law, and Ho Chi Minh had been educated in Paris. This social-class position fits innumerable cases, such as V. I. Lenin in the Russian Revolution, Robespierre in the French Revolution, and our own American founding fathers. The reason for this is really not so mysterious if we think back to what has already been said about the nature of politics. Radical politics may be abnormal and possibly illegal, but it is still politics and it is bounded by many of the same constraints as conventional politics. It also requires the resources of talent, knowledge, organization, time, money, and the political orientation, sophistication, and temperament that comes with a certain class position in society. Revolutions are often made in the name of the common man but that does not mean that they are made *by* the common man.

This point particularly struck home in the United States, where opposition to the draft and the Vietnam war was centered among college students of frequently privileged social and economic circumstances, and the civil rights movement for blacks was often instigated by Protestant ministers like Martin Luther King Jr., and Jesse Jackson in the black community. Why do people who are so successful, particularly compared to the average man, or who at least have great prospects for rewarding careers and material comforts, turn to the risky, disreputable business of political resistance? The answer is not so difficult to unravel if, as we have suggested, the politics of the reformer and the revolutionary does not consist essentially or even primarily of a struggle for personal power or economic advantage but a struggle over the very authority of the state. Social position may have given the revolutionary the tools of political power but, for whatever reasons, he finds himself estranged from the guiding values of the state. Thus, the best picture of the agent of change is not that of the "downtrodden" but that of the "outsider." He is one who is pursuing ideals and political principles out of step with the prevailing system of rule.

A matter of considerable fascination to some political scientists and social psychologists is the question of why and how the agents of political change come to adopt their role; that is, why does the outsider become an outsider? The search for a good explanation has even led to psychoanalytical probing into the early childhood development of revolutionaries. For purposes of general understanding, however, it should be kept in mind that the very sources of change that create a disequilibrium in the social system touch the processes of early socialization themselves. The forces of modernization in Africa, for example, expose the younger generation of the traditional culture to competing views of the world which create the opportunity and the possibility of abandoning or turning against the attitudes and culture of their parents' generation. We can therefore look for things in the life experience of the revolutionary that draw his attention and loyalty to cultural and political values that are out of favor or in conflict with the existing regime.

This question of adopting a role forces us to confront a very basic dispute concerning the nature of resistance behavior. Our analysis portrays this behavior as rational and calculated action directed toward a goal. Yet it also has been explained as irrational behavior, not very purposeful, and more the product of the individual's personal problems, emotional and psychological, than of larger political issues. The rebel is thus viewed as an "oddball" who is using the forum of politics to relieve personal anxieties and frustrations and give vent to purely emotional impulses. This irrationalist view to a great extent derives from an association of resistance with violence, and from the study of rioting, assassination, and seemingly uncontrolled destruction. This ignores the fact that not all resistance uses violence, and it rests on the questionable assumption that all violence is irrational. Aside from the ethical questions involved, the rage and anger that feed violence in society may be perfectly human reactions to what is looked upon as injustice; indeed, it is just as fair to say that those who confront injustice in a docile, submissive, and complacent manner are the ones displaying irrationality and dehumanization. There is particular reason to feel rage over political injustice, for the injustice is man-made and not naturally determined; it is by its very character something that man feels he ought to be able to affect.

The really important thing to note about these irrational, psychologically oriented explanations of resisters is that they serve a certain political purpose in denigrating the importance and relevance of resistance. In the 1960s, protesters on American campuses were said to consist of students with too much time on their hands desiring to avoid the military service which would take them away from the luxury and comforts of the campus. Ghetto rioters were often viewed as malcontents, criminals, and social deviants. These explanations portray the root problems as personal and individual and not political, and it has always been in the interest of public authorities to so portray rebellion. As one study of the 1965 riots in Watts (Los Angeles, California) observes, "The basic issue—whether the rioters were socially pathological or whether the riot revealed something amiss with society and the political system— was the central battleground of the various theories of participation or interpretations of the riot. . . . The political implications of each view differed enormously. If the rioters were socially pathological, they would have to be ostracized or corrected. No major changes in society, or in the distribution of power, would be necessary."[5] Thus, the ability to picture the rebel or the rioter as a deviant may be a political tactic as much as a serious social-psychological explanation.

The view that we take here is simply that the resister *may* be irrational and merely indulging in the expression of personal frustrations, but his behavior is not irrational or politically pointless merely because it is resistance, and where deviancy or irrationality does enter in it is not fundamentally different from the irrationality that may characterize a bureaucrat, a general, a judge, or a legislator. One's personal orientations are a factor in all political experience, and in looking at the agents of change we are interested in the political functions they serve, the values they bring to bear on public affairs, and the changes they instigate. From the point of view of political analysis it makes more sense (and at the same time does not deny the existence of the irrational) to account for the behavior of the agent of change in terms of his values, goals, strategies, and tactics, for it is in terms of these that his resistance takes on political significance, becomes a focal point for the action of others, and generates political change. In short, the early upbringing and psychological state of Lenin do not negate the fact that he changed the course of Russian political history and won a struggle over the authority of the state.

The mass of average citizens, those more directly the victims of relative deprivations, also play a role in the movement for political change. As we will see, their role will vary depending on the tactics of political resistance. But once a sense of relative deprivation takes hold, they are susceptible to being mobilized for resistance. However, as our comments about radical leadership suggest, it is not essential that one be the direct victim of deprivation in order to be oriented to such political movements; the issue of justice goes beyond or transcends individual circumstances. Often it is the sensitive, perceptive observation of injustice experienced by others that motivates the resister.

## THE TACTICS OF RESISTANCE—NONVIOLENCE

Political change is a result of the act of resistance to public authority on the part of those in society seeking change. This is not to say that all acts of resistance work; some are ineffective, successfully suppressed, or abandoned. In the early part of the nineteenth century in England, there was a group known as the Luddites who tried to resist the movement toward industrialization by smashing and tearing apart the machines in the factory. They were unsuccessful, and like so many unsuccessful resisters, they are hardly heard of anymore. With the conditions for political change thrust upon society and with the appearance of reformers and revolutionaries, the next question to consider is how people go about engaging in political resistance. In other words, what are the tactics of political resistance?

In general terms, of course, resistance behavior is explained in the same way as any other type of political behavior—by reference to the individual's orientations, the constraints imposed on him by the government and the social system at large, and the political goals and values that are at stake. Yet in the case of resistance behavior these circumstances are rather special, since what is being challenged is the very way decisions are made, the values that are used to legitimize them and, in the ultimate sense, the very structure and design of the system itself. Resistance behavior can be viewed as "abnormal" politics which is resorted to when "normal" politics has broken down or is rejected. To say that it is abnormal does not necessarily mean that it is wrong but merely that it invokes standards of right or wrong that go beyond or are in conflict with the existing norms of the political system.

The forms that resistance takes can be distinguished according to whether violent or nonviolent means are employed. The choice of means is not totally up to the resister, and in part it reflects the character of the system that is being challenged. Techniques of nonviolent resistance to bring about political change have developed and been most frequently applied in political democracies. The ability of nonviolent resistance to work as a political tactic rests on the assumption that even though the breaking of laws is typically involved, the state will not use the ultimate force available to it to oppose this resistance. In other words, it is assumed that the slightest appearance of such dissent will not lead to people being instantly or permanently imprisoned or shot on the spot, because the government is constrained to operate through the rule of law which requires a hearing of charges, trial by peers, and an appropriate sentence. If this assumption cannot be made, as in the case of Nazi Germany, the prospect of nonviolent resistance as a useful tactic is virtually eliminated.

Nonviolent resistance may take many forms, though as a political tactic it usually has one of two objectives. Its most common objective is to draw public attention to the political issues involved for the purpose of increasing public support and sympathy for the protestors. This was a central objective of the methods employed by Martin Luther King Jr., in his leadership of the civil rights movement in the American South. At one time in the South, blacks were permitted to ride only in the backs of buses and to sit only in restricted areas at lunch counters. As means of protesting such unjust discrimination, blacks would organize to sit in white areas in buses and lunch counters. The act of protest itself involved no damage to person or property and was carried out in an orderly fashion, but it would lead to a confrontation with white officials and citizens. King believed that the conflict resulting from such nonviolent actions would so visibly dramatize the injustices of segregation and their inconsistency with the ideals of freedom and equality that the conscience of the community at large would be stirred to action and effectively directed toward changing the law.

The other objective of nonviolent resistance (keeping in mind that the two objectives could operate together) is to assert individual claims to a right against public authority. Imagine the case of a draft-age American who claims he is a conscientious objector, that is, that his personal moral beliefs prohibit him from fighting in war. His draft board refuses to recognize his claim and when he is finally called up to be drafted he refuses to appear. In this instance the objective is not to generate public support or perhaps not even to encourage mass resistance, for the conscientious objector may feel that people who do not hold to his moral views ought to accept the draft. In this example, the prime objective is getting the state to recognize what the individual considers to be a just claim against a particular action of the state.

The tactic of nonviolent resistance to authority thus spans the whole range of resistance behavior, including purely individual action, organized group action targeted at the legitimacy of particular policies or at the system as a whole. One of the most dramatic events in the history of nonviolent resistance, which has served as a model for others, was the movement led by M. K. Gandhi in India against the British colonial government. This was perhaps the most massive use of such tactics, for its goal, ultimately achieved, was an alteration in the form of government through the removal of a colonial power. Nonviolent resistance typically has not had such lofty objectives, or if it has they have been difficult to achieve. The widespread use of nonviolence is a relatively recent phenomenon in history, most likely because it depends upon a certain tolerance on the part of the political regime that is being resisted. In many democratic systems, particularly the United States, the techniques of nonviolence have become a common form of resistance behavior with a fair record of political success.

The theory behind the use of nonviolent methods of political change justifies their use when all other legitimate and conventional means of change have proven not only ineffective but unjustly prejudicial to one's cause. The assumption is that the reliance on resistance is a last resort. Thus, King did not turn to resistance merely because blacks were being discriminated against but because the normal channels for seeking a legal and democratic solution to the problem were effectively closed off. Another characteristic of nonviolence is that it is a highly planned, disciplined tactic which does not occur spontaneously. The main reason for this is the need to maintain a nonviolent approach in the face of what is frequently a violent response to the protest action. All resistance contains a potential for the outbreak of violence, and where a nonviolent act of protest is not sufficiently well organized and planned, there is a greater possibility of the action degenerating into violent struggle for which the protesters themselves are likely to be ill prepared. The resisters, therefore, accept arrest by the authorities and limit themselves to defensive or protective response to outbursts of violence against them, and their arrest and subsequent legal action against them actually become a continuation of their protest. The protesters will frequently attempt to "politicize" their trial. Though the technical grounds on which they were arrested might be trespassing or marching without a parade permit, they will use the forum of the courtroom to explain the political reasons for the action. A dramatic example of this is found in the transcript of the "Chicago Seven" trial,

in which seven leaders of the antiwar movement were accused of violating the law in connection with demonstrations in Chicago at the time
of the 1968 Democratic National Convention. The following excerpt is
taken from the point where one of the defendants, David Dellinger, is
given the opportunity to address the judge prior to being sentenced for
contempt of court, and it shows the conflict between the defendant's
attempt to politicize the trial and the judge's attempt to treat the issues
on the narrowest legal grounds:

MR. DELLINGER: . . . Now I want to point out first of all that the first two
   contempts cited against me concerned, one, the moratorium action
   and, secondly, support of Bobby Seale, the war against Vietnam, the
   aggression against Vietnam, and racism in this country, the two issues that this country refuses to solve, refuses to take seriously.
THE COURT: I hope you will excuse me, sir. You are not speaking strictly
   to what I gave you the privilege of speaking to. I ask you to say what
   you want to say in respect to punishment.
MR. DELLINGER: I think this relates to the punishment.
THE COURT: Get to the subject of punishment and I will be glad to hear
   you. I don't want you to talk politics.
DEFENDANT DELLINGER: You see, that's one of the reasons I have needed
   to stand up and speak anyway, because you have tried to keep what
   you call politics, which means the truth, out of this courtroom, just
   as the prosecution has.
THE COURT: I will ask you to sit down.
DEFENDANT DELLINGER: Therefore it is necessary—
THE COURT: I won't let you go on any further.
DEFENDANT DELLINGER: You want us to be like good Germans supporting
   the evils of our decade and then when we refused to be good Germans and came to Chicago and demonstrated, despite the threats
   and intimidations of the establishment, now you want us to be like
   good Jews, going quietly and politely to the concentration camps
   while you and this Court suppress freedom and the truth. And the
   fact is that I am not prepared to do that. You want us to stay in our
   place like black people were supposed to stay in their place—
THE COURT: Mr. Marshal, I will ask you to have Mr. Dellinger sit down.
DEFENDANT DELLINGER: —like poor people were supposed to stay in their
   place, like people without formal education are supposed to stay in
   their place, like women are supposed to stay in their place—
THE COURT: I will ask you to sit down.[6]

The specific techniques of nonviolence are varied, and the choice of
techniques will depend on the circumstances. Where the target is an
unjust law, the nonviolent act may consist simply of openly violating the
specific law itself; thus, legally supported segregation of blacks and

whites in public places was protested by public violation of such policies. When the protest is aimed at stopping the government from doing
something, various types of interference are used: New Yorkers used
their cars to disrupt traffic around Kennedy Airport in protest against
the granting of landing rights to the Concorde supersonic jet which
they considered excessively noisy; protesters in New Hampshire waged
a sit-in at the construction site of a proposed nuclear energy plant. Such
interference tactics are not necessarily designed to stop the implemen-
tation of government policy at the moment—sitting in front of troop
trains to protest the Vietnam war could not really keep the trains from
running—but, again, to dramatize the importance of the issue. The full
assortment of nonviolent techniques has included hunger strikes, burning of draft cards, destruction of draft records, refusal to pay taxes,
boycotts, sit-ins, and "mill-ins."

As a method of political change, nonviolent resistance has redirected
public policy and has led to the political respectability and influence of
previously ignored, repressed, or disenfranchised groups and interests.
In the United States, the present power of the labor movement and of
racial minorities and the present state of civil liberties must be attributed in large part to the successful use of such methods. The most
obvious advantage of such methods is that they channel resistance away
from the more destructive and uncontrollable techniques of violence,
yet the self-conscious discipline and training that are required for their
effectiveness make them somewhat elitist techniques difficult to use in
mobilizing masses of politically frustrated and angry people lacking
political skills.

## THE TACTICS OF RESISTANCE—VIOLENCE

More often than not in history, resistance to public authority and the
attempt to bring about political change have involved the use of violent
tactics, including internal war (revolutionary struggle), sabotage, terrorism, assassination, coup d'etat, and rioting. Some of these tactics, such
as internal war or sabotage, are as systematically planned as the techniques of nonviolence, and there is no question of their being politically
directed. But violence also results from the outburst of human emotions
and passions, and this has led to the question of whether certain acts of
violence should be treated as having political significance. Violent tactics should be looked at individually to explore their political significance and usefulness in bringing about political change.

## Terrorism

The use of terror tactics is one of the most sinister and frightening forms of political violence because it involves the use of such seemingly senseless violence frequently against innocent people. Terrorism consists of sporadic acts of violence against people and property—bombing, airplane highjacking, kidnapping, murder—that attack public authority at its very foundation by challenging the ability of government to maintain law and order and insure the security of its citizens. Though terrorism is hardly new in history it has become a disturbingly widespread tactic in political struggles throughout the contemporary world. It has been used by the Irish Republican Army against the British in Northern Ireland, by the Algerians in their war of independence against the French, by the Viet Cong in their fight against the government of South Vietnam, by Russian anarchists in the nineteenth century against the czar, and by both sides at one time or another in the continuing political struggle in the Middle East. Though acts of violence may be aimed at public officials themselves, through attacks on the police or assassination of leaders or the bombing of government installations, terrorism may just as well serve its purposes through attacks on innocent civilians.

A disturbing trend in recent terrorism is the use of such methods as a device for gaining attention and publicity for one's political cause. The worldwide impact of mass media and the instant attention available to previously unknown movements have increasingly enticed people to use terrorism as a vehicle for political recognition. Unfortunately, this objective makes it even less important whether the victims of terrorism are innocent bystanders. In May 1977 a group of South Moluccan radicals took a group of one hundred Dutch school children as hostages and instantly drew the attention of the world to their previously ignored movement for the independence of their small Pacific island country. It may seem preposterous that publicity is the ultimate goal of such actions, particularly since the publicity is virtually all negative, but what is disturbing is the effectiveness of terrorism in this regard. Though it is a difficult admission, the influence and recognition of the pro-Palestinian movement have been greatly built on the use of terrorism.

By its very character, terrorism is a highly secretive, conspiratorial tactic engaged in by small, tightly knit groups of people trained in military skills and operations. Though one of its purposes is to weaken people's attachment to the established regime and possibly even build up sympathy among the larger group that they claim to be acting in the name of, terrorists are really cut off from mass-based organizing. Terrorism draws people with a certain fanaticism or blind loyalty to the cause; such commitment and subordination of one's personal interests to the movement is called for not only by the severity of terrorist actions themselves but by the fact that the terrorist may likely become, in effect, an international outlaw.

## Rioting

The term is used here generally to refer to various types of incidents in which more or less spontaneous violence against property or persons is engaged in by groups of people. Though rioting is not as planned or controlled as terrorism and is not limited to participation by a radical elite, riots may be instigated and inspired as a political tactic. We include under this term such incidents as slave rebellions in the American South before the Civil War, peasant uprisings in Europe under feudalism, riots of industrial workers (such as in the American coal and rail industries in the late nineteenth century), and the more recent urban riots in American cities. Though it is difficult to generalize about rioting throughout history, the dispute over its political significance is a continuing and unsettled issue, particularly since the issue itself is not merely academic but a manifestation of the political differences between rebels and public authorities. Rebels portray riots as vivid testimony of the people's inherent sense of political injustice and evidence of their potential for greater revolutionary action; the authorities portray the rioters as criminals and malcontents whose only political significance is that they have allowed themselves to become the pliant subjects of rabble-rousers. These two explanations are exaggerated by their respective proponents, and more objective versions may show them to be somewhat reconcilable. Rioting is to some degree spontaneous and unorganized, and this necessarily makes it a product of the emotions of the moment, but this is not to say that it lacks political significance but merely that it lacks the tactical structure and sophistication of nonviolence or internal war. This spontaneity does not mean that the rioters' feelings of anger and disgust at injustice and their treatment at the hands of the authorities are any less important politically.

This fundamental dispute over the meaning of rioting carries over to the question of how and why riots occur. The authorities tend to favor the theory that riots are the product of agitators who play upon the emotions of the people so that the riot spreads like a cantagion. Thus, attention is completely turned to the question of who started the riot and to the search for "leaders" to punish. Consistent with this view, much was made of the oratory of H. Rap Brown, a radical black spokesman, as the cause of riots in Maryland, and great effort and attention was devoted to Brown's capture. A somewhat different view is that riots result from the convergence of people with similar sympathies and attitudes who, in effect, find each other and reinforce each other's inclination to action. The implication of this second view is that the rioters do not merely get caught up in the events of the moment but are quite predisposed to violent action already. The effect of rioting on political change is not very easy to determine, but as a general observation it is probably the case that rioting will not have much effect unless it occurs as part of a larger political movement employing a greater variety of tactics. Both the civil rights and labor movements in the United States were accompanied by the outbreak of rioting, though the impact of the rioting is a source of ongoing dispute.

## Coup d'Etat

This term, taken from the French and often called simply a *coup*, refers to the swift and forceful takeover of a government. It is sometimes thought of as a revolution, but it differs from a revolution in that it does not involve a transformation of the political system nor is it based on a mass uprising of the people. The coup itself consists of the forceful displacement of the ruling elite by a new elite though the new elite, upon acquiring power, may institute changes in policy and even attempt more substantial political change by government direction. As a political tactic, a successful coup requires the ability to capture and use the very sources of power that should be at the disposal of the government itself. This is why the central actor in the coup is the military, part or all of which may lead the coup or support civilian leaders of such action. The coup itself is carried out by capturing or killing top civilian and/or military leaders and swiftly moving to control important government buildings and installations, particularly systems of mass communication and transportation. It is important in the execution of a coup that the action be sufficiently quick and decisive as to foreclose the possibility of a counter-coup—the government must not be given time to respond—and that popular worries and concerns be overcome and the people's acceptance be achieved. The very nature of this tactic is such that the masses are relatively passive bystanders in what is essentially a struggle for power between different factions of the elite. If the coup is well organized and executed it actually may involve little violence, producing a so-called bloodless coup in which the show of force is sufficiently impressive to avoid the need for its use.

The coup has become a common feature of contemporary politics, a mode of political change short of full revolution in political systems lacking the ability for more homeostatic change. Among the more prominent coups that have shaped the politics of major modern systems have been the 1952 military overthrow of the Egyptian monarchy which brought to power what might be described as a modernizing oligarchy; the 1967 overthrow of constitutional democracy in Greece by a group of top military leaders which lasted about seven years until political pressures forced a return to civilian rule and the call for elections; and the military overthrow of the Chilean government in 1973, in which President Salvador Allende was murdered. It would seem that the only cure for the possibility of a coup is either an extremely strong democratic tradition, which would provide other means for discontented elites to bring about change and minimize the prospect of a coup's receiving popular acceptance, or a thoroughly repressive regime which would effectively foreclose the possibility of such internal conspiracies. Thus, tutelary democracies and oligarchies that have not fully employed totalitarian means are more susceptible to this type of political change.

## Internal War

When conflict over the control of government breaks out into organized mass struggle with the motivation of changing the very character of the political system, we have a situation of *internal war* which is the characteristic method of revolution. Internal war represents the ultimate breakdown of public authority. Authentic revolution is still a sufficiently unique and rare political phenomenon that it is difficult to generalize about the methods used; to a great extent they reflect the special circumstances of the particular revolution. Internal war may take the form of a fairly sudden overthrow of government through mass actions and thus take on the appearance of a coup with mass support. The initial stages of the French and Russian revolutions appear this way; however such overthrows are followed by extended periods of conflict between opposing segments of society only after which is the revolutionary regime successfully consolidated. The revolutionary struggle may also take the form of a civil war with standing armies, lines of battle, and fighting for control of territory much like conventional international war. The Communist Chinese revolution more closely resembled this form.

The form of internal war that is most common in revolutionary struggles in the world today is the guerrilla war in which the military objectives of subversion and sabotage against the government are directly tied to building political loyalty among the people for the revolutionary movement. The Viet Cong movement in South Vietnam and Fidel Castro's movement in Cuba were of this type. Guerrilla warfare has become very much the doctrine of communist movements in Third World countries. Mao Tse-tung gave great encouragement to it as a means of spreading the ideals and goals of the Chinese Revolution, and Che Guevara, after the success of the Cuban Revolution, attempted to recreate the struggle in other parts of Latin America.

The tremendous dimensions and consequences of internal war as a political tactic reflect both its monumental purposes and the depth to which the existing political order has become weakened as a viable system. A successful revolution is not a momentary event; it brings about a convulsive dislocation in society that can last for as long as a generation. It is not only an extended but a totally absorbing struggle which, being neither as sporadic nor as limited as other violent tactics, sooner or later touches virtually the whole population, giving practical significance to the revolutionary maxim that "if you are not with us, you are against us."

Returning to the issue we raised earlier, not all violence against society is political in nature, even though violence is a classic tool of political resistance and radical change. A certain amount of ordinary crime will not be considered a political threat to the legitimacy of the state even though it involves the use of violence against the public. As we saw in the case of rioting, the determination of whether violent acts are political is often open to question, particularly so when the violence appears spontaneous and unorganized. A curious case in this respect is assassination. Is the assassin of a governmental or political leader a crazed, disturbed individual or is he consciously engaging in an extreme political act? There is no issue when assassination is used in conjunction with a coup or revolution, but assassinations in American history have been unrelated to larger political actions. The singular political change is the removal of a specific leader which may be enough motive for the assassin. Many American assassinations would seem to be politically motivated and deranged acts at the same time; that is, they often seem to be the products of irrational and disoriented political impulses. President Garfield was killed by a "disappointed office seeker," President McKinley by an anarchist, and President Kennedy by a person who had spent his life in confused political activity.

In comparing violent and nonviolent tactics of resistance, it is interesting to note the connection between the choice of tactics and the character of the existing regime against which the resistance is aimed. Repressive regimes virtually necessitate the ultimate reliance on violence for the purpose of any serious resistance to authority; indeed, the dependence on force seems to be mutually reinforcing between the authorities and the rebels. For this reason the successful leaders of a coup or revolution will often be as repressive in their use of the power of government as the regime they have overthrown because of the need to establish and maintain control in a highly charged, polarized situation. Though violent revolution has had great effect in transforming social and economic systems, it does not have a very persuasive record in achieving advances toward political democracy. On the other hand, the pacifist defenders of nonviolent resistance have contended that their methods are universally applicable, though they seem to have flourished only in countries in which the arbitrary and capricious use of governmental power has been restrained. Where these conditions are not present, nonviolent resistance is more likely to lead only to individual martyrdom. While nonviolent resistance has become refined in democracies, this is not to say that democracies are immune from political violence. Indeed, democracies are caught in an ironic situation: while their openness and permissiveness remove much of the motivation for political violence, these very same considerations allow the implements of violence to be easily available and make it difficult to decisively suppress violence when it does arise. Loose gun-control laws (if any), protection of individual rights, limitations on the ability of government to engage in surveillance and wiretapping, lack of restrictions on individual travel, all make democratic systems peculiarly vulnerable to those who have turned toward violent tactics. It is in response to this dilemma that democratic systems when faced with such stresses often turn to stricter measures than would usually be acceptable, such as "martial law" under which the government gives itself special police powers to deal with violent disturbances.

Another important difference between these two kinds of tactics is that nonviolence is an open and public form of resistance, whereas violent methods are clandestine and conspiratorial in nature. For this reason, if mass-based violent resistance is to be organized at all, it invariably relies on elitist forms of internal organization. Internal democracy is not viable and an active revolutionary movement may be organized along almost military lines. Nonviolence, though it depends on discipline and the inspiration of resistance leaders, need not be as hierarchically organized. By virtue of being a public demonstration of resistance, it is not truly subversive as a tactic; it does not depend on secrecy and surprise and, in fact, a nonviolent demonstration is frequently known about in advance and is quite predictable in its execution.

# DOCTRINES OF RESISTANCE AND THE ROLE
# OF THE MASSES

In discussing political resistance as the source of change, one should place emphasis on the struggle for power and the role of radical elites. But the point of view we have taken here considers the question of justice as the central issue in political resistance and public authority as the main object of change. Power, whether of violence or nonviolence, is not the main objective of resistance but the tool of resistance. If it is legitimacy that is called into question then it is not only the ability to control the machinery of government that is at stake but also the allegiance of the people. Thus, a balanced analysis of political change must account also for the role of the masses and the alternative doctrines offered by resisters to gain the support of the masses.

An important part of resistance, of whatever form, is political education and propaganda. The spreading of dissenting views among the public, raising public awareness of injustice, and the promotion of alternative conceptions of political order are essential elements in resistance. Particularly in the initial stages of resistance, the political struggle becomes a war of words and ideas. The peace movement's use of "teach-ins," the Communist party's emphasis on the political education of the workers, the control of public communications that is so central to the successful coup, the nonviolent objective of publicly dramatizing issues, the reliance on books, pamphlets, "underground" newspapers as a means of acquiring the support of the average citizen, and the corresponding efforts of the government to suppress and condemn the spread of such ideas, all attest to the fact that the battleground of political change is the hearts and minds of the people. The masses must either be organized in support of the movement for change or convinced to accept it after it is accomplished. They may not be capable of spontaneously initiating such movements, but their power derives from the fact that their allegiance is so critical to success.

In examining the role of doctrines and ideas in respect to political change, we encounter one of the most fundamental ironies of politics. While no form of government accepts the principle that it can be legitimately resisted and assumes an unquestioned right to preserve itself, many modern forms of government derive from political doctrines that have been the basis for revolution and have been used to justify the citizens' resistance to authority. The three major political doctrines of contemporary Western history—democracy, communism, and fascism—all have revolutionary origins and implications that we can look to as a way of gaining insight into the revolutionary appeals that have stirred people in history.

## Democracy and the Right of Self-Determination

One of the principles associated with political democracy is that the individual has the right and the ability to determine his political fate. This was originally expressed by the philosophical idea that political association is the product of a unanimous agreement among men, a "social contract" as it was known, which determines the basic scheme of government and system of law by which people are ruled. This idea contained radical implications for European society of the seventeenth and eighteenth centuries in which authority was based on ancient traditions and inherited rights. If the sound principles of government are the product of man's reason and independent ethical judgment, why grant legitimacy to a government which runs counter to reason and ignores the weight of popular will? It is in these terms that Thomas Paine attacked British monarchy at the time of the American Revolution for lacking historical origins that in any way demanded the respect and loyalty of British subjects. A critical shift occurred in the attitudes of the American colonists when they moved from proclaiming their rights as *Englishmen* against the actions of the king and Parliament to proclaiming their rights as *human beings.* As in the American case, the democratic argument for popular sovereignty became a powerful force in the early revolutions and rebellions of the modern period.

The democratic tradition has continued to serve as a doctrine of rebellion either by promoting the idea that the voice of the people contains more basic authority than government itself or, consistent with the social contract, the idea that there are natural standards of justice and law that government cannot violate and that, when violated, provide legitimate grounds for resistance. Such ideas have inspired nonviolent civil disobedience, conscientious objection to war, and popular rebellion against government. The claim to restore constitutional government as symbolized through the calling of elections by the leaders of a successful coup also relies on the power of democratic ideas. The revolutionary power of democratic ideas is perhaps best attested to by the fact that so many regimes in the world, whether really democratic or not, proclaim themselves to be forms of popular rule. Popular self-determination may not be widely applied but it certainly seems to be widely valued as heralded by the use of such political labels as "People's Republic," "Popular Front," "Populist Movement."

## Communism and the Mission of History

Of all modern political doctrines, communism is the most systematically and explicitly revolutionary in its view of the world. It is based on the notion that historical change does not occur through random events or result merely from human will and purpose but that it follows definite laws which give to these currents of change a distinct pattern. According to Communists, the dynamics of political change are rooted in inevitable conflicts over the material goods of life which have divided all societies in history into distinct classes according to whether people are engaged in the mere production of wealth or whether they control the means of such production and thereby reap the material benefits of others' labor. The various successive social systems in Western history have all been so divided, whether it be into master and slave, nobleman and serf, or worker and capitalist. The struggle between economic classes sets up a basic tension that dictates the general moral, political, and cultural shape of the society. Class conflict ultimately reaches a point where it breaks out into a revolutionary struggle of the lower class against the ruling class. This struggle and the subsequent transformation of society which it brings about account for the fundamental shifts that have occurred in history. History is thus seen as a progressive development of man toward increased freedom through an extended series of revolutionary stages ultimately terminating in the overthrow of capitalism and the establishment of a classless, socialist society.

The revolutionary appeal of communism rests on the idea that one is engaging in a political movement of historical importance, that one is part of a historical mission. To make revolution is to recognize the more profound historical forces that are operating on society. In broad terms, the revolution is thought of as a course of action that is not chosen but is inevitable and not to be a part of it is to be overtaken by events, caught in a past that does not have a future. Such a doctrine has been tremendously influential among the economically and politically repressed people's of the world. In it they have seen an explanation of their own plight, attributing responsibility to the ruling class and the forces of class struggle, and an expression of hope that the future is theirs. Communism has, in practical terms, been the most widespread and successful revolutionary doctrine of the modern era, implanted as the governing ideology of such countries as the Soviet Union, China, Cuba, Vietnam, and the nations of Eastern Europe.

In the development of communist ideology, an early dispute arose over the question of whether or not the transformation of society from a capitalist to a socialist form had to occur through the means of a violent political revolution. Some argued that the theories of Karl Marx, on which communist doctrine is based, allowed for the possibility that under the right conditions socialism could be achieved through peaceful democratic means. In this regard, an interesting contemporary development is the prospect that in certain democratic countries

Communist parties could achieve power through free elections. In fact, Salvador Allende's victory in the presidential elections in Chile has been referred to as the first instance in which a Marxist has won national office through free elections. There is serious speculation that in countries like France or Italy the Communists, possibly in alliance with various socialist parties, could also win national elections. What is of great concern here and what will be closely watched is whether or not such regimes will continue to preserve democratic methods in pursuing what are, in effect, revolutionary goals or will use electoral victory to attack the very foundations of democratic politics. It has been argued that under the influence of such Western democracies, communism has become a less militantly revolutionary doctrine. Whether this is true or not, it would certainly seem that it has entered a very critical stage in its own development.

## Fascism and the Passion for Order

We are inclined to think of political revolution as invariably a matter of the downtrodden rising up against their rulers—the image conveyed by democratic and communist revolutions—yet, as we saw, the more accurate image of the revolutionary is the "outsider." It may even be that revolutions are engaged in for the purpose of reasserting the values of conservative oligarchy. It is in this respect that we can gain an appreciation of the role of fascism in transforming society.

Fascism is the most recent revolutionary doctrine of the modern age, being first recognized in the 1920s and receiving its main expression in the form of the Nazi movement in Germany and the Fascist movement in Italy. The central appeal of fascism is for order and direction in public life and the promised relief from the conflict and turmoil associated with the open and free-wheeling politics of democracy and the pervasive class struggle envisioned by communism. It bemoans the lack of leadership and heroism in politics and calls for the appearance of an elite which will rid society of divisive ideas. The function of the elite is to build a unified society by appealing to nationalistic and sometimes racist impulses and removing the influence of the masses from politics. The Fascist belief in the idea that "might makes right" and that the stronger and more courageous elements in society should be given the mantle of leadership is used to justify the forceful overthrow of weak, debilitated democratic regimes. In meeting people's need for a sense of political order, fascism is responding to a political need as fundamental as the need for liberty or equality which, when severely denied, can provide the conditions for a Fascist movement. For all of its exaggerated elitism and conservatism, it is no less revolutionary in its impact on society. Once gaining power, such movements have decisively and thoroughly swept away any semblance of democracy or rule of law by the uninhibited use of state power.

These three doctrines, as we noted, are not only the ideas that have fueled modern revolution, they also are the ideas by which societies have been governed and defended against change. Though this may seem paradoxical, it results from the fact that the very arguments used to create new forms of government are relevant to the defense of the new form of government when it is achieved. Democracy, thus, fights under the banner of self-determination and then defends its own authority on the ground that it is the will of the people; communism interprets attacks on its regimes as "counterrevolutionary" attempts to turn back the clock of change; and Fascists, we might almost say, fight revolutions in order to give themselves the power to put an end to revolutions.

## SUMMARY

Political change has its romantic side; it is stirred by hope and the search for justice. Most of the political regimes of the modern period have their origins in revolution or coup d'etat. Yet we must remember that in studying radical political change we are examining politics in its most fundamental form and in the most severe convulsion that society can experience. The reason for this is not merely that political change so often involves violence, for it need not be violent and violence need not be political. Society also suffers through waves of crime and natural disasters from plague to earthquakes. The real reason is that political change disrupts the very norms that people live by. Ordinary politics depends on a core of values that need not be questioned—tradition, laws, constitutions, ideology—and this stable core serves a very real human need to know that though this fabricated experience of politics may be man-made, it is reliably anchored by a social ethic that gives pattern and meaning to people's life together in society. It is this that is shattered by the forces of revolution, creating what it would not be an exaggeration to call a collision of two different worlds. As the German novelist Herman Hesse has said, in giving expression to this plight of society,

Every age, every culture, every custom and tradition has its own character, its own weakness and its own strength, its beauties and ugliness; accepts certain sufferings as matters of course, puts up patiently with certain evils. Human life is reduced to real suffering, to hell, only when two ages, two cultures and religions overlap. A man of the Classical Age who had to live in medieval times would suffocate miserably just as a savage does in the midst of our civilization. Now there are times when a whole generation is caught in this way between two ages, two modes of life, with the consequence that it loses all power to understand itself and has no standard, no security, no simple acquiescence. Naturally, every one does not feel this equally strongly. A nature such as Nietzsche's had to suffer our present ills more than a generation in advance. What he had to go through alone and misunderstood, thousands suffer today.[7]

If the dynamics of political and social change bring a special kind of suffering to society, it should be added that they reveal the truly human character of political experience. This is shown not so much by the increase in human reason and freedom that we expect and hope for but by the very fact of historical novelty and creativity, the very fact that politics is a realm of human experience that can be renewed. Thus, in the study of change we see political experience in all of its contradictions—its dangers, greatness, nobility, violence, and tragedy.

## NOTES

[1]Harold Lasswell, *Politics: Who Gets What, When, How* (New York, 1958), p. 14.

[2]Ibid., p. 47.

[3]Charles Tilly, "Collective Violence in European Perspective," in Hugh Davis Graham and Ted Robert Gurr, *Violence in America* (New York, 1969), p. 28.

[4]James C. Davies, "The J-Curve of Rising and Declining Satisfactions as a Cause of Some Great Revolutions and a Contained Rebellion," in Graham and Gurr, p. 671.

[5]David Sears and John McConahay, *The Politics of Violence* (Boston, 1973), p. 19.

[6]*Contempt: Transcript of the Contempt Citations of the Chicago Conspiracy 10* (Chicago, 1970), pp. 71–72.

[7]Herman Hesse, *Steppenwolf* (New York, 1963), pp. 24–25.

## FOR FURTHER READING

Bell, David V.J. *Resistance and Revolution.* Boston: Houghton Mifflin, 1973. A useful review of the general topics of revolution and rebellion which stresses the role of the question of justice in the process of political change.

Brinton, Crane. *The Anatomy of Revolution.* Englewood Cliffs, N.J.: Prentice-Hall, 1965. A well-known, highly readable analysis of four major revolu-

tions—the English, American, French, and Russian. Good treatment of the
stages of revolution.

Graham, Hugh Davis, and Ted Robert Gurr. *Violence in America.* New York:
The New American Library, 1969. A collection of articles that represents
the results of the National Commission on the Causes and Prevention of
Violence. The analysis and data it contains make it a basic source in studying political violence.

Johnson, Chalmers. *Revolutionary Change.* Boston: Little, Brown, 1966. An
attempt at a comprehensive theory of revolutions focusing on the processes
by which systems become destabilized.

Paynton, Clifford T., and Robert Blackey, eds. *Why Revolution?* Cambridge,
Mass.: Schenkman, 1971. A collection of historical and contemporary essays
exploring the causes and processes of political change. A good general
source of views on revolution.

# 7

# Political Thinking

Politics has been not only one of the perpetual activities of mankind, it has also been a continuing object of thought and reflection. By virtue of the fundamental mission of politics in creating and maintaining the means by which people live together in society, the political experience has always confronted man with a rich and demanding set of issues for intellectual inquiry. Thus, the tradition of political thought can be traced back to the earliest period of recorded history and active philosophical speculation. The host of questions that has drawn the attention of political thinkers is vast. How are governments created? How is order maintained? What is the basis of public authority? What is the best form of government? What is freedom? How much of it is good or necessary? Should all people be treated equally, or is it more just to recognize their differences? Why do people do what they do in politics?

In one sense, the development of political thought is merely an extension of man's general interest in trying to understand himself and his natural and social environment. Man is a thinking animal, and he extends his thinking to politics just as he does to biology, chemistry, physics, economics, psychology, and ethics. However, there is another dimension to political thinking, for politics is not only the *object* but it is also the *product* of intellectual energies. Political life is a human construction and it thereby reflects our ideas being put to work, being used and applied. Political thinking is itself a form of politics; one of the things people do in politics is articulate, debate, exchange, and share ideas and values. This is why Aristotle thought of politics as peculiarly related to the human capacity for speech and why the ancient Romans thought of oratory as a very special political skill. Pericles, speaking of the quality of public life in ancient Greece, captures a sense of the relationship between political thought and action:

> We alone regard a man who takes no interest in public affairs, not as a harmless, but as a useless character; and if few of us are originators, we are all sound judges of a policy. The great impediment to action is, in our opinion, not discussion, but the want of that knowledge which is gained by discussion preparatory to action. For we have a peculiar power of thinking before we act and of acting too, whereas other men are courageous from ignorance but hesitate upon reflection.[1]

This is not to say that politics is a fully rational enterprise or to deny the fact that people are moved by events, circumstances, or environment, but merely to suggest that, to one degree or another, in studying politics we are studying the results of human thought operating in the world.

Contemporary political thought has taken a variety of forms and will be treated here under three general headings—political science, ideology, and political philosophy. Though all three deal with a common subject matter, they deal with it in different ways and with different objectives. Many concepts, terms, and ideas are shared among them and overlap the boundaries separating them, yet they have become relatively independent types of political thinking best examined separately.

## POLITICAL SCIENCE

One objective of political thought is the development of an "empirical science of politics." Unfortunately, to define precisely what this means requires defining what *science* is, itself a source of intellectual dispute. For our purposes it should suffice to identify the objective of political *science*, which is the systematic description, explanation, and, perhaps, prediction of political phenomena. By *empirical* we mean the development and use of ideas and principles that can be tested for their validity against the real world of experience. Thus, the task of the political scientist is to develop general concepts, principles, and theories about how politics works and to test these ideas against direct evidence that he is able to collect. One of the goals of this "empirical science of politics" is to be objective, or "value free," which means that the political scientist is not interested in how politics *ought* to work but how it *does* in fact work. He attempts to leave aside his own personal values and political interests in approaching his subject matter so that the results of his thinking are an accurate representation of reality, not a reflection of his personal preferences.

Thus, political scientists deal with many of the very questions we have raised here. Who governs? How is power distributed? How are public decisions made? What causes political change? Why do some people vote and others not vote, and why do they use their vote as they do? Many of the ideas we have employed in introducing the subject matter of politics derive from the work of political science: roles, power relationships, homeostatic change, relative deprivation, systems analysis, among others. Our treatment has necessarily been introductory and general, but in the larger work of political science the goal is the achievement of an exact, precise, rigorous knowledge bound together by general theory.

Perhaps the best way to begin understanding what political scientists do is to consider the way in which they test their knowledge by linking it to the evidence of political reality. An initial element in doing "empirical research" is to develop ideas which can be defined in terms of the evidence; these are referred to as "operational concepts." For example, if we were to define political participation as "activity directed toward influencing public decisions," our concept might be informative and accurate but not operational. To operationalize the concept we would define it in such a way as to be able to identify exactly when participation is or is not occurring by looking at people's behavior. If we are studying a population and wish to sort out those who participate in politics from those who do not, we might want to define participation as consisting of attendance at political meetings, contribution of time or money to a political campaign, membership in a political group, and/or attempts to change the political attitudes of friends or associates. Employing the concept in this way, exact information can be collected about the activities of the people in our population, through public records or actually questioning them directly, and the amount of participation going on in the group can be determined with considerable precision and reported quantitatively. It may be discovered that 15.5 percent of the group has contributed time or money to a campaign or that 6 percent has attended a political meeting.

This process of exact, statistical description of phenomena is a basic building block of political science, and it reflects the typical approach to the accumulation of much knowledge about what is going on in politics. But the larger purpose of political science is to find out not only what is going on but why—that is, not merely to describe political experience but to explain it. In the study of participation, for example, we may wish to know why some people get involved in politics and others do not or why those who get involved do so in different ways. Lest we get the impression that the scientific enterprise is dry and

mechanical, we should appreciate that such questions demand judgment and imagination. Here the facts will not speak for themselves, and
it is incumbent upon the scientist to create possible explanations for
testing. These possible explanations, called *hypotheses,* are formulated
by examining the range of factors that might serve as explanations. This
process is necessarily subjective and selective; speculation about likely
explanations should rest on general familiarity with the subject matter
and may derive from general theories. It may be hypothesized that
people who participate more are better educated or more socialized
into the norms of good citizenship or more influenced by the political
stakes in question. In formulating concepts and hypotheses a number
of factors may actually have to be taken into account; no single type of
behavior will define participation and no single element explain it.
Groups, patterns, or clusters of factors will be looked for.

Once formulated, the hypothesis requires testing against evidence. In
some scientific activity this testing is done through experimentation. In
an experiment the scientist recreates under controlled conditions in a
laboratory the situation he is trying to explain. If the scientist wants to
test how particular diseases are caused in a type of animal, he can bring
the animal into the laboratory and expose it to those agents which he
has hypothesized cause the disease. The value of the laboratory experiment is not only that cause and effect can be so carefully manipulated
but that the effects produced are themselves controlled and insulated
from the real world, thus providing the scientist with the ability to
tamper with nature without changing it. From this derives one of the
frequent devices of popular fiction, the mad scientist creating mon-
strous potions and beasts in his hidden laboratory surrounded by an
unsuspecting community. But not all science uses experimentation or
is veiled in the mystique of the laboratory. Astronomy and geography
are exceptions and so is political science. These scientific activities, by
the nature of their enterprise, study the world primarily by going out
into the world and replacing work in the laboratory with work in the
field. The attractions of the laboratory have still been strong, however,
and even political science has tried to study some behavior through
controlled reconstruction of situations. The use of games and simula-
tions is an example of this. A group of individuals is brought together,
assigned specific roles to play or given a particular task, and provided
with certain ground rules. The game might involve the "players" as
members of a legislative body or voting population or party convention.
The activities they engage in are intended to reveal something about
the real world.

Despite such attempts at experimentation, the practice of political
science necessarily draws one into the field, that is, into the observation
of politics itself where events cannot be so easily manipulated or effects

controlled. From the complex and intricate array of human relationships and the maze of interconnected events, the political scientist must
ferret out explanations. He needs to test his hypotheses by finding out
which events are connected and which are not. This sorting out and
analysis proceed by controlling certain factors, not by using the boundaries of the laboratory but by manipulating the data that are collected.
For example, the political scientist will seek correlations among events
that follow a certain pattern. Voting is a type of behavior that follows
a pattern; it is an act that is replicated by large numbers of people all
doing the same thing—making a decision—at the same time, by choos-
ing among the same alternatives—the ballot. What does one's vote
correlate with? In other words, what characteristics of the voting population will best distinguish those who vote Republican versus those who
vote Democratic? Age, economic status, party affiliation of parents? An
empirical study can show what traits best explain the vote for different
parties. If it reveals that there is a higher ratio of blacks voting for one
of the parties but that people of higher socio economic status tended
to vote for one party and people of lower status tended to vote for
another, regardless of race, it would indicate that one's wealth and
social status better explain one's voting decision. By examining a variety
of statistical information about people it is possible to provide an exact
picture of the inclination of a voting population. A good measure of the
effectiveness of such analysis is the fact that national elections in the
United States can now be predicted with great accuracy, and the skills
of the trained voting analyst are in great demand by the contemporary
politician.

There are certain tools that are depended upon to be able to make
such a precise analysis. Survey research, one of the more commonly
used tools, involves the carefully designed questioning of those people
being studied. Since the group of people being studied may be so large
as to make it impossible to survey all of them, it is necessary to draw
a sample of people from the larger population. There are statistical
techniques that insure as close a resemblance as possible between the
sample and the population from which it is drawn. The design of the
questionnaire administered to this sample is guided by the questions
the investigator is asking, the need to generate answers in a form that
can be handled statistically (what students like to call "objective questions"), and the need to get the most direct and frank response. Thus,
there are innumerable practical skills required of the political re-
searcher: the framing of hypotheses, the designing and administering
of questionnaires, the selection of a good sample, the statistical analysis
of the resulting data, and the use of computers for the managing and
computation of such information.

The actual tactics and mechanics of inquiry—concept formation, hypotheses, testing, data gathering, statistical analysis—represent a technical and sophisticated body of knowledge in their own right. The point of our brief observations is to refer to these tactics only as examples of the kind of thing that the political scientist sets out to do. Yet they can also help reveal certain characteristics and problems of the scientific enterprise. For example, science assumes that events follow discernible patterns and that these patterns can be rendered as laws or principles that explain phenomena. It might be quite difficult to explain or predict my vote or your vote, but it is not nearly as difficult when dealing with the pattern of votes among thousands or millions of people. One result of this is that the precision and exactness of the scientific analysis of politics are greater when studying similar forms of behavior among large numbers of people. The precision of science is most challenged by events that are less routine and patterned, such as the outbreak of riots, revolution, or the influence of a specific political leader. It should not be surprising that the most sophisticated application of scientific techniques has occurred in connection with such things as mass voting behavior. This leads, in turn, to the further observation that the political scientist must be prepared to develop and adapt his methods of investigation to the subject matter he is studying and the kinds of questions he is asking. Precise statistical conclusions are highly valued in science, but they do not define what science is and they may not be possible under some conditions. It is the systematic and rigorous analysis of empirical propositions that is the mark of a scientific approach even where strictly quantified results are not possible. Another way of putting it is that the questions that are asked define the scientific enterprise more than the kinds of answers that are produced. The mechanics of science are not ends in themselves but means to an end. They should be looked upon as tools and resources, not as limitations on inquiry.

Another attribute of science is that it is highly analytical, that is, it approaches its subject by breaking it down into its component parts and examining each part separately, thereby producing specialized bodies of knowledge. It is further analytical in carefully distinguishing the various elements of the discrete events or behavior under investigation. Scientific knowledge can be broken down into very fine areas of study, making refined treatment of a subject more manageable. Specialized bodies of literature and research can be found on American voting behavior, childhood political socialization, roll-call votes in the House of Representatives, the recruitment of party leaders, and the formation of coalitions on the Supreme Court. The reason for the analytical quality of science is its dependence on inductive knowledge—knowledge derived from direct observation. The world of political experience is vast, and inductive knowledge requires drawing our attention to some part of it, to focusing in on one aspect of it, a specific political system, function, institution, or process.

Beyond the fine analysis of politics and the mechanics of testing particular ideas, science also involves a synthesizing and pulling together of knowledge. The ultimate objective of science is the development of general theory, the reduction of phenomena to the simplest and most efficient general explanation, not unlike Newton's famous laws of motion. Though empirical science should be firmly grounded in evidence, the culmination of scientific inquiry is found in highly abstract theoretical constructions. The search for a comprehensive scheme for explaining political experience that is reasonably simple, clean, and all-encompassing has produced such results as general systems theory, discussed earlier. Though competing general theories in political science may differ in the emphasis they place on particular approaches—stressing perhaps a psychological, environmental, or institutional approach—in one form or another, the "systems" idea has dominated contemporary Western political science. It is important to understand that in judging the worth of such theories it is misleading to think of them as either true or false. The relevant issue is not whether a theory is true but whether it is good, and it is a good theory if it is useful to us. Like statistics and survey methods, a theory is a kind of tool also; it is supposed to do a particular job for us. The theoretical enterprise should not be looked upon as an attempt to discover *the* theory that will explain all but to create good theories that do their job. Theories are always open to alteration, refinement, and, at times, scientific revolution analogous to those in the political realm. Theories thus constitute definite points of view, selective ways of examining reality and determining what is important and what is not.

Aside from the more comprehensive explanatory value of general theory, there are other particular functions theory performs in the scientific enterprise. First, it functions as a kind of map directing the political scientist to the kinds of data that are most important. If we are trying to explain the decision of a legislative body, systems theory directs our attention to the kinds of demands and supports impinging on the legislators or to the possible feedback effect of other decisions and actions. A different theory might direct us in a different way. Classical theory often took a teleological approach to explaining politics, which means, roughly, that it explained events or actions in terms of the ends to which they were moving. Teleologically, man was defined as a "rational animal" not because people always acted rationally but because the full development of rational powers was understood to be the characteristic end to which human nature was drawn. From such a theoretical perspective as this, inquiry into political behavior would draw our attention to very different kinds of data—perhaps an investigation of the political values and goals of political leaders. The point is that we do not look for relevant information by aimlessly wandering about political experience but by employing a theoretical perspective of some sort that helps tell us where to look.

Second, in a similar way theory assists in formulating hypotheses to be tested. Again, though imagination and perceptiveness are required, this is not a random, purely hit-and-miss process. Theories suggest the kinds of explanations that should work in regard to a particular area of investigation. Our theoretical point of view regarding revolutions would lead us to seek explanations for revolutionary activity not in the objective conditions of people's lives but in the relative deprivation that they experience. Our theoretical point of view concerning political roles would lead us to formulate hypotheses about an individual's socialization. Finally, theory ties together the analytically disparate elements of scientific investigation. We might say that where research analyzes, theory serves to synthesize. Each discrete area of investigation must be put into a larger context in order to explore its full meaning. The process of analysis makes somewhat artificial distinctions for reasons of necessity and convenience, but while we isolate parties, individuals, institutions, or specific policies for purposes of study, we cannot ignore their actual connection with the rest of the political system. It is the relationship between specific analysis and the larger framework of theory that makes this connection for us.

Some mention should be made of two interrelated disputes that have been much at the forefront of contemporary political science. One concerns whether or not the discipline of political science is actually objective and value free, and the other concerns the extent to which the discipline should be directed toward the influence of public affairs. In recent years it has become increasingly popular to argue that the traditional idea of scientific objectivity, in which the scientist supposedly is able to examine the world without reference to his own values and political outlook as a citizen, is a dangerous myth. Such objectivity cannot be achieved realistically, and the perpetuation of the idea that it can be will only mislead people about the meaning and significance of scientific results. Beyond the psychological impossibilities of preventing one's biases from creeping into professional research, it is argued that the very concept of objectivity is itself quite meaningless. It derives from the mistaken notion that reality is completely external to and unaffected by the person studying and observing it and that truth results from the observer's directly formulating in his mind ideas that conform to this reality. However, the very processes of inquiry and reflection involve the observer's imposing his own subjective way of thinking on the thing he is studying; the very choice of a theory involves a somewhat subjective judgment that the theory is valuable. If these charges are true—and to a great extent I think they are—there is no cause therefore to throw science out the window. More important than trying to fulfill the unrealistic expectations of the mythical "neutral observer" is honestly appraising the limits and the possibilities of science and being rigorously conscious and responsive to the kinds of subjective intellectual commitments it does demand. As the American philosopher John Dewey correctly observed many years ago, the modern fascination with science has perhaps placed too great a stress on the value of absolute certitude, science being viewed as the way to certain knowledge and certain knowledge being the only kind that is worth anything. The scientist was more than happy to try to meet this cultural need. But in a practical sense, if man limited himself to knowledge that was objectively certain he would not know very much and would certainly limit his usable store of knowledge. Ultimately man's quest for knowledge is not determined by the rules and methods of science but by his practical need for knowledge, and the role of science ought to be defined by the attempt to meet this need as effectively as possible. The objective is not to see how scientific we can be but to see how intelligent we can become, a task for which science ought to be a superb tool.

This issue naturally leads to the second, the relationship between political science and the world of public affairs. If we were to accept the simplistic view of scientific objectivity, it would seem that the political scientist could tell the politician about how politics works but could not tell him what to do politically. The latter issue brings into play the values of the politician and goes beyond the enterprise of science. Here intellectuals have always been caught on the horns of a dilemma. At the same time that they understandably feel their accomplishments should be of some worth to society, they wisely fear the prospect of politics exploiting science and interfering with the pure search for truth. Conversely, political actors are not always comfortable with the role of the intellectual. The citizen becomes justifiably impatient with the contradictions among government reports all prepared by "experts." Citizens and politicians have their own worries about the extent to which the influx of science seems to remove power from their hands into the hands of unelected experts. It is also not altogether comforting to reflect on the political uses of science, such as Hitler's attempt to muster scientific support for his claims about the inferiority of Jews. Thus, going all the way back to the warnings of the ancient Greek philosopher Plato, there has been an uncomfortable relationshp between intellectual and political pursuits.

I do not propose any solution to this long-standing problem but I think it does provide insight into an important aspect of politics: information and knowledge are themselves vital forms of power in society. (It may be this above all else that makes the neutrality of science illusory.) An important question is what types of research government will spend its money on, i.e., what kinds of problems will it want science to solve for it? The answer to this question will greatly affect the mobilization of resources and talent in the scientific community and the priorities of scientists themselves. One must certainly wonder whether the proliferation of experts in military strategy, nuclear deterrence, and "war gaming" as opposed to the methods of pacifism is really the result of cool academic detachment from the pressures of politics. Having a certain kind of knowledge, the kind that politicians want, is a vehicle for personal influence and being able to manage the distribution of knowledge is a lever of political control.

These are serious problems, but they need not pervade our more ordinary experiences with political science. Taking science down from the pedestal on which modern society has tried to put it, we can begin to appreciate it as a commonplace set of methods by which we develop an understanding of reality. It is an exacting activity but it need not be mysterious. Much of what we have done in this book is an initial exercise in political science, a review of the kinds of questions that are asked and the kinds of approaches taken.

## IDEOLOGY

Political thinking is aimed not only at the scientific understanding of political experience but at the effective practice of politics itself. Science, as we saw, presumes to be value free and is not intended to direct the individual as to what he should do in politics. Scientifically derived information can be very useful in making decisions and choices, but it cannot by itself dictate those decisions. Science can be said to be conditional—if you do $x$, then $y$ should follow—but it is not in a position to conclusively determine that you should choose or not choose $x$. Science should reveal cause and effect; it should yield explanations; it should be able to give us some fair idea of what the results of our actions *will* be, but it cannot tell us how to do politics or what our objectives or goals *should* be. But this need for direction and purpose in politics, the need for norms to guide behavior, is also the object of political reflection and thinking. In the contemporary world the systems of political thought that fulfill this need are called ideologies.

A shorthand definition of *ideology* might be "an applied system of political beliefs." The definition suggests that ideologies are more than just casual opinions or assorted feelings about politics, but political beliefs that follow a more or less coherent or logical pattern. It further identifies the most distinctive trait of ideologies as forms of political thinking—that they are "applied" beliefs, that is, beliefs directly related to political goals and actions. One other characteristic that might be added is that ideologies are forms of *social* belief; their significance and influence depend on widespread social promotion of and adherence to them. A more technical definition of ideology which sums up some of these points is offered by Willard Mullins:

> ... I would define ideology as a logically coherent system of symbols which, within a more or less sophisticated conception of history, links the cognitive and evaluative perception of one's social condition—especially its prospects for the future—to a program of collective action for the maintenance, alteration or transformation of society.[2]

That is a rather imposing description for what is actually the most familiar form of political thinking, for in speaking of ideologies we are speaking of doctrines that have become the common currency of modern politics: communism, liberalism, socialism, conservatism, nationalism. Ideological ideas represent the one form of political thought that the average person is most likely to encounter; it likely constitutes one's initial consciousness of political values and beliefs.

Ideologies serve two practical functions in our political experience: a knowledge function and a value function. By the knowledge function we mean that ideologies provide people with practical frameworks of thought that guide their everyday comprehension of politics. Without some such framework for organizing his thoughts, the average man would see in politics only a senseless and incoherent sequence of events, but equipped with an ideological point of view he comes to politics with a set of categories, concepts, and principles that give shape, form, and meaning to his observations of reality. The concept of a "Cold War" as a description of international relations after World War II was just such an ideological point of view. According to the Cold War concept, relations among nations were dominated by the struggle between two great superpowers, the United States and the Soviet Union, and international incidents were to be appraised in terms of their effect upon this larger struggle. For many people the function of the Cold War doctrine was to assist them in making sense out of what was happening in foreign affairs by relating events to the general scheme of struggle in the world. In much the same way the doctrine of capitalism directs people to see in economic relations the competition and interaction of various economic interests in a free market, while the doctrine of socialism draws attention to the underlying class differences in society as the explanation of political and economic forces. In short, people not professionally engaged in the pursuits of political science or political philosophy gain a significant practical grasp of what is going on in politics mainly through reliance on an ideology.

The value function of an ideology consists of the norms and values it provides as ethical guides to action. Ideology helps answer for the individual questions about what government should be doing for him, what his own political objectives are, what behavior is allowed in politics and what is not. Democratic ideology, for example, tells of the importance of tolerating divergent political opinions, of the value of individual freedom from government constraint, rule under law, and the opportunity to influence government decisions. Thus, democratic ideology provides people with the norms by which they go to the polls and vote in elections—peaceably accepting the results—express their concerns about government through contacts with public officials, and openly criticize the government.

The point of view taken here is that the use of ideologies is a perfectly ordinary part of political experience and that, in fact, anyone who engages in politics to any significant extent most likely has developed some ideological bearings in his thinking. But this is not a universally accepted point of view and we often encounter the use of the term *ideology* to refer to unhealthy or perverse forms of political consciousness. According to this view, belief in an ideology makes one dogmatic, intolerant, and doctrinaire; the ideologue is concerned solely with the perfection and application of abstract principles to the exclusion of any appreciation for practical politics. It is further argued that ideology is the cause of fanatical political movements like revolutionary Marxism and fascism, and the cause of irreconcilable polarization and violence. Ideology is seen as a dangerous and harmful force in politics as embodied in the anarchist, the Fascist dictator, the bomb thrower, and the terrorist. Though much of this characterization points to legitimate political dangers, it is mistaken in pinning the responsibility on ideology as such. Our position is that ideologies may become fanatical and dangerous but that there is nothing inherent in the idea of ideologies that means that it must be this way. What the critics are talking about is not ideology as such but certain types of ideology that are adhered to in certain ways, and their criticism should best be directed toward certain personality types or specific systems of belief. Fascism is a fanatical and rigid doctrine not because it is an ideology but because it is fascism, whereas one of the main supports for the relatively moderate brand of politics in the United States is the very widespread belief in the ideology of liberal democracy.

Perhaps one explanation for such a critical attitude toward ideologies is the feeling that they represent beliefs only slightly removed from the realm of mere opinion and are lacking in any method of verification or standards of truth such as those found in the realms of science and philosophy. Ideologies are accepted and disseminated through social-ization and propaganda; they are forms of mass political beliefs, not the product of intellectual reflection but of the need for popular political ideas. Ideas that cannot be tested and judged cannot be controlled. However, though the average citizen may not acquire or test his ideas in the same manner as the professional theorist, this does not mean that ideologies are merely elaborated opinions. They can be evaluated as more or less logical and coherent, as more or less accurate in their picture of reality, and as promoting more or less worthwhile political values. There are also practical grounds for testing them; any ideology ought to be held accountable for the conditions it produces. Does the Stalinist dictatorship reveal a flaw in the doctrines of Marxism? Did the historical plight of blacks in America attest to a weakness in liberal democratic principles? Again, ideologies should not be viewed as inher-ently rational or irrational; this will depend on the behavior of the people who adopt and promote them.

It is a curious feature of ideologies that in historical terms they are relatively new. The very term *ideology* was only coined in the late eighteenth century by the French thinker Destutt de Tracy, and the popular belief systems that are encountered throughout modern poli-tics are no more than a couple of hundred years old at the most. This observation would seem to be in conflict with the view that ideological thinking is a characteristic of politics in general. Perhaps more accu-rately it should be said that all politics requires a system of operating beliefs and values and that ideology constitutes the modern form such beliefs take. This naturally leads to the question of why ideologies ap-peared in history. The general explanation for this has to do with the very character of modern politics, the main feature of which is the inclusion of increasing numbers of people into politics. Prior to the modern age, politics was an activity strictly marked off for a narrow, closed elite in society. The mass of average men and women, if they were conscious of their relationship to government at all, saw them-selves as mere subjects. By virtue of a number of factors—increase in literacy, the demise of feudal aristocracy, industrialization, the rise in the general standard of living, urbanization—modern society became what has been called a *mass society*. The greater inclusion of the masses into politics does not mean that society became more democratic, though democracy has been related to the growth of mass society. It means that the mass of average citizens became a political force that would have to be dealt with in whatever form of government developed. Whether by independent action or by having their allegiance contested over by competing elites, the mass of average citizens in the modern state have become an integral factor in modern politics. One sign of this development is the appearance of the political party, which is not so much a peculiarly democratic institution as it is a peculiarly modern one. The political party is a device by which the mass of citizens is organized for political purposes, and it is found in modern dictatorships as well as modern democracies.

The development of ideology, like the appearance of political parties, is another result of mass politics. In the aristocratic politics of feudal Europe, operative beliefs and values reflected the political consciousness of a distinct, closed class which thought alike, passed its ideas down from generation to generation with a reassuring continuity, and rooted its thinking in the permanent principles of theology. Contention over differing political beliefs occurred only among members of the small, educated elite and was ultimately subjected to the settlement of some proper authority. But with the coming of mass politics, beliefs now had to be tailored to mass consumption and use. If the average man was to partake of politics, if his loyalty was to be won and his energy mobilized for action, he also needed a framework of principles and values. It is the development of competing ideologies in modern politics that serves this vital function; ideological persuasion becomes an essential political tool.

Along with the rise of mass society there is a closely related factor in the appearance of ideology. With the coming of the modern age political thinking becomes increasingly independent of other realms of thought, particularly religion. Political ideas are no longer merely derived intellectually from the higher reaches of philosophy and theology; they take on a life and meaning of their own and they both derive from and shape the world of action. In this sense ideology is a part of one of the most pervasive new outlooks of the modern age—the notion that the problems of social organization can be solved through the application of rational ideas. At the end of the Middle Ages, the birth of modern natural science opened up great areas of discovery and invention capable of changing the quality of people's lives. This led to the powerful new idea that man could put an end to the perpetual turmoil, instability, hardship, and injustice that he saw around him in society by a similar application of human intelligence that was concrete, practical, and unfettered by the myths and dogmas of the past. This produced numerous attempts to change or reform society through the spread of ideas, of new ways of thinking that had both a scientific soundness about them and what Mullins has called a "program of collective action." This included assorted socialists, communists, and democrats all offering popular accounts of the inherent principles of the political order and each proclaiming rational or scientific grounds for their visions. It is ironic that while we see science and ideology as opposed forms of thinking today, ideology was initially understood as the applied arm of science in the service of social man.

The following review covers some of the major ideologies that have appeared in the modern period and shaped political experience.

## Liberal Democracy

The guiding political value in liberal thought is the freeing of individual enterprise and energy from the restrictions of government. Liberalism portrays society as an amalgam of more or less independent, self-reliant individuals who join together in political association only for the limited purpose of basic governmental services, protection of individual rights, and the orderly resolution of conflict among divergent social interests. Government is thought of as the creation of a contract among citizens, and public authority is embodied not in the majority but in the rule of law. The government's tampering with individual decisions and the private affairs of citizens is looked upon as an interference with natural rights and natural relationships among people. One such natural set of relationships is that of buyer and seller operating in an open market regulated by the laws of supply and demand, and liberalism defends free-enterprise capitalism as the economic system most in line with its political views.

The central objective of liberalism is the avoidance of tyranny, of the arbitrary use of government power. This is accomplished by limiting the overall powers of government in the first instance through explicit legal restrictions (the constitution and its subsequent legal embellishment) and through allowing sufficient power to reside in the private sector outside government. It is further accomplished by fragmenting those powers that are given to government in such a way that it will be difficult for the powers of government to be consolidated in the hands of any one group or individual. The avoidance of tyranny is preserved by the free-wheeling interplay of countervailing political forces. Individuals and minority groups are afforded the opportunity of influencing governmental decisions, and politics typically takes the form of bargaining and compromise among opposing interests.

For the liberal, justice is considered "justice under law"—all people are to be treated equally in the eyes of the law and in their relationship to the state and the bureaucracy. In addition to legal equality, the liberal also defends the principle of equal opportunity, by which people are to have the same chance to pursue their personal objectives. Liberalism limits itself to these conceptions of equality and does not contend that people are necessarily equal in ability, intelligence, ambition, or personal drive nor that they need to end up the same in their accomplishments. The reason for this is the commitment to individual freedom which, it is assumed, will necessarily bring about some degree of unequal achievement. Thus, actual social and economic inequality is to some degree looked upon as the consequence of a free society. As in any ideology, the general framework of thought is open to differences in specific interpretation and application, and liberals will typically debate what is required to insure equal opportunity, how individual rights should be protected, what rights are more important than others, and the extent to which the maintenance of freedom may actually require the direct intervention of government.

Liberal ideology developed throughout Europe and North America, but has been most influential in Anglo-American countries. It is one of the oldest of modern ideologies having its philosophical roots in the seventeenth and eighteenth centuries and serving at the forefront of the early modern struggle against aristocratic privilege. Its greatest appeal has been in economically strong capitalist societies having a fairly large middle class. As in any ideology that has endured for some time, there have been adaptations and adjustments in liberal beliefs over the years both to refine the ideology and meet changed historical circumstances. For example, traditional liberalism had always been intensely individualistic, whereas contemporary liberals recognize that people do not relate to government or participate in politics as lone individuals but as members of groups within the society and that politics is really a struggle among various organized group interests. Another adjustment in liberal thinking involves a changed conception of the proper role of government. Originally, liberal doctrine perceived government to be the main threat to individual freedom and went to great lengths to control governmental power, yet more recently it has become apparent that the government may often be used as an ally of the individual in the defense of his rights against their infringement by powerful interests outside government. The civil rights movement in the United States represents a case of the application of liberal values

—right to vote, nondiscrimination in public accommodation and employment—mainly through appealing to government for effective enforcement of laws. Such alterations help show how ideology can adjust
to political reality.

## Radical Democracy

Also called *direct* or *participatory democracy*, radical democracy
places greater stress on the collective power of the people to govern
than on limited government and the balance of private interests. The
radical democrat looks at political association not as a mere aggregate
of individuals with divergent interests but as a community of citizens
each of whom contributes to the definition and pursuit of the public
good. The citizens are bound together not merely by the formalities of
legal obligation but by a shared sense of public values and purposes. The
people, it is argued, ought to be able to govern as directly as possible,
and government ought to be designed in a simple and straightforward
manner so that the average man can comprehend it. Given the proper
conditions envisioned by the radical, strict majority rule should serve
for the making of public policy and the basis of public authority. Thus,
the radical rejects the liberal idea of limited government on the
grounds that since the people are the government, to limit government
is to limit the popular will. So also the liberal balancing of interests is
thought of as interfering with the operation of majorities. The radical
design of government stresses the preeminent position of popular assemblies and rejects the notion that their power should be checked by
less democratic institutions, such as the courts.

Radicals necessarily must promote a broader concept of equality than
liberals, for direct popular rule would be endangered among a population with vast differences of wealth, education, and social position. Radicalism also assumes a certain homogeneity of outlook among the
citizens if the majority is going to be able to effectively give voice to the
public interest. For these reasons radical democracy may bear a certain
resemblance to socialist doctrines discussed below. For all his stress on
equality and the importance of the public interest, the radical does not
ignore the issue of freedom. Individual liberty beyond the range of
public concerns is still defended, though the radical adds to this a
somewhat different conception of freedom. Freedom is not thought of
as a condition of being unrestrained from action, which can be achieved
by government merely leaving you alone; it is thought of as a positive
ability or power to act. Thus it is the very principle of popular rule
which provides people with political freedom; they are free because

they can govern themselves, because political power has been put in the service of popular needs.

Radical democracy has had some influence in almost all Western democracies. It also appeared fairly early, and was a prominent force in France at the time of their revolution in 1789. Its modern philosophical origins are often attributed to people like Jean Jacques Rousseau in France and Thomas Jefferson in the United States. Radical democratic ideology in the United States has appeared in the form of the traditional New England town meeting, the Populist movement, and the call for "participatory democracy" by the student movement of the 1960s. The modern influence of radicalism has been limited by the fact that it is not well suited to the political realities of the large nation-state in which the practical problems of effective direct popular rule are insurmountable. Radical ideology is naturally tailored for small-scale political units, which is why, in its purest form, it has appeared mainly as a doctrine in support of "local control" and had only marginal influence on the organization of national politics. But even at the national level, radical thought has had some measurable effect on institutional design and legal principles and practices.

## Socialism and Communism

Because of their close affinity, these two ideological systems are treated together, though they cover a very broad part of the ideological spectrum. Socialism is the more general term, and communism may be viewed as a more specific version of socialism. Where democratic ideology begins with the assumption of self-reliant, rational individuals willfully shaping their own destiny, socialism begins with the assumption that people are the product of their environment and accumulated experiences. You cannot improve conditions of life merely by handing power over to people and leaving them to their own devices. Indeed, the attempt to do this has turned liberal democracy into an elaborate justification for a system in which the potential of human beings is stifled and economic competition becomes destructive. The socialist argues that human beings are creatures of society; society makes them what they are by creating the conditions under which people grow, develop, and learn, and by defining the legal, economic, and political boundaries of their capabilities. For the socialist, this explains the incongruity of political and legal rights existing side by side with poverty, injustice, and economic oppression. Early socialists were particularly influenced by the harmful effects of early industrialization which seemed to cause so much human suffering despite the appearance of constitutional democracy.

If people are social beings shaped by the environment that society has created, it is argued that the means of reforming society and bringing real social justice must be found in the conscious, systematic, and organized rearrangement of the conditions under which people live. Society should be purposefully designed and structured so as to create the most favorable circumstances for people to maintain a healthy standard of living and the development of their full human potential, and the state should be the vehicle for accomplishing this. This process of social design should be guided by the application of rational moral principles and a humane understanding of human behavior and needs. The initial pursuit of these ideas was carried out by a diverse assortment of European thinkers known as utopian socialists. The utopians were intrigued with the idea of creating society from scratch along rational, socially cooperative lines, and they actually produced a number of experimental communities. Among the most famous of these early ventures was New Lanark, a community in Scotland founded by Robert Owen and built around a textile mill. Through Owen's personal inspiration it was possible to reorganize the work of the mill in a manner that was healthier, less oppressive, and at the same time more productive. Many such experiments proliferated in Europe and America—including New Harmony, Indiana; Oneida, New York; and Brook Farm, Massachusetts—but what they contributed by way of social innovation they lacked in endurance.

The most influential version of socialism is communism, the principles of which were originally worked out by Karl Marx and Frederick Engels in the nineteenth century. They found socialist ideas appealing, and they agreed that the democratic idea of self-reliant individuals was a harmful myth. They insisted, however, that the patterns of human development be examined according to a rigorous and systematic science of history and that this "scientific socialism," as Engels called it, guide man in bringing about political change. The major determining factor of social and political relationships was the means by which material wealth was produced and distributed. The economic factor determined the fundamental class conflicts that pervaded social life and culture and were so basic to the structure of society that they were altered only through periodic revolution. Ideologically, the communists set about the task of trying to convince workers that any significant alteration of their condition of life required the overthrow of capitalism and the rejection of the doctrines of liberal democracy which gave support to it. The capitalist had a vested interest in maintaining the existing economic system, and attempts to bring change through the very institutions that he controlled and that had brought him his power would prove futile. Communist ideology aimed not at merely organizing workers to improve their conditions of life but at organizing the working class for the fundamental transformation of society.

In accord with their scientific theory of society and history, the communists' objective is to gain control of government, presumably through revolution, and to use the power of the state to reshape the economic foundations of society. The ideological goal is the achievement of a classless society in which basic economic needs will be met and the material basis of social conflict removed. A critical element in understanding the communist conception of government is the idea of "true and false consciousness." Where democratic ideologies tend to assume that an individual is capable of defining his own interests and goals, communism contends that the lower class in society adopts the outlook and beliefs of the upper class, failing to appreciate that these attitudes are in direct conflict with the real interests of their class. This is described as "false consciousness" on the part of the worker, and it is a state of mind that inhibits him from understanding his class interests. The oppression of the capitalist class, though basically economic, carries over into the realm of ideas and thought as well. Communists argue that an important political task is the achievement of authentic class consciousness on the part of the worker, and that this cannot come about through the liberal device of an open interplay of ideas but only through the exclusive direction by revolutionary elites already possessed of true consciousness. Only by grasping the importance of this ideological position can we make sense of the communist commitment to the one-party state, the intense politicization of education and culture, and the strict limits on political dissent and literary expression.

It should be quite apparent that socialist ideologies have had a tremendous impact on the modern world. Communism itself has become the ruling ideology of such major world powers as the Soviet Union and China and a host of smaller nations in Eastern Europe and various parts of the Third World. Many democracies have Socialist and Communist parties that compete for power in open elections, with varying degrees of success. The socialist concept, broadly defined and variously interpreted, has been an influential ideology in developing nations because of both the socialist ideal of controlled social progress and the fact that the culture and traditions of such countries do not fit as comfortably with the individualism of Western-style democracy. The mixture of democratic methods and socialist objectives has also combined to produce a distinct ideology of "democratic socialism" which is not radically experimental and utopian like early socialism and not revolutionary like communism. Sweden is often pointed to as an example of social democratic principles at work.

## Conservatism

Conservatism is a difficult ideological point of view to pin down, especially since it tends to reject the very idea of a formal worked-out political doctrine. The central theme of conservatism is the idea that the good and just political order results from a careful preservation of a society's traditions. Contrary to popular impressions, the true conservative is not opposed to change but only to abrupt or radical change; he believes that change should consist of a gradual, evolutionary extension and refinement of the past. The conservative is opposed to the presumption of other ideologies that the good society can be rationally designed on paper and created from scratch. Human wisdom is not to be found in the reflections of any single individual or group of individuals but in the accumulated efforts of several generations, and to turn one's back on the past, as the revolutionary does, is to pit the modest dimensions of one's own intellect against the wisdom of the ages. The sound principles of good government are best found in the heritage of generations, and they are most likely to be passed down not by the average man or the majority but by those in society particularly educated in and sensitive to the importance of that heritage. Thus, inherent in conservative ideology is the justification of conservative elites.

One of the accusations that conservative ideology has been open to is the charge that it deals with matters of form without regard to content. In other words, conservatism may defend tradition without regard to the quality or character of the tradition itself. In this way it is possible to speak of conservatives in the Soviet Union as well as conservatives in the United States; any political system or ideology can be supported in a conservative manner if it happens to constitute the prevailing tradition in the particular situation, whether it be monarchy, democracy, or communism. Since conservatism is relative to the particular political context in which it arises, an American, British, Chilean, and Russian conservative might not find much common basis of political agreement. The strength of conservatism derives from the universal impact of tradition on politics; even revolution can be thought of, from one perspective, as an attempt to establish traditions that will serve into the future. Not surprisingly, the main source of support for conservatism comes from established elites; this attitude initially was given expression in the modern period by those spokesmen of the old regime, like the eighteenth-century Englishman Edmund Burke, who wrote against the increasing waves of revolutionary change. But the appeal of conservatism need not be confined to established elites; it may symbolize a measure of satisfaction with the existing state of affairs and provide a refuge from the challenges and pressures of change for all classes of people in society.

## Nationalism

If there is any ideology that can be said to have dominated the political consciousness of the modern period it would not be democracy or communism but nationalism. The phenomenon of the modern nation-state has necessarily spawned its own supportive ideology which has accompanied, if not outweighed, the impact of other belief systems. Even communism, which traditionally claimed to be internationalist and attacked the nation-state as an outgrowth of capitalism, has succumbed to the pressures of nationalist thinking and action. In a broad sense, nationalism may simply refer to feelings of loyalty to and identity with one's country; it is an expression of the feeling of political community at the national level, also called *patriotism* or *chauvinism*. In a more formal, ideological sense nationalism is a doctrine which contends that the purposes and goals of the nation-state transcend in importance the goals of private individuals and groups in society and that the nation should become an object of political loyalty greater than loyalty to group, class, or self.

For nationalists, the state is viewed as the concrete expression of the values and ideals of a national community. The consolidation of nation and state is vital to the maintenance of political life, and a nation or a state existing without the other is an aberrant condition. The impact of nationalist thinking helps explain not only the drive for independent statehood on the part of populations that view themselves as distinct national groups but also the pressures the state applies to stamp out loyalties to ethnic or cultural groupings that may threaten allegiance to the nation. The greatness of the nation-state is defined in terms of its power, its ability to preserve itself, and its ability to expand its control. In relation to other nations in the world, one's country is considered absolutely sovereign and incapable of surrendering any authority or control to another country or supranational entity (such as an international organization). Because of its stress on the unity of the state and the nation, the stronger nationalism becomes the more opposed it is to those ideologies, such as democracy and communism, which legitimize or encourage the surfacing of social conflict. Internal conflict is inherently dangerous to the strength and unity of the state, and nationalist thinking therefore tends to work in support of the interests of established elites who articulate national goals and are looked upon as having overcome the enticements of personal rewards for dedicated service to the state. Nationalist thinking surfaces particularly during wartime, when the nation is being directly threatened, when political unity is critical to the military venture, and when the average man is being called upon to give his life for his country.

With the consolidation of the modern nation-state in the nineteenth century, there developed an identifiable body of nationalist writing by such figures as Giuseppe Mazzini in Italy and Heinrich von Treitschke in Germany. In the twentieth century there has been a tremendous swelling of nationalism not only in the form of fascist fanaticism but as a result of the large-scale proliferation of nation-states produced by the efforts of decolonization in Asia and Africa. The intensity and scale of international warfare in the past one hundred years have also functioned as both cause and effect of nationalist thinking.

## Fascism

Fascism is the newest ideological movement for, though it builds on certain political beliefs and attitudes with deep historical roots, it does not appear as an identifiable ideology until after World War I. Fascism may be thought of as a fanatical extension and embellishment of nationalism committed to the worship of nationalistic values, the leadership of a heroic dictator, and the rigid and militant imposition of hierarchical order on society. Fascism is thought of as an extreme manifestation of conservatism, but more precisely it is a reactionary doctrine which is not interested in harnessing and controlling the forces of change but in reacting against them by employing a romantic appeal for the restoration of society's past periods of triumph and greatness. It is this that the fascist has in mind in claiming a support for spiritual values over the crass materialism of other ideologies.

Fascist ideology is characterized by a peculiar conception of state organization, adopted from classical political thought, called *organicism*. According to the organic theory of the state, political association is characterized by a type of unity analogous to that found in biological organisms. In other ideologies the whole (the state) is a mere artificial aggregate of parts (individuals, groups, classes) and the parts have a certain significance or self-sufficiency independent of the whole. Accordingly, the problem of politics has been defined as a problem of maintaining a particular kind of just order in the face of inherent human conflict. The fascists, however, imagined that the component parts of society should be so organized that they are not in conflict but mutually supportive of each other, just like the parts of the human body. Agriculture, industry, education, the arts, and numerous other functional divisions within society involve no more inherent mutual struggle than do the heart, arms, kidneys, and head of our bodies. Carrying the analogy further, they observed that as in an organic system, the value and significance of any single part could be understood only in its relationship to the whole; our hand is living and useful not as a separate piece of tissue but as a functional part of the body. The civic duty of the individual was to serve the state through the contribution of his special skill, profession, or form of labor. Political leadership itself was thought of as one such special function with a specific class of people to exclusively perform it. In his memoirs, the former Nazi leader Albert Speer gives us some idea of the impact of this ideological principle on the organization of German society under Hitler's rule:

> The ordinary party member was being taught that grand policy was much too complex for him to judge it. Consequently, one felt one was being represented, never called upon to take personal responsibility. . . .
> Worse still was the restriction of responsibility to one's own field. That was explicitly demanded. Everyone kept to his own group—of architects, physicians, jurists, technicians, soldiers, or farmers. The professional organizations to which everyone had to belong were called chambers (Physicians' Chamber, Art Chamber), and this term aptly described the way people were immured in isolated, closed-off areas of life. The longer Hitler's system lasted, the more people's minds moved within such isolated chambers. If this arrangement had gone on for a number of generations, it alone would have caused the whole system to wither, I think, for we would have arrived at a kind of caste society. The disparity between this and the *Volksgemeinschaft* (community of the people) proclaimed in 1933 always astonished me.[3]

This organic concept helps explain much of the behavior of fascist regimes, including the resort to political violence. Like a diseased or irreparably harmed organ of the body, subversive elements were best dealt with by being destroyed and removed. German propaganda portrayed Jews as "poisonous vermin" infecting the body politic. The organic metaphor further explains one of the singular traits of fascism, the appearance of the personal dictator. Society's unity must be displayed and manifested at the very top of the government structure through the leadership of a single individual. This heroic leader is considered to be possessed of attributes far surpassing those of the average man; his position at the head of the state is destined.

Fascism burst forth as a great political shock wave between the first and second World Wars, its most significant political successes being in Germany and Italy, with somewhat more moderate versions appearing in Spain and Argentina. An important question, given the seemingly bizarre and extremist character of such doctrines, is why they ever arose in the first place and how they were able to mobilize popular support. The absolute ruthlessness and opportunism of fascists cannot be dismissed as an important explanation for their temporary success, but they also needed a population sufficiently receptive to their ideological rhetoric to make their grab for power work. Defeat in war, social and economic disarray and instability, the difficulties of coping with the pressures and insecurities of change, all conspired to create an atmosphere in which fascism could appear to people not as a cruel and irrational ideology but as a source of security and relief from chaos.

## Anarchism

Since all of the various ideologies we have reviewed can be said to have had some impact on the shape of modern politics, it is perhaps worth giving some mention to at least one ideology which, in practical political terms, must be judged a failure. Anarchism might actually be called an antipolitical ideology, for its central principle is that all forms of government are illegitimate since they necessarily rely on the ultimate use of force in order to maintain control. The stereotype of the anarchist in the popular mind is often that of a wild-eyed, crazed radical bent on indiscriminate violence and destruction. There have probably been such types in the colorful history of anarchism, but the typical anarchist is more likely a kind of nonviolent humanist. Ideologically, anarchism bears a certain resemblance to extreme liberalism and utopian socialism. If liberals think of government as a necessary evil, anarchists will agree that it is evil but cannot agree that it is necessary. As with the early socialists, human behavior is considered alterable through changing the circumstances and conditions in which people live; if people are quarrelsome, corrupt, and egotistical it is not the fault of human nature but the fault of the social and political system in which they were made to grow up. Aside from the absence of coercive government, anarchists may disagree widely about the dimensions of the good society and the means of achieving it. Many anarchists believe that relatively sophisticated forms of social organization can be achieved through purely voluntary agreement; others adopt an extreme individualistic attitude toward their relationship to society. Communism is also a form of anarchism in that the ultimate achievement of a classless society is supposed to bring about what they like to call "the withering away of the state."

If the achievement of the anarchist society at anything above the level of a community the size of an extended family has been an elusive vision, anarchist beliefs have nonetheless been a persistent source of dissent against established government. Individual anarchists have, in fact, won a measure of notoriety, such as Mikhail Bakunin, Emma Gold-man, and more recently, the American writer Paul Goodman.

Unlike science and philosophy, ideology is not merely a form of re-flection on political experience but a tool for political action, making ideology itself a part of what we study when we study politics. The political scientist will be interested in what role ideology plays in deter-mining political behavior, in the extent of ideological agreement or disagreement in a particular political system, and in what effect this has on political performance and on the causes for the rise and fall of particular ideologies in history. Ideology is thus a vital link between the world of speculation, theory, and empirical science and the real world of politics itself.

## POLITICAL PHILOSOPHY

If the character of modern culture and education makes the ways of science familiar to most of us, and if ideological consciousness of some sort is an inevitable result of serious political participation, political philosophy is by contrast an alien and exotic mode of political thought. The function of philosophy is restricted neither by the inductive meth-odologies of science nor by the practical political objectives of ideology, and its speculative inquiry into the most basic concepts and ideas of politics removes it from more commonplace forms of political thinking. Yet science and ideology are both, in a sense, rooted in philosophy. The very principles of science rest on certain philosophical theories of knowledge, and any general theory in science is ultimately accepted or rejected on philosophic grounds. The ideologies reviewed above all derive in one way or another from the contributions of political philoso-phers such as John Locke (liberal democracy), Jean Jacques Rousseau (radical democracy), Karl Marx (communism), and Edmund Burke (con-servatism). It should also be pointed out that while the idea of a science of politics has had its ups and downs in Western history and the appear-ance of ideology is relatively recent, philosophy has served as a perma-nent and ongoing tradition of thought and reflection through the ages.

Defining philosophy is a risky and difficult business, the word itself conjuring up images of phlegmatic academics asking ponderous ques-tions having little visible bearing on real life. But one way we can gain an understanding of what philosophy is all about is to think of it as formal inquiry into the meaning of and justification for our basic intel-lectual orientation to the world. All forms of knowledge, no matter how closely tied to scientific verification, proof, or practical application operate on the basis of some "world view," a basic set of assumptions about the nature of reality and the meaning of experience. These world views are adopted and used in various forms of knowledge and fields of study, often without any regular examination of them. This is understandable since only by making some intellectual commitment to such world views is it possible for more ordinary human inquiry and thought to proceed, but when we turn attention to a direct examination of world views themselves we have entered the realm of philosophical investigation. If we look at the scientist again we will see that his methods of inquiry assume a particular viewpoint: that the ideas in our mind are traceable to our encounters with reality through the mediation of our senses and that the meaning and truth of ideas are contained in their correspondence with real sense experience. These assumptions allow the scientific enterprise to go forward as it does, yet these assumptions pose philosophical questions in their own right. Do ideas really only derive from sense data or are there modes and structures of thought that are universal to humanity and inherent in human intelligence? What is the meaning of truth and is it accurately described by the correspondence of idea and sense data? What does an explanation consist of, and what do we mean when we say that one thing causes another?

The role of philosophy can also be understood in somewhat more specific terms. It assists in exploring and clarifying the meaning of concepts. The operationalizing of concepts, discussed earlier, represents only one way in which we attach meaning to our ideas, but there is a broader range of meanings and connotations that concepts may have. People use ideas not only to describe observed reality but to describe unrealized possibilities and give expression to values and preferences. Taking the concept of participation used earlier, the operational definition of it allows us to pin down what we mean by participation when describing what people are actually doing in politics, but we may just as well wish to convey some idea of forms of involvement that have not yet been realized. Those who have spoken of "participatory democracy" do not necessarily mean that we should get more people to vote but that new avenues of participation should be opened up, that we should explore new ways in which people can be involved in the making of public decisions. Used in this way, *political participation* is an abstraction which may or may not correlate with our direct experience but should still be useful as an expression of political intentions, criticism, and values. This abstraction may mean variously that important public decisions should be put to a referendum, that small-scale local communities should be politically organized to control their own destinies, or that citizens ought to be directly consulted about administrative decisions in government that touch their lives. These larger meanings of the term are not established operationally but philosophically, and some such clarification has to occur before dealing with ideas operationally.

If we ask whether or not people are free, the answer would seem to involve at least two stages: first, considering what we mean by freedom when we ask the question (explaining ourselves) and, second, exploring the possible meaning of the term *freedom* itself (philosophical clarification). Indeed, there has been an ongoing philosophical dispute over the meaning of freedom which affects how we answer the question of whether people are free. One point of view, *negative freedom,* claims that freedom occurs where there are no obstacles to a person's speaking or acting as he wishes. Thus, I would say I am free to speak my mind openly, decide whether I want to go to college, or buy the kind of house I want to the extent no one is stopping me from doing these things or putting restraints on me (such freedom is obviously a matter of degree). Political liberty is achieved by removing as many obstacles as possible. *Positive freedom,* in contrast, considers freedom to be not an absence of constraint but a positive ability or capacity to pursue objectives. Accordingly, one might be considered free by virtue of his ability to express himself coherently not merely because no one is stopping him from talking. The achievement of political liberty would thereby consist of insuring that people have the resources that will allow them to realize their greatest potential. In the one case freedom describes a condition in which the individual finds himself; in the other case freedom is an attribute of the person's activity. These different ways of thinking about freedom represent distinct philosophical positions that, in turn, affect our empirical analysis and our ideological evaluation of political freedom. Thus, the problem of determining whether or not people are free is not just a question of how best to operationalize the concept but a question of which philosophical meaning we give it. It is the job of philosophy to explore the issues involved in defining various critical terms we use in politics, such as justice, order, equality, law, power, authority, and citizenship.

Philosophy also provides for the formal investigation of ethical or normative questions raised by our political experience. Why should we obey government? Is it right for government to use force against us? Should people be treated equally? According to what standards or criteria should public decisions be made? And also, that underlying question that has so fascinated and driven political theorists through history: what is the best form of government? In practical terms we turn to ideology to answer many of these questions for us but each of them is also the subject of philosophical scrutiny leading to even more basic questions about the nature of man and of politics.

In addition to providing a world view, a clarification of general ideas, and an exploration of political values, philosophy has also served man in another vital respect. It has been through developments in the realm of political philosophy that man has been able to explore the possibility of alternative ways of organizing political life. Through the activity of philosophy, thinkers have woven models of new and different political systems guided by their sense of the possibilities of human life and unfettered by the immediate concerns of politics in their own day and age. Plato devised a scheme of communal organization under the guidance of the wisest members of society; Aristotle described his "polity" as a system of mixed institutional structures balancing the interests of an active and informed citizenry; John Locke portrayed the rational society as a product of an original agreement or contract among men; and Karl Marx envisioned the beneficent possibilities of a society in which economic class distinctions had been removed. It is this aspect of political philosophy that has led to the popular image of the philosopher as a dreamer with his "head in the clouds." The practical man of action wonders how any of these visions can be taken seriously and how any of these imagined societies actually could be created. But in historical terms this is a very narrow-minded point of view, for much of today's political experience has been shaped by principles and ideas having their origin in philosophical systems worked out in a previous age and criticized by contemporaries as impractical schemes. How many people three or four hundred years ago could have imagined the prospect of successful national systems in which diverse religious beliefs would be freely tolerated, the basic law of the land approved by consent, and the adult population given regular opportunities to elect public officials and even pass laws? The irony of the question is that it is probably difficult for us today to imagine a time when those ideas were only the vision of a small handful of people.

History has a way of making yesterday's ideals today's reality, and it is no idle task to speculate on the yet uncovered and unexplored possibilities of human organization. Thus, one of the important features of philosophical inquiry, beyond being abstract and normative, is that its concern is not limited to immediate political experience, that is, not limited to studying what politics is but what it might be or could be or will be. When thinkers like John Locke a few hundred years ago toyed with the idea that "all men are created equal," they were not saying that people as they knew them were actually equal or that they were being treated as equal. What they were suggesting was the possibility that man could organize society on the assumption that all people *should be* treated as equal, that it would work to so organize society. They were projecting the possibilities of new forms of political life based on different assumptions than were accepted up to that time and on appraisals of the unfulfilled and unrealized capacities of human nature.

One way of familiarizing ourselves with the realm of political philosophy is to look briefly at some of the central issues that have regularly appeared in the development of philosophy and that have defined competing views of political experience. Our objective in doing this is to convey an appreciation of the relevance and impact of the questions raised more than to point out a definitive direction toward answers.

## The Nature of Man

To a great extent our general outlook on politics is influenced by our view of human nature. Is man inherently selfish and egotistical? Is he capable of acting rationally, or is he inclined to follow his impulses? Does he have an inherent sense of right or wrong, or is this imposed on him from without? Is he the product of his own will and effort, or is he the product of his experiences as a social being? The position one takes on these basic questions can have much to do with the kind of political system one feels is possible and justifiable.

In the history of political thought there have been a number of cynical views of human nature portraying man as basically selfish and irrational, enmeshed in the pursuit of self-preservation and gratification of his own emotional wants. One of the more famous such accounts was offered by the English philosopher Thomas Hobbes, who imagined that life outside society would consist of a constant state of warfare among people and an existence which he described as "solitary, poor, nasty, brutish, and short." Politics is thought of as fundamentally a struggle for power; political values and principles of authority and law are mainly devices for holding in check the destructive inclinations of human nature. A variation on this view is the idea that man's nature is two-sided, or dualistic. There is an irrational or emotional side which is in a continuing struggle with the capacity for reason and ethical conduct. In the theories of Plato and some modern conservatives, the difference between these two sides of man's nature corresponds to different personalities or types of people in society. The result is a kind of class theory in which the key to good government consists of properly distinguishing those who have the ability to rule from those who do not and insuring that the leadership of government is put in the hands of the former. Leaders in society are those who, through education, training, birth, or strength of character, have mastered the less noble part of their nature to which average men ordinarily succumb. Cynical views of human nature seem to lead invariably to elitist conceptions of government and to be incompatible with at least the more radical forms of democracy. Politics is relied upon to mitigate the quarrelsome and competitive inclinations of human nature, and this is used to justify not only the rule of elites and the resort to coercion but even, at times, the political imposition of specific systems of belief and the intolerance of misguided "heresies" among the people.

An opposite view, which we have already seen in its ideological version, contends that man is basically good and possessed of a kind of native wisdom and intelligence. Evil and irrationality in the world are interpreted as a corruption of man's nature for which social and political institutions are primarily responsible. Even where a person might be instinctively inclined toward a cooperative style of social relationships, society imposes a variety of economic and legal conditions on him that encourage the individual to look upon others as threats to his own liberty and interests. Thus, the good society is achieved by tapping man's better nature and replacing political relationships based on power and force with the cohesive influence of shared values and ideals. The optimist argues that the ability to organize society in this fashion will diminish the need for highly formalistic, elitist, hierarchical relations and make possible the more radical versions of popular rule.

There are other, more moderate variations of these positions, but this should suffice to show that philosophical disputes over human nature are of no small importance to our view of political life. Is politics an expression of man's basic sociability and goodness or is it a check on his passions? Indeed, you may recall that this book began with just such a dilemma, for the nature of politics was defined in terms of both the pursuit of the public good and the resolution of conflict among different interests. We attempted to blend both positions together, though one's opinion about man might lead to rejecting one outright in favor of the other. Politics is one measure of what we think about human nature.

## The Unity of Political Association

Political association is, by definition, a collectivity of individual persons, but what kind of collectivity is it? In what way is the whole related to its several parts? Is it a natural and total unity of which the individual is merely an extension? Or is it an artificial combination of distinct and independent parts? In the case of the organic theory of the state, promoted by fascists, we saw a rather exaggerated theory of political unity. It is the task of the state, according to such a view, to achieve political perfection by developing a conformity of values, ideals, and behavior. Differences among factions in society are taken to be weaknesses or flaws in the social system, a real deficiency that it is the job of politics to correct. The unity of political life ought to mirror the unity, balance, and coordination in nature itself.

Against this view it has been argued philosophically that the unity of politics is quite different from what we find around ourselves in nature. Politics is an association of individuals who have an integrity of their own aside from their membership as citizens in a state. The state is what Aristotle called a *compound,* by which he meant that politics achieves and should only achieve a partial coordination of individual thought and energy. The drive for an excess of political unity is destructive of politics; indeed, the very reason for the art of politics, with all the accommodation, discussion, joint decision making, and give-and-take that it involves, is to deal with the inevitably partial and limited unity of the political system. Individuality is recognized as a value in its own right which politics should not destroy but actually attempt to preserve and maintain. By any account, political disunity may reach a point where it is positively harmful and a source of great strain on the social system, but the price of stability ought not to be the stifling of human uniqueness. Lest we think that this second position has a natural appeal to us because of our own liberal heritage, we should reflect on the difficulty people experience in tolerating views divergent from their own and the frustration they feel with the apparent lack of decisiveness and leadership when politics is thrown open to all the various factions in the community.

## Freedom versus Determinism

Though the meaning of freedom has been much debated by political philosophers, an even more profound dispute has taken place over the question of whether or not there is such a thing as human freedom at all. In one way or another it has been up to the defenders of freedom to contend that events in the political world are the result of human action, that human will and purpose make a difference. Contrary to this, it has been argued that freedom is only an illusion and that human action is really determined by forces external to and beyond the control of man. The stricter versions of such determinism contend that were man able to sufficiently master his knowledge of man and society, it would be possible to develop a theory capable of predicting human behavior. Incidents that would seem to testify to the presence of freedom operating in the world actually represent a gap in our knowledge of the determining factors acting on man.

One version of determinism, called *dialectics*, portrays the forces acting on our lives as laws of historical development. G. F. Hegel, the German philosopher, formalized this view, which was subsequently adapted by Karl Marx. A highly technical theory, dialectics in essence argues that human history is the product of inherent conflicts within the social system which periodically burst forth in a revolutionary form, transforming society into a new condition with a new set of tensions and conflicts. This pattern of change recurs in history and is guided by principles or laws of human development which point the process in a particular direction. Curiously enough, the end to which this dialectical pattern is supposed to be moving is the realization of freedom, though the processes of historical change are not themselves amenable to free human intervention. Another version of determinism is *behaviorism*, its best known spokesman B. F. Skinner. According to behaviorism, all human action can be explained by reference to stimuli impinging on the person from his environment; we are all the direct products of the conditions under which we have lived and the experiences we have had. Though one's conduct may appear novel or unpredictable, it is only a lack of complete information about the individual and his environment that keeps us from anticipating and accounting for such phenomena. There are various types and degrees of determinism, including attempts to blend the principles of freedom and determinism in the same theory, yet they all represent some challenge to the popular liberal notion of politics as the expression of autonomous human will.

Presumably the effect of this philosophic issue on our view of politics is that if we accept some version of determinism, the achievement of the good political order rests on the discovery of the determining principles shaping our lives. Here determinism encounters some difficulties, for admittedly many people are unaware of such principles and the resulting effect on their behavior. Is their behavior any different from that of the person who *is* aware? If it is not any different, does it matter if they are aware? If it is different, is there some freedom to ignore or run against the grain of such forces? If some significance is attached to special knowledge of the laws of history, is the resulting theory of politics necessarily going to be elitist? Antideterminists argue that man makes the decisive difference in politics and that social and political conditions are what we make of them. But despite the strong appeal of the doctrine of freedom, it is necessary to account for the fact that in practice, the plight of many people hardly seems amenable to change merely through their own efforts and that their own beliefs, values, and behavior reveal the impact of the social milieu in which they live. The doctrine of freedom can also have its harsh side if full moral responsibility is placed on each individual without any recognition of the limits and constraints that he suffers. From this standpoint it has been concluded by some that the poor are poor because of a lack of initiative and that criminals are criminals because of personal flaws in their sense of morality. If there is any truth to determinism, such conclusions place altogether too much weight on the assumption that people are fully in control of their actions or that they are really doing what they want to do.

The problem of freedom is one of the thorniest in political philosophy. What does it mean? Is it real? Can people be made free through politics? Does freedom imply unrealistic responsibilities for the individual? For that matter, do we really desire complete freedom with all that it involves?

## The Basis of Authority

Political man defines standards of right and wrong and applies these standards to the behavior of citizens and the conduct of government. These standards form a system of public authority which, as we have seen, is a crucial element in the design and maintenance of the political system as a whole. But where do these standards come from? Who defines the rules and values that make up public authority?

The philosophical positions taken on such questions are extremely varied, but two general approaches can be identified in the history of Western political thought. First, it has been argued that ethical principles in general are universal and absolute and that the principles of public authority, as a particular aspect of general human ethics, are also common to all cultures and all societies. There is a specific set of true standards for public authority, and the diversity of actual standards in the real world simply attests to the fact that many societies have not discovered the "political good." One function of philosophy is to assist political man in his search for and understanding of universal moral truths. How these universal truths are known is quite another question. One theory is that knowledge of them requires a sufficient exercising of man's rational faculties that they will not be known to everyone but only to those with the wisdom and energy to seek the truth. Yet it has also been argued that these universal ethical truths are somehow ingrained in all of us by nature and that knowledge of them requires only an ordinary amount of reflection and common sense available to everyone. Though the argument in favor of a universal standard for public authority has often been used to justify the exclusive political power of elites, who are presumed to possess insight into such ethical questions, it may also be used to support more democratic theories if it is assumed that such knowledge is not unattainable for the common man.

The contention that the basis of public authority can be discovered in a universal ethical standard has been challenged by the idea that the principles of authority are devised by men themselves out of common agreement. In the modern period this idea has been conveyed by the concept of a "social contract" according to which it is imagined that men existing in a natural condition without any form of social organization create society and a corresponding form of government by entering into a contract or agreement with one another to abide by certain basic rules and recognize certain duties, rights, and responsibilities. Authority is not discovered but it is created and supported by mutual consensus. It will not be surprising if different societies arrive at different forms of the social contract, and political differences from system to system may be viewed as reflections of cultural and historical differences. Taken strictly, this position denies the ability to define a single universal system of political values. Applying this position, we might say that we support the Constitution because it is what our society has historically agreed to, not because it derives from some universal standard. Certain philosophers have explored mixtures of these two positions, such as John Locke, who thought of society as formed out of a social contract but imagined that the sole purpose for entering into the contract was to establish a government that could preserve and protect principles of natural reason known in the natural state but in constant danger of being ignored or violated.

If the first theory runs into the problem of how ethical truths are to be known, the social-contract theory encounters the practical problem of determining how any agreement has taken place. Who has actually consented? When did we ever consent? One answer to this is contained in a somewhat more cynical version of the theory that the basis of authority is relative and conventional. It may be argued that public authority represents a consensus among those in society who are powerful enough to impose their views on the rest. There is an agreement but it is an agreement among the elite requiring only the acquiesence of everyone else. This is the basis for the view that "might makes right."

## SUMMARY

If nothing else, this brief review of some of the questions that have interested political philosophers should show that while politics may appear reasonably comprehensible at first glance, a more penetrating inquiry suggests that in political experience we confront the most basic questions of human values and of man's relations with others in society. This is so because politics is one of the most purely human enterprises we engage in; in its purest form it engages us as acting, thinking, judging, speaking, and creating beings. It is so because of the paradoxes of political experience: the incredible violence and repression that have occurred in its name combined with its central function in creating security and social order; the fear of government as a threat to human freedom combined with the seeming total lack of necessity of dictating how politics should operate. It is so because political experience is critical in determining the rest of our relationships in society—whether they will be free or equal or just—and in making it possible to imagine a future that will not be thoroughly beyond our control.

Finally, it should be pointed out that the argument that any analysis or understanding of the political world is based on some philosophic "world view" also applies to this book. This examination of political experience began with the somewhat presumptuous attitude that a direct and unvarnished account of the basics of politics was going to be presented. But this account, like any other you will read, has its own "world view," its own philosophical slant. Among other things, it is committed to the notion that the state is a compound rather than a total unity, that the political task of man can be understood in reference to the public interest, and that there is such a thing as freedom and one of the places we should find it is in the activity of politics. What has been presented is not merely an operational conception of politics but a distinct position on the very nature of politics. It might be said that the author's political experience has also found its way into this book.

## NOTES

[1]Pericles, "Funeral Oration," in *Communism, Fascism, and Democracy*, ed. Carl Cohen (New York, 1972), p. 538.

[2]Willard A. Mullins, "On the Concept of Ideology in Political Science," *The American Political Science Review* 66, no. 2 (June 1972):510.

[3]Albert Speer, *Inside the Third Reich* (New York, 1970), p. 65.

## FOR FURTHER READING

Benn, S. E., and R. S. Peters. *The Principles of Political Thought.* New York: The Free Press, 1965. A very useful overview of the central issues of political theory, such as justice, freedom, and authority. The analysis of these issues is related to historical developments in political thought.

Cohen, Carl, ed. *Communism, Fascism, and Democracy,* 2d ed. New York: Random House, 1972. A substantial collection of the more prominent original writings that have served as the basis for modern ideologies.

De Crespigny, Anthony, and Jeremy Cronin, eds. *Ideologies of Politics.* Cape Town: Oxford University Press, 1975. A collection of essays by prominent contemporary thinkers, each describing a particular ideological point of view.

Sabine, George H. *A History of Political Theory,* 3d ed. New York: Holt, Rinehart and Winston, 1961. For years a standard historical survey of Western political thought from the ancient Greeks to nineteenth-century Marxism.

Van Dyke, Vernon. *Political Science: A Philosophical Analysis.* Stanford, Calif.: Stanford University Press, 1960. A useful examination of the methods and approaches involved in the practice of political science. Deals with how political scientists collect, organize, and use information and develop theories and explanations.

Wolin, Sheldon S. *Politics and Vision.* Boston: Little, Brown, 1960. An historical treatment of Western political thought. Unlike Sabine, Wolin is more interpretive and explores certain major thinkers and issues in greater depth.

# Index

## DATE DUE

| | | | |
|---|---|---|---|
| | | | |
| | | | |
| | | | |
| | | | |
| | | | |
| | | | |
| | | | |
| | | | |
| | | | |
| | | | |
| | | | |
| | | | |
| | | | |
| | | | |
| | | | |
| | | | |
| | | | |

DEMCO 38-297